AF327350

TRUTH *from the* TRENCHES

TRUTH *from the* TRENCHES

USING GOD'S WORD
TO ILLUSTRATE
TIMELESS TRUTHS

COMPILED BY

DR. PETE CHARPENTIER

AMG PUBLISHERS
ADVANCING THE MINISTRIES OF THE GOSPEL

Truth from the Trenches
Using God's Word To Illustrate Timeless Truths

Copyright © 2014 by Pete Charpentier
Published by AMG Publishers, Inc.
6815 Shallowford Rd.
Chattanooga, Tennessee 37421

All rights reserved. Except for brief quotations in printed reviews, no part of this publication may be reproduced, stored in a retrieval system, or transmitted in any form or by any means (printed, written, photocopied, visual electronic, audio, or otherwise) without the prior permission of the publisher.

Print Edition: ISBN 13: 978-0-89957-368-7
EPUB Edition ISBN 13: 978-1-61715-358-7
Mobi Edition ISBN 13: 978-1-61715-359-4
PDF Edition   ISBN 13: 978-1-61715-360-0

First Printing—December 2014

Cover designed by InView Graphics, Chattanooga, TN.
Interior design and typesetting by PerfecType, Nashville, TN.
Edited and proofread by Agnes Lawless Weaver and Rick Steele.

Printed in the United States of America

LSI

To Joseph and Joshua
I thank God for you both, and may Jesus lead and guide you
through the trenches of life.
Love Dad

ACKNOWLEDGMENTS

Nothing in life is accomplished alone. This is a core truth learned in life's trenches. So I want to acknowledge several people God used to help me in writing *Truth from the Trenches.*

Thank You, Lord Jesus, for speaking to me through the pages of Your Word. Your truth sets me free, indeed (John 8:32).

Wendy, I thank God for your love. You are the most genuine person I know, and you've helped me see God's truth more clearly in the trenches of life.

I want to express my gratitude to my parents, Jr. and Cheryl Charpentier. You have loved and sacrificed so much for me, and I'm still reaping where you have sown into my life. Also, I want thank my brother, Jessie Charpentier, Sr., for generously giving of his time to read and offer helpful comments on the manuscript of this book. Thanks for your partnership in the Gospel (Philippians 1:3-11; Philemon 7).

I also want to thank my "other parents", Bruce and Donna Pourciau (better known as "Papa and Mimi"). Your love and support in the trenches of life have helped Wendy and I in more ways than you'll ever know, and Mimi, thanks for offering to proofread and edit the manuscript as well. But please, do not expect "mercy" in our Super Bowl games!

I'm grateful as well to my students in the Caskey School of Divinity and at Grand Canyon University. Your thoughtful interactions in classes have and continue to sharpen my understanding of Scripture. May we grow in how to rightly divide God's Word of truth (2 Timothy 2:15; 4:2).

Lastly, I want to thank Rick Steele and his team at AMG Publishers. Your expertise and hard work have been such a blessing to me over the course of this project, and I trust our collaborative effort will now be a blessing to others for God's glory.

CONTENTS

INTRODUCTION

Truth from the Trenches is a simple title. The word *truth* refers to God's truth as revealed in His inspired Word. The words *from the Trenches* emphasize that much of Scripture is communicated through narratives—real-life stories of struggle and sin.

God did not simply convey His Word through propositional statements or poetical sayings. Rather, He communicated many of His principles in the crucible of life's difficulties. In other words, believers learn that David is a man after God's own heart (1 Samuel 13:14; Acts 13:22). However, the Lord's portrait of David includes his sinful warts as well (see, for example, 2 Samuel 11:1–27).

So God's people glean insights from David's writings, such as Psalm 23, but they also understand something of the Lord's discipline from Nathan's rebuke of David in 2 Samuel 12. Furthermore, God not only teaches His people about His chastening hand through this story, but He likewise shows His gracious compassion by including a mention of Bathsheba and her second son with David, Solomon, in Jesus's genealogy (Matthew 1:6).

Simply put: *Truth from the Trenches* is a focus on learning God's truths through the real-life stories of Scripture. This resource can help those who share God's Word with others to teach it more effectively. As those who proclaim the Lord's Word through preaching and teaching use biblical stories to illustrate biblical principles, God's people will grow in Christlikeness. They will deepen their understanding of who God is. They will grasp more firmly all He has accomplished for them in Christ, and they will learn more of what it means to walk in ways that honor Him. All aspects of Scripture, both narratives and propositional statements, dovetail to convey God's truth powerfully.

An Overview of the Book

If you are a preacher or teacher committed to handling the Scriptures accurately, *Truth from the Trenches* is just for you. Most people who study God's Word carefully and who seek to communicate its truth effectively know that the best commentary on the Bible is the Bible. This applies to various aspects of studying the Scripture, especially when using biblical stories to illustrate biblical principles. Yet, some expositors may struggle with how to apply this axiom of sound interpretation in their regular study time. Or they may want a resource to help them along this line. But now the wait is over.

Truth from the Trenches is a practical study tool that ministry leaders will welcome. It is a user-friendly collection of biblical illustrations from the narrative sections of both the Old and New Testaments. For instance, if a pastor is preaching on the importance of forgiveness from Ephesians 4:32, he could use *Truth from the Trenches* to show how Joseph forgave his brothers in Genesis 50:15–21. From this biblical story, he could explain how God worked for good even through pain. Or if a Bible teacher is elaborating on God's absolute sovereignty from Proverbs 19:21, she could use *Truth from the Trenches* to show how the Lord worked even through Paul and Barnabas's conflict in Acts 15:36–41 to expand His mission.

With an extensive Scripture index and subject index, *Truth from the Trenches* is a valuable and versatile resource for preachers and teachers alike. By using this study aid, they will not only agree that the best commentary on the Bible is the Bible, but they also will have a handy reference work to put this principle into practice. Furthermore, the practice of illustrating Scripture with Scripture will equip those who listen to their preaching and teaching to learn more of God's Word and to live more aligned with His truth.

The Thesis and Argument of the Book

As already alluded to above, the thesis of *Truth from the Trenches* is straightforward: The narrative sections of Scripture are biblical illustrations for biblical truths. The argument underlying this thesis is that God gave scriptural stories to reveal His truth more fully and how it applies to life (Romans 15:4).

Consider the following examples from within the pages of Scripture itself. In Joshua 22:1–20, the Israelites referred to an event in their past (see Joshua 7:1–26) as an illustration of a principle they had learned about God and His dealings with them. Also, in 1 Corinthians 10:8–10, Paul alluded to Old Testament events (see Numbers 25:1–9; 21:4–9; 14:1–38 respectively) in order to issue sober warnings based on biblical stories to fellow believers.

In an effort to accomplish its focus and purpose, *Truth from the Trenches* contains four special features. First, every chapter includes a section dealing with the context of each biblical story. This brief discussion serves to help expositors avoid hermeneutical errors that typically result from a violation of a narrative's original setting.

Second, each chapter overviews the main contours of its respective illustration.

Third, all chapters conclude with several suggestions for how the particular illustration in view could be used in preaching and teaching.

Fourth, the two indices in the resource combine to make it beneficial to ministers and teachers on a regular basis. The Scripture index provides an easy way to locate any and all verses and passages referenced in the book. The subject index furnishes readers with a quick way to find a scriptural story related to a particular topic.

Pointers for Using the Book

Pastors and teachers who use biblical illustrations in their preaching and teaching need to keep three important pointers in mind.

Avoid Allegorizing Scriptural Narratives

First, they must avoid allegorizing the text. The best way to prevent inappropriate allegorization from occurring is to pay close attention to a story's original context. This is why the first section of every chapter focuses on background issues. Frequently, those who violate the integrity of a text with allegorization pay little if any attention to the original setting of a passage or how it fits into the overall redemptive theme of Scripture.

For example, in their classic book on biblical interpretation, Fee and Stuart cite a well-known instance of allegorical interpretation from Augustine. Here is how they identified the details of Augustine's allegorical approach to the parable of the good Samaritan:

A certain man went down from Jerusalem to Jericho = Adam
Jerusalem = the heavenly city of peace, from which Adam fell
Jericho = the moon, and thereby signifies Adam's mortality
thieves = the devil and his angels

> *stripped him* = namely, of his immortality
>
> *beat him* = by persuading him to sin
>
> *and left him half-dead* = as a man he lives, but he died spiritually, therefore he is half-dead
>
> *The priest and Levite* = the priesthood and ministry of the Old Testament
>
> *The Samaritan* = is said to mean "Guardian"; therefore, Christ himself is meant
>
> *bound his wounds* = means binding the restraint of sin
>
> *oil* = comfort of good hope
>
> *wine* = exhortation to work with a fervent spirit
>
> *beast* = the flesh of Christ's incarnation
>
> *inn* = the church
>
> *the morrow* = after the Resurrection
>
> *two-pence* = promise of this life and the life to come
>
> *innkeeper* = Paul[1]

Although the above example of allegorization focuses on a parable as opposed to a scriptural narrative, other examples of how both non-Christian and Christian figures from the past allegorized biblical stories are readily available. For instance, Philo, a Jewish philosopher from the time of Jesus, believed "a Bible passage was like a human being; it had a body (i.e., a literal meaning) and a soul (an allegorical meaning)."[2] In light of this line of reasoning, Philo viewed the various rivers that flowed through the garden of Eden according to Genesis 2:10–14 in the following way: "The Edenic river represented goodness, while the other

---

1. Gordon D. Fee and Douglas Stuart, *How to Read the Bible for All Its Worth: A Guide to Understanding the Bible*, 2nd ed. (Grand Rapids: Zondervan, 1993), 136.

2. William W. Klein, Craig L. Blomberg, and Robert L. Hubbard Jr., *Introduction to Biblical Interpretation* (Nashville: W Publishing Group, 1993), 26.

four represented the four great virtues of Greek philosophy—prudence, temperance, courage, and justice."[3]

Another noted proponent of allegorical interpretation in the early church was Origen. "In his extensive writings, Origen argued that just as humans consist of body, soul, and spirit, so Scripture has a threefold meaning."[4] His approach to Old Testament narratives from an allegorical perspective is exemplified in his explanation of Genesis 19:30–38:

> As an example, consider Origen's interpretation of the sexual relations between Lot and his daughters (Gen 19:30–38). According to Origen, the passage has a literal sense (it actually happened). But its moral meaning is that Lot represents the rational human mind, his wife the flesh inclined to pleasures, and the daughters vainglory and pride. Applying these three to people yields the spiritual (or doctrinal) meaning: Lot represents the OT [Old Testament] law, the daughters represent Jerusalem and Samaria, and the wife represents the Israelites who rebelled in the wilderness.[5]

It should be obvious from the above examples that when the door is flung open to allegorical interpretations, there is no limit to how far preachers and teachers can wander astray from the meaning of the text in terms of its original context and the overall redemptive theme of God's Word. Those who seek to rightly divide Scripture must pay careful attention to the context of biblical narratives. To quote one contemporary author: "*Remember that context is king.* Always consider the context of the passage that you are studying. 'Context' means 'that which goes with the text.' Ripping verses out of context, and using

---

3. Ibid.
4. Ibid., 34.
5. Ibid., 34–35.

them in a way that does not represent the intended meaning of the Holy Spirit, is irresponsible and inexcusable."[6]

Commit to Study God's Word Thoroughly

A second important pointer to keep in mind follows closely on the heels of the prior emphasis on context. Expositors must be devoted to a thorough study of God's Word in order to grow continually in their grasp of the context of Scripture. For example, a passage's literary context (its location within a certain section of Scripture) is vital. Also, a scriptural story may include cultural references that are crucial for correct interpretation. Lastly, every text must be understood in light of Scripture's overall thrust of God's redemptive plan in Christ. These multifaceted aspects of context must not be viewed from an either/or perspective but from an appropriate both/and perspective when necessary.

For this reason, pastors and teachers will want to focus on the various aspects of context for each biblical illustration at the beginning of each chapter. However, they will not want to rely exclusively on these introductory overviews. These brief discussions should not be used as substitutes for a more thorough analysis of the contexts for each narrative. Ministry leaders who focus on the background of a passage will further safeguard themselves from misinterpreting the intent of the biblical authors.

Focus on Christ and Not Moralizations

The third important pointer for pastors and teachers to remember when using biblical narratives to illustrate biblical principles is to refrain

---

6. Tony Merida, *Faithful Preaching: Declaring Scripture with Responsibility, Passion, and Authenticity* (Nashville: Broadman and Holman Academic, 2009), 63.

from moralizing Scripture to the exclusion of a concentration on the Christological focus of all Scripture. Fee and Stuart once again provide helpful insights for those who want to handle God's Word correctly, especially as this relates to the interpretation of biblical narratives. They first of all explain how scriptural narratives are useful in several ways to convey God's truth. For instance, they write, "Bible narratives tell us about things that happened—but not just any things. Their purpose is to show God at work in his creation and among his people. The narratives glorify him, help us to understand and appreciate him, and give us a picture of his providence and protection. At the same time, they also provide illustrations of many other lessons important to our lives."[7]

In addition to this overview of biblical narratives, Fee and Stuart basically assert the thesis of *Truth from the Trenches* when they write, "An Old Testament narrative usually illustrates a doctrine or doctrines taught propositionally elsewhere."[8] However, it is precisely at this point that they also alert students of Scripture to the dangers of taking this thought to an extreme. Fee and Stuart argue that biblical narratives were not intended to teach morals but to highlight God's storyline of redemption woven throughout Scripture. For instance, they explain that "the fallacy of this approach [moralizing] is that it ignores the fact that the narratives were written to show the progress of God's history of redemption, not to illustrate principles. They are historical narratives, not illustrative narratives."[9]

Yet, preachers and teachers might wonder if the above warning erects a false dichotomy. In other words, is it true that a focus on God's

7. Fee and Stuart, 79.
8. Ibid., 83.
9. Ibid., 92.

redemptive plan in Christ prevents biblical narratives from also being useful in illustrating other biblical truths in light of the message of the gospel? As long as expositors maintain a proper balance between these two points, it would appear that the stories of the Bible can oftentimes serve a multipurpose function. One purpose is always to emphasize God's ongoing plan of redemption. Another purpose is to show examples of how the Lord worked in and through the trenches of life to reveal Himself to others, namely, to teach and reinforce His truths, which are also expressed in biblical principles.

The aforementioned balance is what Scripture itself seems to argue. For instance, as Paul wrote to Timothy, he emphasized how all of God's Word was profitable for both salvation and sanctification: "But as for you, continue in what you have learned and have firmly believed, knowing from whom you learned it and how from childhood you have been acquainted with the sacred writings, which are able to make you wise for salvation through faith in Christ Jesus. All Scripture is breathed out by God and profitable for teaching, for reproof, for correction, and for training in righteousness, that the man of God may be complete, equipped for every good work" (2 Timothy 3:14–17).

Guidelines for an Appropriate Christological Focus

In light of this third important pointer, pastors and teachers should view every biblical narrative through the lens of God's redemption in Christ. This will yield several important guidelines. First, every scriptural story is ultimately about God. It's been well said that the main person in the book of Jonah, for example, is not Jonah; it's God. If anything, even though Jonah is the Lord's prophet, he is an example of what behavior to avoid rather than what to embrace. Paul appears to make this very point in 1 Corinthians 10:1–14 when he wrote:

For I do not want you to be unaware, brothers, that our fathers were all under the cloud, and all passed through the sea, and all were baptized into Moses in the cloud and in the sea, and all ate the same spiritual food, and all drank the same spiritual drink. For they drank from the spiritual Rock that followed them, and the Rock was Christ. Nevertheless, with most of them God was not pleased, for they were overthrown in the wilderness.

Now these things took place as examples for us, that we might not desire evil as they did. Do not be idolaters as some of them were; as it is written, "The people sat down to eat and drink and rose up to play." We must not indulge in sexual immorality as some of them did, and twenty-three thousand fell in a single day. We must not put Christ to the test, as some of them did and were destroyed by serpents, nor grumble as some of them did and were destroyed by the Destroyer. Now these things happened to them as an example, but they were written down for our instruction, on whom the end of the ages has come. Therefore let anyone who thinks that he stands take heed lest he fall. No temptation has overtaken you that is not common to man. God is faithful, and he will not let you be tempted beyond your ability, but with the temptation he will also provide a way of escape, that you may be able to endure it. Therefore, my beloved, flee from idolatry.

Paul here stressed a Christological focus as he referred to several biblical stories (*see* verses 4, 9); however, he also saw these Old Testament narratives as instructive for believers. His words signal his obvious belief that God wanted to teach His people lessons about how to walk aligned with His truth as revealed through Israel's negative example on these occasions.

Second, every narrative should be viewed in light of God's plan of salvation. For instance, the story of Joseph in Genesis was not only written to teach lessons about God from the life of Joseph; rather, the historical account of Joseph's painful journey into a powerful position is meant to emphasize how the Lord is a covenant-keeping God. He preserved His people from the ravages of a famine because, although no human being knew that it was coming, God did. And He positioned one of His servants in a place of influence so that He could fulfill His covenant promise to His people (Genesis 15:13–16).

Also, Israel's suffering in Egypt set the stage for the Old Testament's greatest expression of God's deliverance—the exodus event. This also included the account of the first Passover meal (Exodus 11:1–15:21). Thus, all these stories should be viewed in light of how the Lord delivered His people in ways which pointed forward to how "Christ, our Passover lamb, has been sacrificed" through His "exodus" or death on the cross (1 Corinthians 5:7). (*See* Luke 9:30–31 where Moses and Elijah talked with Jesus on the Mount of Transfiguration about His impending departure or "exodus.")

Third, believers should read every biblical narrative (especially Old Testament stories) in light of their salvation in Christ. In other words, when a positive example occurs in a story, Christians should not resolve to emulate this behavior. Instead, they should rest in God's indwelling Spirit to empower them for godliness (2 Peter 1:3).

An instance where the above point might surface is in the story of Joseph and Potiphar's wife. Although Joseph resisted her continual sexual advances (Genesis 39:6-18), believers should not read this story and resolve to be strong like Joseph in resisting temptations. Rather, Christians should desire to be like Christ. Joseph was not a perfect example; only Christ is a perfect example (Hebrews 4:15–16). In fact, without Christ, believers can do nothing (John 15:5). The power of the Holy Spirit alone strengthens them to walk in victory over sin (Romans 8:9–11; Galatians 5:16–25).

However, it is true that Joseph is a positive example in this case. After all, he stressed his focus on God when he responded to his temptress: "How can I do this great wickedness and sin against God?" (Genesis

39:9) Of course, others in Scripture presented their lives as examples for believers to follow as well. Paul, for instance, urged believers in Philippians 3:17, "Brothers, join in imitating me, and keep your eyes on those who walk according to the example you have in us" (*see* also 1 Corinthians 4:16).

Obviously, Paul was not trying to present himself as a substitute for Christ. In fact, he wrote in 1 Corinthians 11:1, "Be imitators of me, as I am of Christ." Peter also exhorted suffering believers to follow Jesus who "suffered for you, leaving you an example, so that you might follow in his steps" (1 Peter 2:21). While the writer of Hebrews cited a long list of Old Testament figures in Hebrews 11 who demonstrated lives of faith, he ultimately challenged Christians with these climatic words: "Looking to Jesus, the founder and perfecter of our faith, who for the joy that was set before him endured the cross, despising the shame, and is seated at the right hand of the throne of God" (Hebrews 12:2).

All of this means that believers are called to focus on Christ who is their salvation and their only perfect example in sanctification. Jesus wants His followers to follow His example. In relation to service in particular, Jesus told His disciples after He washed their feet, "For I have given you an example, that you should do as I have done to you" (John 13:15).

Of course, this idea must be understood in light of the third important pointer mentioned above—the danger of an exclusive moralizing view of Scripture. Christianity is not merely about following Jesus's example in life. Instead, Christianity is about the fact that every person is dead in sin and in desperate need of salvation through Christ alone. Only Jesus lived and died as the perfect sacrifice. He shed His blood to satisfy God's just wrath against sinners, and He rose again to set them in a right standing before the Lord. Once people repent and trust in Jesus by God's grace through the Spirit's power for the forgiveness of sins, they are God's workmanship in Christ—created for every good work to the glory of the Father.

Therefore, moralizing Scripture to the exclusion of focusing on God's redemption in Christ sends a wrong message. It falsely implies that people can become believers by simply trying to live according to Jesus's example. The truth is that Scripture first exhorts sinners to look to Christ for salvation, and then it calls them to follow His example by the Spirit's power.

In the final analysis, biblical stories are useful in illustrating biblical principles, assuming the following three ideas are kept firmly in mind: 1) All narratives must be understood against the backdrop of their contextual aspects. 2) All stories must be viewed in light of God's overall story of redemption in Christ. 3) All historical accounts must teach Christians how to walk according to God's truth with Christ as their ultimate focus and by the Spirit's power. As long as these important points are clear, pastors and teachers can effectively use *Truth from the Trenches* to illustrate the Bible with the Bible.

1

God's Perfect Work through Imperfect People

~ Genesis 12:10–20 ~

For everyone who reads the Bible carefully, the following message is clear: Only God is perfect, and yet He uses imperfect people to accomplish His plans. This point is best seen in one of the most climatic events of all Scripture—the crucifixion of Christ.[10] Peter wrote that Jesus died as "the righteous for the unrighteous" (1 Peter 3:18). Peter also declared that Christ was "crucified and killed by the hands of lawless men" (Acts 2:23). So the cross is the ultimate picture of how God accomplished His perfect plan of salvation by using even sinful men. Of course, this point recurs throughout Scripture, and it first surfaces in the story of how God fulfilled His perfect plan through imperfect Abraham.

---

10. Millard J. Erickson, *Christian Theology*, 2nd ed. (Grand Rapids: Baker Academic, 1998), 423.

Context

The context for Genesis 12:10–20 should begin with the ending of Genesis 11. In Genesis 11:31–32, Terah, Abraham's father, left Ur of the Chaldeans for the land of Canaan. He took along his son Abram (Abraham), his grandson Lot, and his daughter-in-law Sarai (Sarah). But Terah never completed his journey to Canaan. He only made it as far as Haran, where he died.

So God issued a call to Abram in Genesis 12:1–3 to finish the journey to Canaan that his father Terah began. But the Lord's call to Abram contained more than simply an invitation to enter a new geographical territory. His call outlined His perfect plan for Abram and his descendants. Among other things, God promised to make Abram into a great nation. Also, God made it clear that He would fulfill His plan Himself. This is evident from His words in Genesis 12:2–3. In these verses the Lord mentioned the words *I will* five times to emphasize His power to accomplish His plan.

Therefore, the preceding context of Genesis 12:10–20 reveals that the fulfillment of God's perfect plan was dependent upon His power. This point is essential to understand because the biblical story which follows in Genesis 12:10–20 emphasizes both God's power and Abram's imperfections. Although Abram obeyed the Lord's call and wanted to honor Him (Genesis 12:7–8), he nevertheless showed his imperfections by acting in fear in Egypt. Yet, God still used Abram because His perfect plan didn't depend on Abram and his imperfections. It depended upon Himself.

The Illustration

Genesis 12:10 opens the scene for this biblical illustration. A famine had ravaged the land of Canaan, the land God promised to give to Abram and his descendants (Genesis 12:1–3). At this point, an obvious tension began to build in the story. Not only was Abram's wife, Sarai, barren (Genesis 11:30), but now the very lives of Abram and his wife were threatened by a famine. The tension next intensifies as Abram and his wife left Canaan and journeyed into Egypt, because on this sojourn Abram revealed his imperfections.

Whether or not readers wonder if Abram exposed his fear by leaving Canaan in the first place, he clearly acted in fear once he arrived in Egypt. He basically instructed Sarai to lie about being his wife because he feared the Egyptians would kill him in order to take her. While some may be tempted to call this lie a half-truth since Abram and Sarai were apparently half-siblings (Genesis 20:12), the fact remains that Abram acted in fear instead of faith.

Nevertheless, God protected Abram's life and preserved Sarai's purity. The Lord also began to fulfill His plan to make Abram into a great nation because during his stay in Egypt, he acquired sheep, cattle, donkeys, servants, and camels (Genesis 12:16). The Lord began to accomplish His perfect plan even though Abram was an imperfect person.

Suggestions for Use

As noted above, God is perfect, but people are imperfect. Still God uses imperfect people in accomplishing His perfect plans. Although Abram failed at times because he acted in fear, the Lord was always faithful to fulfill His promises.

This biblical illustration provides tremendous encouragement to believers who seek to obey God's call in their lives. Even though all Christians fail at times, God never fails them. His perfect plan depends upon His power—not upon the imperfections of His people. In fact, Paul wrote in 1 Thessalonians 5:24, "He who calls you is faithful; he will surely do it."

This general principle of Scripture can be used in a wide variety of ways. For instance, teachers can use the biblical illustration of Abram's sinful fear as an example of how those who seek to follow God still stumble in many ways. In other words, if a preacher is dealing with how the Lord used Peter and David with all their imperfections, he can also illustrate his point by sharing how God worked in a similar way to accomplish His perfect plan through Abram and his imperfections as outlined in Genesis 12:10–20. Also, if a teacher is presenting a lesson on the fact that believers still struggle and fail at times (Galatians 6:1–5; James 3:2), he or she can draw attention to the story of Abram to encourage others to understand that God still uses imperfect people as He accomplishes His perfect plan.

2

ANGELS, PROVIDENCE, AND PRAYER

~ Genesis 24:1–27 ~

The inner workings between God's providence and the prayers of His people are mysterious. When the involvement of the Lord's angelic hosts is added to this mix, all these realities become even more incomprehensible for believers. Yet, Scripture is clear that God works providentially in the lives of His people in order to fulfill His purposes (Proverbs 16:33). Also, He invites His servants to bring their petitions to Him in prayer (Matthew 7:7–11). And, lastly, His angels are sent to minister to His children (Hebrews 1:14) as they do His bidding (Psalm 103:20–21). All of these points are powerfully presented in the story of how the Lord supernaturally led Abraham's servant to find a wife for Isaac in Genesis 24.

Context

Like many passages throughout the book of Genesis, God's covenant with Abraham provides the theological context for Genesis 24:1–27.

Of course, the Lord's covenant with Abraham would extend to future generations through Abraham's offspring. Genesis 17:8, for example, makes this point clear when the Lord promised, "I will give to you and to your offspring after you the land of your sojournings, all the land of Canaan, for an everlasting possession, and I will be their God."

But so far in the book of Genesis, at least since chapter 15, suspense has mounted. How would God bless Abraham and his descendants? Abraham and Sarah had been aging more and more beyond their child-bearing seasons with each passing year. God said Eliezer of Damascus would not be Abraham's promised successor (Genesis 15:2–4). Also, the Lord declared that Ishmael would not be God's promised son either (Genesis 16; 17:15–19). But the Lord fulfilled His promise in a miraculous way. He blessed Abraham and Sarah with a child in their old age. He promised the birth of Isaac and extended His covenant blessings to Abraham through him (Genesis 17:19, 21; 18:9–15; 21:1–7).

Yet, the suspense continued to mount in Genesis 24. Abraham was moving off the scene of this life, and Isaac was moving into a more prominent position as the successor to the blessings of God's covenant. In light of this, the selection of Isaac's wife became critically important. But just as the Lord proved faithful thus far, He continued to show Himself strong. In short, He answered Abraham's prayer to guide Abraham's servant to find a wife for Isaac within the Abrahamic line as opposed to a wife from among the Canaanites.

The Illustration

While Scripture is abundantly clear that God answers prayer (Matthew 7:7–11), the precise ways by which He answers prayer is shrouded in mystery. However, glimpses of God's providential workings in response to prayer surface in the Scripture at various points. One of the ways the Lord moves in answer to prayer, for example, is through angels.

This point is also clear in other biblical stories. For instance, Daniel learned that from the beginning of a long season of struggling through prayer, God dispatched one of His angels to answer his request (Daniel 10:2–14). Also, Jesus mentioned both prayer and angels when He faced the cold shadow of the cross in Gethsemane. Christ explained in Matthew 26:53, "Do you think that I cannot appeal to my Father, and he will at once send me more than twelve legions of angels [approximately 72,000]?"[11]

And it is likewise clear in Genesis 24:1–27 that the Lord used an angel to answer Abraham's prayer concerning the selection of Isaac's wife. In fact, Abraham plainly indicated that God would "send his angel" before his servant in order to answer his prayer (Genesis 24:7, 40). And as the story unfolded, the Lord obviously orchestrated events in several ways according to His perfect timing.

First, while Abraham's servant journeyed to the right city of destination, settled his camels by a well, and arrived at this location during a time when the women of the city would be going to the well (Genesis 24:10–11), he was nevertheless dependent upon the Lord in prayer (Genesis 24:12–14).

Second, just as Abraham's servant finished praying, Rebekah was on her way to the well (Genesis 24:15). Of course, some would perhaps label this as coincidence but not those who are familiar with this text and the God of Scripture. With the Lord's sovereign power already displayed throughout the book of Genesis in general and with Abraham's words that God would "send his angel" before his servant in particular, the timing of these events are indelibly marked with the Lord's providential fingerprints.

One could almost imagine an angel nudging Rebekah at just the right time to start her walk to the well as Abraham's servant settled

---

11. Craig L. Blomberg, *Matthew*, vol. 22 of *The New American Commentary* (Nashville: Broadman and Holman, 1992), 399.

with his camels. Also, one could visualize how an angel gently directed Rebekah to the particular well where Abraham's servant was waiting and praying for God to answer both his prayers and the prayers of his master Abraham.

Third, Rebekah's offer to furnish water for both Abraham's servant and his camels in response to his prayerfully planned request absolutely confirmed God's power at work (Genesis 24:14, 17–21). Again, since the mention of the Lord's angel occurs at the beginning and ending of this text (Genesis 24:7, 40), it seems clear that this story is a powerful illustration of how God can providentially use His angels when answering the prayers of His servants.

Suggestions for Use

While the Lord doubtlessly uses members of His heavenly hosts in answering prayers, He is always the only One who receives glory for His providential workings. In fact, angels would not even exist without God who created them (Psalm 148:1–5).[12] The Lord's preeminence always overshadows angels because they do His will (Psalm 103:20–21), and they always correct people who attempt to worship them (Revelation 22:8–9).

Yet, it is helpful to learn about how God may utilize angels at times when answering prayers. Although angels may not be involved in every answer to prayer, some circumstances seem to make more sense when their involvement is considered. In light of this, the above biblical illustration could be used in several ways.

To begin with, an expositor could appeal to Genesis 24:1–27 as support for the general truth of Scripture mentioned in Psalm 103:20–21, namely, angels fulfill God's will. Also, the story of how God identified

---

12. Erickson, 462.

Rebekah as Isaac's chosen wife reveals the intermingling of such theological truths as God's providential power and human prayer. A Bible teacher could refer to this narrative to emphasize the biblical balance between God's providence and human actions. In addition to these truths, both the timing and the details of the events recounted in Genesis 24:1–27 highlight the perfect precision of how the Lord accomplishes His will. While a pastor would want to be careful in qualifying language on this point (*see* the words *imagine* and *visualize* used above under "The Illustration" section), it seems obvious from the text that God did indeed send His angel ahead of Abraham's servant, and the Lord's angel was involved in how the miraculous timing and details of the events unfolded.

3

GOD'S PURPOSE
AND HUMAN PAIN

~ Genesis 37; 39–50 ~

One of the oldest questions in human history focuses on the relationship between God's purposes and human pain. Actually, the first and most fundamental question is: Is there a purpose in pain?

The Scripture is clear in both the Old and New Testaments that God is accomplishing His perfect purpose even in the midst of pain. For example, the psalmist realized that his personal affliction led to a deeper realization of his sinfulness and God's goodness (Psalm 119:67–68). Also, when the prophet Jeremiah penned a letter of comfort to God's people in exile, he shared these immortal words of hope:

> For thus says the Lord: When seventy years are completed for Babylon, I will visit you, and I will fulfill to you my promise and bring you back to this place. For I know the plans I have for you, declares the Lord, plans for welfare and not for evil, to give you a future and a hope. Then you will call upon me and come and pray

to me, and I will hear you. You will seek me and find me, when you seek me with all your heart. I will be found by you, declares the Lord, and I will restore your fortunes and gather you from all the nations and all the places where I have driven you, declares the Lord, and I will bring you back to the place from which I sent you into exile (Jeremiah 29:10–14).

The New Testament likewise emphasizes God's purpose in human pain. For instance, when the disciples asked Jesus why a certain man was born blind, He explained, "It was not that this man sinned, or his parents, but that the works of God might be displayed in him" (John 9:3). Of course, Paul taught that personal pain postures people to receive God's comfort and then to pass it on to others (2 Corinthians 1:3–7). He also learned how to depend more on the Lord's all-sufficient grace as he experienced a relentless "thorn in his flesh" (2 Corinthians 12:7–10). Lastly, Paul plainly emphasized that God is accomplishing His perfect plan through every season of life—both pleasure and pain—when he wrote, "And we know that for those who love God all things work together for good, for those who are called according to his purpose" (Romans 8:28).

So, it is clear: In this life, pain is inevitable, but God accomplishes His purposes in the midst of it. The ancient words of Job give voice to the reality of pain: "But man is born to trouble as the sparks fly upward" (Job 5:7). Yet, Jesus's words give hope in the face of human suffering: "In the world you will have tribulation. But take heart; I have overcome the world" (John 16:33).

Context

The Scripture's message about how God uses pain for His good purposes is evident in the story of Joseph in Genesis 37, 39–50. God first promised to make Abraham into "a great nation" (Genesis 12:2). In time He blessed Abraham with a son named Isaac (Genesis 21:1–3), and then the Lord gave twin sons to Isaac, Esau and Jacob (Genesis 25:21–26). Of course, God eventually gave Jacob the name *Israel* (Genesis 32:24–28), and he had twelve sons who became the twelve tribes of Israel (Genesis 35:22–26). So God continued to fulfill His promise to Abraham by increasing His people.

This is the background for the story of Joseph. As the Lord's people flourished, He preserved them. But God knew a famine was coming that would ravage the ancient world, threatening the very existence of His people. So He positioned Joseph in Egypt to provide for His covenant people during the upcoming years of famine (Genesis 41:25–36; 45:1–11). In this way, God fulfilled His promise to Abraham and accomplished His good purposes even in the midst of Joseph's incredibly painful journey to Egypt. (*See* "The Illustration" section below.)

The story of Joseph is not really about Joseph; it's about the faithfulness of Israel's covenant-keeping God. Even beyond this, the Lord later used the pain of Israel's Egyptian slavery to set the stage for His greatest Old Testament act of deliverance—the exodus event (Exodus 1:1–15:21). God once again used human sufferings in a sinful world to point toward His ultimate deliverance through Christ's death, burial, and resurrection (Romans 5:6–11).

The Illustration

As indicated above, one of the most well-known biblical illustrations about how God accomplished His purposes in the midst of pain is the story of Joseph in Genesis 37, 39–50. While space does not permit a detailed study of the entire Joseph narrative, a survey of its major contours underscores this central theme. For instance, Genesis 37 begins with a mention of Joseph's dreams. Here the Scripture clearly points to the fact that God gave Joseph his dreams to signal His unique purposes for Joseph's life (Genesis 37:1–11). However, Joseph's dreams quickly turned to nightmares when his brothers sold him as a slave (Genesis 37:12–28). As a result, the conclusion of Genesis 37 describes how Jacob, Joseph's father, mourned over what he thought was the death of his beloved son (Genesis 37:29–36).

The Joseph narrative resumes in Genesis 39, and although Joseph is a slave in Egypt, the Scripture is again clear that God was still at work even in Joseph's painful struggles: "The Lord was with Joseph, and he became a successful man, and he was in the house of his Egyptian master" (Genesis 39:2). Of course, Joseph's troubles did not end when he arrived as a slave in Egypt. In fact, in some ways, his troubles only began there. After being falsely accused by Potiphar's wife, her husband threw Joseph into prison. Yet, God was still accomplishing His purpose in the midst of this painful season of struggle. The Scripture echoes this truth in Genesis 39:20–21: "And Joseph's master took him and put him into the prison, the place where the king's prisoners were confined, and he was there in the prison. But the Lord was with Joseph and showed him steadfast love and gave him favor in the sight of the keeper of the prison."

At this point in the story, the theme of dreams resurfaces. However, this time Joseph is not the one having the dreams; he is the one interpreting the dreams. The idea of dreams at this juncture in the narrative explicitly emphasizes God's work. This is clear as Joseph explained to both Pharaoh's imprisoned workers (Genesis 40:8) and eventually to Pharaoh himself that the interpretation of dreams comes from God alone (Genesis 41:16). Of course, God gave Joseph insight and wisdom to interpret Pharaoh's dreams, and through this process, the Lord elevated Joseph to second-in-command in Egypt (Genesis 41:37–57).

After God positioned Joseph in a place of power and gave him wisdom to provide food during the famine, the Lord's good purpose in the midst of his pain became clear. This is a classic example in Scripture of the old adage: *Hindsight is 20/20.* Through a series of interactions with his brothers, Joseph revealed his identity to them (Genesis 42–44), and he explained to them how God used his pain to fulfill His covenant promises to sustain His people (Genesis 43:4–13). This is essentially the message Joseph spoke to his brothers at the close of his story in Genesis 50:20, "As for you, you meant evil against me, but God meant it for good, to bring it about that many people should be kept alive, as they are today."

Thus, Joseph realized this theme in Scripture through his painful journey: God's purpose is fulfilled even in the midst of human pain. While there is no guarantee that people will always see in this life all God accomplished through their pain, they can nevertheless be sure that His purpose is threaded even through the tattered fabric of their pain. Perhaps only the brilliant light of eternity, shining back over the steps of earthly journeys, will be sufficient to reveal more of the ways God worked to fulfill His purposes through pain.

Suggestions for Use

The Joseph narrative is useful in illustrating many obvious and subtle truths from Scripture. For example, the consequences of the sin of parental partiality surface in this story (Genesis 37:1–8). The devastating impact of jealousy is unmistakable as well (Genesis 37:1–28). The need for wisdom when sharing with others is also apparent from the fact that even Joseph's father chastised him at one point because of his dreams (Genesis 37:9–11).

Some of the other ways this story could be used to illustrate biblical truths are as follows: Even though Joseph was forced to live the painful life of a slave, God prepared him for leadership. In other words, before Joseph managed an empire, he managed an estate.[13] Also, even

---

13. Pete Charpentier, *Reaching the Next Level: Partnering with Others for Spiritual Growth,* Leader Guide (Rapid City, SD: CrossLink Publishing, 2010), 12.

when other people falsely accuse (Genesis 39) and forget God's people (Genesis 40), the Lord Himself never abandons them (Genesis 39:20–21; *see* also 2 Timothy 4:9–18). Lastly, God desires for believers to forgive others even when they are hurt because He accomplishes His purposes in the midst of sinful schemes (Genesis 50:15–21).

Of course, all of the multifaceted opportunities for biblical illustrations from the Joseph narrative center on the core truth of God's purposes and human pain. Whether it is the sin of parental partiality, jealousy, lack of wisdom, false accusation, or abandonment, God is working to prepare His people to embrace His purpose by His power and for His glory. The Lord desires for His people to surrender to His lordship as they walk in His grace. They become free from the bitterness that flows from focusing on their pain because they gaze more on the light of His perfect purposes.

4

FORGIVENESS

~ Genesis 50:15–21 ~

The message of forgiveness is relevant to everyone for two reasons. First, all have sinned against God and are in desperate need of His forgiveness (Romans 3:23; Ephesians 1:7).

Second, believers will be hurt or offended by others in life, and they will need to forgive others. Simply put: Christians are called to forgive others (Ephesians 4:32). Interestingly, the two biblical references above show how these two points are interconnected. In other words, since believers have experienced God's forgiveness in Christ (Ephesians 1:7), they are called to extend forgiveness to others by the power of Christ (Ephesians 4:32). Again, these two realities show why the message of forgiveness touches the life of every Christian.

Context

The account of how Joseph forgave his brothers is a powerful scriptural portrait of forgiving others. The context for his words to his brothers in Genesis 50:15–21 is the entire Joseph narrative (Genesis 37, 39–50). Joseph had been sold into Egyptian slavery because of his brothers' jealousy over their father's special love for him and over his dreams (Genesis 37). Also, Potiphar's wife falsely accused Joseph, and her husband sent him to an Egyptian prison (Genesis 39). In addition to all this pain, Joseph interpreted the dreams of Pharaoh's cupbearer and baker in prison (Genesis 40), but after the chief cupbearer was released from prison and went back to work, he forgot Joseph (Genesis 40:23).

The brief sketch of Joseph's major trials in the previous paragraph shows that he had plenty of opportunities to forgive others because many people had wronged him. Yet, Joseph's words to his brothers in Genesis 50:15–21 reveal that his heart was not bitter; instead, it was forgiving. And Joseph's forgiveness did not only surface at this point in his narrative. His forgiveness was also revealed after he initially revealed his identity to his brothers in Egypt (Genesis 45:4–8). Clearly, then, Joseph learned to forgive others, even though they inflicted great pain on him. Since Joseph's suffering began with the jealousy of his brothers, it is fitting that the climatic expression of his forgiveness was expressed specifically to them.

The Illustration

As mentioned above, Joseph experienced pain from several people over the course of his story, including his brothers, Potiphar's wife, and Pharaoh's chief cupbearer. Nevertheless, Joseph learned to forgive others. This is why his interaction with his brothers, his very first offenders, was presented at two points in his story (Genesis 45:4–8; 50:15–21).

Joseph's words to his brothers in these two passages reveal several insights concerning how Joseph could forgive those who hurt him so deeply. First, Joseph's initial words to his fearful brothers in Genesis 50:19 demonstrated that he was surrendered to God's lordship. When he responded to his brothers with the question, "Am I in the place of God?" Joseph acknowledged that vengeance was not within his jurisdiction.

Second, Joseph said in Genesis 50:20, "As for you, you meant evil against me, but God meant it for good." His words here emphasize that he learned to focus more on God's goodness than on his brothers' sinfulness.

Third, Joseph's closing words in Genesis 50:20, "God meant it for good, that many people should be kept alive, as they are today," point to the reality that Joseph understood how God's plan was bigger than himself and his pain.

Fourth, his final words and actions recorded in Genesis 50:21 describe his provision for his brothers and his kindness towards them. They powerfully confirm that Joseph's forgiveness was not confined to mere words. They were a genuine expression of his heart.

While this biblical illustration focuses on Genesis 50:15–21, the other expression of Joseph's forgiveness toward his brothers in Genesis 45:4–8 highlights two similar points. For instance, Joseph's repeated mention that God sent him to Egypt as opposed to his brothers (Genesis 45:5, 7–8) parallels the truth that he understood how God's good plan was accomplished even in the midst of his brothers' sinful actions. Also, Joseph's focus on how God saved many lives from the devastation of the famine (Genesis 45:7) aligns with his appreciation for the broad scope of God's plan. In other words, Joseph realized that God was fulfilling His covenant promise to preserve His people and their future generations through his painful struggles (Genesis 12:1–3; 15:1–6; 17:1–21; 26:1–5; 35:9–12).

Suggestions for Use

The story of how Joseph extended forgiveness to his brothers in Genesis 50:15–21 is an excellent illustration of the Scripture's general call to forgiveness. Both Jesus and Paul challenged believers to exercise forgiveness. For example, in the Sermon on the Mount, Christ taught His followers: "Love your enemies and pray for those who persecute you, so that you may be sons of your Father who is in heaven" (Matthew 5:44–45). Later, Jesus explicitly emphasized forgiveness when He expanded on His own model prayer in Matthew 6:14–15: "For if you forgive others their trespasses, your heavenly Father will also forgive you, but if you do not forgive others their trespasses, neither will your Father forgive your trespasses."

Also, Paul exhorted his fellow Christians to forgive others when he wrote, "Let all bitterness and wrath and anger and clamor and slander be put away from you, along with all malice. Be kind to one another, tenderhearted, forgiving one another, as God in Christ forgave you" (Ephesians 4:31–32). This is a clear challenge for believers to extend the forgiveness they have experienced in Christ. The emphasis is squarely on the fact that believers cannot forgive in their own power and strength. But since they have been transformed by God's grace, they can share forgiveness with others as children of their heavenly Father.

The connections between the passages above that call for believers to forgive others and the illustration of forgiveness in the Joseph narrative should be obvious. Joseph's expression of forgiveness practically reveals several truths concerning how forgiveness can and should be extended to others.

First, believers should extend forgiveness because they have experienced forgiveness. Just as Joseph understood that he was not in the place of God (Genesis 50:19), so Christians should understand that they are not in God's place, either. Paul touched on this point in Romans 12:19–21: "Beloved, never avenge yourselves, but leave it to the wrath of God, for it is written, 'Vengeance is mine, I will repay, says the Lord.' To the contrary, 'if your enemy is hungry, feed him; if he is thirsty, give him something to drink; for by so doing you will heap burning coals on his head.' Do not be overcome by evil, but overcome evil with good."

As Christ committed Himself to God who judged justly when He was falsely accused and abused, believers are called to follow Jesus's footsteps in this way (1 Peter 2:21–23).

Second, believers should focus on the goodness of God rather than on the sinfulness of others. What Christians focus on will dramatically impact their lives. If they focus on how others have sinned against them, they will seethe with bitterness. However, if they focus on God's good purposes even in the midst of their pain, they will be at peace, knowing that their heavenly Father is in control of all things.

One might imagine that Joseph spent every spare moment on his painful journey concocting ways to inflict bitter revenge on his brothers, but his words and actions in Genesis 45:5, 7–8 and 50:20 point in the opposite direction. While Joseph doubtlessly struggled with extending forgiveness (as any ordinary human being would), he ultimately rested in the peace of knowing that God's good purposes triumphed over his enemies' evil plots. Surely, this simple truth cultivated genuine forgiveness in his heart toward others.

Third, believers must have a focus that is bigger than themselves and their pain. When Christians look inward and dwell on themselves, they become completely self-absorbed. Every offense against them will be magnified in their hearts and minds until an all-consuming whirlwind of anger envelops their lives. Both in Genesis 45:7 and 50:20, Joseph revealed that he understood and appreciated the broad scope of God's plan. He acknowledged that God accomplished His good purpose to save many lives through his personal suffering. While this truth certainly did not remove all of Joseph's pain, it nevertheless positioned him to embrace the fact that his pain was not in vain.

Fourth, believers should do more than merely speak words of forgiveness; they should also demonstrate acts of forgiveness. When Jesus taught about how His followers ought to treat their enemies, He said, "For if you love those who love you, what reward do you have? Do not even the tax collectors do the same? And if you greet only your brothers, what more are you doing than others? Do not even the Gentiles do the same? You therefore must be perfect, as your heavenly Father is perfect" (Matthew 5:46–48). While Christ was not saying that His followers can love others with perfect consistency in this life, He still called them to live lives of supernatural love as expressed through genuine, heartfelt forgiveness. And, of course, Jesus not only preached this message; He lived it. When He hung on the cross, He forgave those who mocked and assaulted Him (Luke 23:34). This is how Joseph responded to his brothers—with generosity, kindness, and comfort.

Although believers cannot respond in genuine acts of love toward their enemies in their own strength, they can surrender to the power of God's Spirit as children of their heavenly Father. And the fruit of the Spirit is love—supernatural love even extended to vicious enemies (Galatians 5:22–23). The Christian life, especially in the area of forgiveness, is not a natural life but rather a supernatural one. It is only possible by the Spirit's power pulsating in and through believers who have been saved and are being sustained by God's life-transforming grace (2 Corinthians 5:17).

5

A Higher Moral Obligation

~ Exodus 1:8–22 ~

Scripture shows that believers owe their highest allegiance to God alone (Exodus 20:2–3; Luke 14:25-33). God's Word also shows that Christians are to submit to governing authorities (Romans 13:1–7; 1 Peter 2:13–17). Yet, conflicts sometime arise between God's will and the will of wicked authorities (Psalm 2:1–3). At these points, a natural question arises: What should believers do when the laws of this world and God's will are mutually exclusive? The biblical illustration in Exodus 1:8–22 describes such a situation. It teaches that those who fear God always have a higher moral obligation to obey Him rather than sinful leaders.

Context

As the book of Exodus opens, the perfect storm gathered for the people of Israel. Joseph, his brothers, and their entire generation exited from the stage of history (Exodus 1:6). Nevertheless, God multiplied Israel so that "the land was filled with them" (Exodus 1:7).

Of course, a growing alien population would make any rulers concerned with safeguarding their empires, and this was the exact situation in the first chapter of Exodus. A new pharaoh who did not know Joseph rose to power and deemed Israel a threat (Exodus 1:8–10). So he decided to oppress them (Exodus 1:11). However, "the more they were oppressed, the more they multiplied and the more they spread abroad" (Exodus 1:12). Pharaoh nevertheless ruthlessly afflicted them with severe slave labor (Exodus 1:13–14).

But for the careful reader of Scripture, Israel's slavery and suffering in Egypt does not come as a surprise. The Lord had already told Abram (or Abraham) in Genesis 15:13–15, "Know for certain that your offspring will be sojourners in a land that is not theirs and will be servants there, and they will be afflicted for four hundred years. But I will bring judgment on the nation that they serve, and afterward they shall come out with great possessions." In other words, although Israel was suffering in bondage, God's promise to deliver them was certain.

One way that the Lord guarded His people in Egypt was through their midwives. Pharaoh ordered Shiphrah and Puah to kill any male children born to Israelite women (Exodus 1:15–16). This was another facet of his sinister plot against the Lord's people. Yet, the midwives defied Pharaoh's order because they held to a higher moral obligation out of their fear of God (Exodus 1:17, 21).

The Illustration

After Pharaoh commanded the midwives in Egypt to kill all the Hebrew boys, Exodus 1:17 simply says, "But the midwives feared God, and did not do as the king of Egypt commanded them, but let the male children live." Two key words in this verse are important for understanding this biblical illustration. First, the introductory conjunction *but* is crucial. To this point in the story, tension had mounted. Pharaoh's first assault against the Hebrews was slave labor (Exodus 1:8–11), but God still blessed His people with an increase in population (Exodus 1:12). Next, Pharaoh intensified his oppressive tyranny over the Hebrews as he hatched a murderous scheme to kill every male Israelite child born in Egypt (Exodus 1:13–16). Yet, the small word *but* points to the fact that God was at work. While Pharaoh had his evil plans, the Lord was working to accomplish His perfect purposes.

Second, the verb *feared* in Exodus 1:17 is a key word. Among other semantic nuances, this word describes reverence for God.[14] The main idea here is that the midwives chose to obey God rather than Pharaoh's sinful command to kill the male Hebrew infants. Of course, this thought brings an important point to the proverbial table for discussion. Some may ask: Did God bless the midwives for defying authority and subsequently lying to Pharaoh? The answer to this question is found in a careful reading of the text. The emphasis in the Scripture appears to be on how the midwives feared God and not on how they defied and lied to Pharaoh. The summary statement concerning the midwives and God's blessing on them appears in Exodus 1:21: "And because the midwives feared God, he gave them families." This verse describes both the Lord's blessing on the midwives and the reason for His blessing, namely, their reverence for God even at the risk of their own lives.

Of course, Exodus 1:8–22 is not the only biblical passage where God's people defied human authority because of their submission to His supreme authority. While the scriptural principle to submit to God-ordained authority is clear (*see*, for example, Romans 13:1–7), there is a higher moral obligation to God's will whenever earthly laws oppose God's laws. For instance, when Nebuchadnezzar issued a command for

---

14. Spiros Zodhiates and Warren P. Baker, eds., *The Hebrew-Greek Key Word Study Bible* (Chattanooga: AMG Publishers, 2008), 1894.

everyone to worship his image, Shadrach, Meshach, and Abednego defied his order with these words: "Our God whom we serve is able to deliver us from the burning fiery furnace, and he will deliver us out of your hand, O king. But if not, be it known to you, O king, that we will not serve your gods or worship the golden image that you have set up" (Daniel 3:17–18). Also, when the religious leaders charged Peter to stop preaching in the name of Jesus, Peter fearlessly defied their threats with these words: "We must obey God rather than men" (Acts 5:29). These biblical examples do not provide Christians with blanket approval to rebel against authority, but they do reveal that believers have a higher moral obligation to adhere to God's Word over the laws of humanity in cases where the two become mutually exclusive.

Suggestions for Use

The scriptural story of the midwives in Egypt can be useful to expositors and teachers in several ways as they seek to handle God's Word with integrity. For example, they could obviously appeal to this account in Exodus 1:8–22 when they teach on passages such as Daniel 3 and/or Acts 5. Also, this text could be utilized in showing a biblical balance for other passages such as Romans 13:1–7, 1 Timothy 2:1–2, and 1 Peter 2:13–17. Christians need to understand the passages which call for submission to authority are not in contradiction to other texts which indicate God's blessings on those who defy authority. Rather, these passages complement one another. They reveal that different circumstances call for different responses in light of the truth of God's Word. While this does not mean that truth or morality is somehow relative to circumstances, it nevertheless does emphasize the need for wisdom in navigating the complexities of living godly lives in an ungodly world.

Furthermore, preachers and teachers could appeal to Exodus 1:8–22 in at least two other ways. First, they could point to this story as an example of how God worked to preserve His people and accomplish His will in the face of sinful attacks. Whether it is the midwives in Egypt (Exodus 1:8-22), the remnant in exile (Jeremiah 29:10–14), or Jesus's escape from the Bethlehem massacre (Matthew 2:13–23), the Lord always fulfills His perfect will even in the midst of every plot against Him and His people.

Second, this text could provide a practical example of what life looks like when God's people live in reverence to Him as opposed to fearing others. The fear of the Lord means that God is honored above all and at any cost. The approval of others or even the value of personal safety does not outweigh the importance of being completely devoted to Him alone. The midwives in Egypt clearly demonstrated this fact in their defiance of Pharaoh. Reverencing God above all else by obeying Scripture is always the believer's highest moral obligation.

6

LEADERSHIP STRENGTH, STRATEGY, AND SECURITY

~ Numbers 11:10–30 ~

Leadership is hard. This is why many people long for the titles of leadership, but they flee from the trials of leadership. They want the accolades of being leaders, but they hide from the adversities of leadership. The reality is that almost anyone can be a leader when the sun is shining, and the world is all as it should be. However, being a leader is incredibly difficult during seasons of turbulence, which are very common in life. During these times, leaders need to learn lessons about strength, strategy, and security from Numbers 11:10–30.

Context

Moses was in a familiar place in Numbers 11. He was once again within earshot of Israel's grumbling and complaining, and he was also an audience to God's just judgment (Numbers 11:1). Of course, Moses was also

41

trying to exercise compassionate patience by crying out to the Lord on behalf of His people (Numbers 11:2).

Yet, just when it seemed the Israelites had learned their lesson, another outbreak of sinful discontentment erupted (Numbers 11:4). This time the people wept about their menu selections or lack thereof. Rather than express gratitude for their freedom and for God's daily provision, the Israelites longed for the food they ate in slavery (Numbers 11:5–6). Interestingly, they described Egypt's food as free (Numbers 11:5), while they complained that all they had in the wilderness was "this manna to look at" (Numbers 11:6).

But after Numbers 11:7-9 describes what manna was like, how the Israelites prepared it for various meals, and when God provided it, Moses reentered the text in verse 10. However, he was not in a stable frame of mind. With the weeping of the Israelites still ringing in his ears, Moses had more than he could take. He vented his sense of despair to God. And in this crucible of crisis, the Lord taught Moses about leadership strength, strategy, and security.

The Illustration

The illustration of leadership strength, strategy, and security in Numbers 11 actually comes from verses 10–15 (*strength*), verses 16–17 (*strategy*), and verses 24–30 (*security*). First, Moses learned the important leadership lesson of God's strength in Numbers 11:10–15. In these verses, Moses offered a brutally honest prayer to the Lord. As he buckled under the crushing weight of his position, the all-too-familiar question of why fired out of Moses' heart and mouth like a blazing arrow into the heavens (Numbers 11:11). Suddenly, God's leader slammed into the reality of his complete inability to fulfill his calling. At the end of his prayer, Moses was ready to die. In fact, the sensitive reader can bend an ear to the pages of the Bible and hear Moses' closing words barely escape through his sobs: "I am not able to carry all this people alone; the burden is too heavy for me. If you will treat me like this, kill me at once, if I find favor in your sight, that I may not see my wretchedness" (Numbers 11:14–15).

Of course, Moses' confession of inadequacy was not a news flash to God. The Lord never relied on His servant. Instead, God called His servant to rely on Him. When God first called Moses, this truth was crystal clear (Exodus 3–4).

Second, God never intended for Moses to shoulder the full weight of his leadership responsibilities alone. This is the leadership lesson of strategy, and it surfaced twice already in Moses's life. When God first called him to lead His people, for instance, the Lord provided Aaron as a partner to complement Moses's weaknesses (Exodus 4:10–17). Also, when his father-in-law Jethro visited him in Exodus 18, he outlined a plan for Moses to enlist help from others.

So God's response to his broken and burdened servant in Numbers 11:16–17 was a practical reminder of what Moses already knew from past experiences. God simply told Moses to gather seventy men who had already demonstrated reliable service so that some of the Lord's Spirit could be distributed from Moses to them. It is clear here how God's Spirit remains the source of strength for His work. The common sense aspect of this leadership strategy is likewise obvious as the Lord explained, the elders "shall bear the burden of the people with you, so that you may not bear it yourself alone" (Numbers 11:17).

Lastly, the Lord taught His servant about leadership security. After Moses followed God's instructions and the seventy elders experienced the power of God's Spirit upon them, a potential situation developed. (As mentioned above, problems always lurk at every turn for leaders.) Two of the elders, Eldad and Medad, did not prophesy at the same location as the others (Numbers 11:26). At this point, Joshua, Moses' faithful assistant, urged Moses to silence Eldad and Medad, but Moses did not do it. He seemed to have truly embraced God's strategy because he finally rested securely in the Lord's work. In fact, Moses replied to Joshua, "Are you jealous for my sake? Would that all the Lord's people were prophets, that the Lord would put his Spirit on them!" (Numbers 11:29). Simply put: Moses realized that God's work was bigger than any one person could handle, and he understood that it would be accomplished only by the power of God's Spirit working through His people in various ways.

Suggestions for Use

A host of leadership lessons are in Numbers 11:10–30. For this reason, Numbers 11 may be one of the most important leadership chapters in the Bible. And the leadership lessons concerning strength, strategy, and security can provide useful biblical illustrations on a wide variety of other teaching texts in Scripture. For instance, any instruction on the essential need for God's people to rely on His strength for ministry finds a vivid example here. If Sunday school teachers are handling John 15:5 or 1 Thessalonians 5:24, they could easily use Numbers 11:10–15 to illustrate the biblical principle about the need for God's strength for His ministry callings.

Also, the leadership lesson on strategy in Numbers 11:16–17 is a powerful portrait of other biblical principles. For example, Paul's teaching in Ephesians 4:11–13 finds an easy link to these words. Just as God instructed Moses to select reliable leaders to serve alongside him in the work, ministry leaders have a biblical mandate to equip others for ministry. Of course, two additional notes are important to emphasize at this point. One is that God led Moses to be careful in his selection of leaders. The elders he chose were to have a track record of prior reliable service among God's people (Numbers 11:16). This text could serve to illustrate various other passages which describe different qualifications of leaders such as pastors in 1 Timothy 3:6 and deacons in 1 Timothy 3:10.

Another important point to underscore is that God's Spirit remains the essential power source for effective leadership. Even though Moses assembled a team, the reality remained that the Holy Spirit was absolutely necessary to empower each person. This biblical illustration brings to mind other texts such as Acts 1:4 where Jesus instructed His followers "to wait for the promise of the Father" because they would "receive power when the Holy Spirit [came] upon [them]" (Acts 1:8). In other words, while God's design is to assemble and use His people as a team, their confidence should be in the Lord alone, not in their team.

Finally, the leadership lesson on security is powerfully relevant to all leaders. It is interesting to note that Numbers 11:16–17 was not the first time Moses heard of God's leadership strategy. As mentioned above, Exodus 18 also showed how Moses's father-in-law Jethro had previously outlined a similar plan. This could simply be an example of how God's servants need many reminders of His principles along the way. But it could also indicate how Moses was not completely broken of his self-reliance nor secure enough in the Lord to release others into ministry service. Many leaders are ineffective and inefficient because they are insecure. They give a token nod to delegation, but they continue to micromanage others because they actually fear the successes of their team members. Their insecurity keeps them trapped under the unbearable weight of trying to do ministry alone.

All of this shows how versatile Numbers 11:24–30 is as a biblical illustration. For instance, this story could be used as a powerful example of how the apostles assembled a team to focus on the growing practical ministry needs of the early church so they could remain focused on their service in the Word and prayer (Acts 6:1–7). This passage also illustrates how one seasoned leader (Moses) used teachable moments to pass along God's practical wisdom to another young leader (Joshua). For this reason, it could be employed as a general example of any sermon or teaching lesson on discipleship (*see* 2 Timothy 2:1–2). Lastly, this story emphasizes the importance of balancing freedom and biblical guidelines in ministry. In other words, Moses released Eldad and Medad to prophesy because they were prophesying by the power of God's Spirit even though their expression of ministry differed from the other elders. The bottom line here is that as long as ministry approaches fit within the Spirit's guidance according to Scripture, leaders should grant freedom to the Lord's servants to minister in unique and creative ways. This will help delegation to be truly effective and for ministry service to flourish among the Lord's people. Another way this story could be used is as a biblical illustration for Mark 9:38–40 where Jesus told one of His disciples not to prohibit others from ministry even though they were serving in different ways.

7

Decisions Sometime Need Adjustments

~ Numbers 27:1–11 ~

Decision making is one of the critical aspects of leadership.[15] While ministry in the church is definitely team oriented, circumstances usually require an individual to make final decisions. Of course, this reality is stressful in many ways. Leaders who desire to honor Christ want to make correct decisions as they lead God's people. However, they cannot allow themselves to become paralyzed by indecision. Furthermore, leaders must understand that they will learn and grow on the job as they walk with the Lord. In light of this, a key point for leaders to keep in mind is that decisions sometime need adjustments.

---

15. Kenneth O. Gangel, *Team Leadership in Christian Ministry: Using Multiple Gifts to Build a Unified Vision* (Chicago: Moody Press, 1997), 127–145.

Context

The biblical illustration in Numbers 27:1–11 occurs toward the end of Moses's story. God taught Moses a great deal over the course of his leadership experiences. Actually, in the very next passage (Numbers 27:12–23), God chose Joshua as Moses' successor to lead the Israelites into the Promised Land. But before Moses passed from history's stage, he demonstrated how decisions sometime need adjustments.

The daughters of Zelophehad surface three times in the book of Numbers. They are first mentioned in Numbers 26:33. This verse occurs in the context of a divinely ordered census list (Numbers 26:1–4). It notes that unlike the others, Zelophehad had no sons to receive his inheritance—only five daughters: Mahlah, Noah, Hoglah, Milcah, and Tirzah (Numbers 26:33; 27:1; 36:11). The daughters of Zelophehad also appear in Numbers 27:1–11. They petition Moses here for an adjustment to the traditional laws of inheritance. As implied by the text (Numbers 27:4), the inheritance of land previously passed only from a father to his sons. However, since Zelophehad had no sons, his daughters asked to receive the land. In this way, their father's name would not fade from existence. Lastly, Zelophehad's daughters surface in the last chapter of the book of Numbers (36:1–12). The focus in this passage is on the interrelated issues of land inheritance and marriage. Basically, if land could pass to daughters because their father had no sons (Numbers 27:1–11), then a regulation must be devised to retain the land within their tribe even if they married. Numbers 36:6–7 recorded this regulation: "Let them [the daughters of Zelophehad] marry whom they think best, only they shall marry within the clan of the tribe of their father. The inheritance of the people of Israel shall not be transferred from one tribe to another, for every one of the people of Israel shall hold on to the inheritance of the tribe of his fathers."

From the above discussion, it is clear that the context for the biblical illustration in Numbers 27:1–11 is twofold. First, a textual context is within the book of Numbers. As one resource notes, "These daughters have already been mentioned (in 26:33) without an obvious reason. Now it becomes clear why they were picked out."[16] Upon first reading Numbers 26:33, it may appear that the mention of Zelophehad's daughters randomly appears; however, the later contexts of both the issues of land distribution (Numbers 27:1–11) and marriage (Numbers 36:1–12) reveal the organic unity of this text with other sections of the narrative flow of Numbers.

Second, a cultural context is within the book of Numbers. As noted above, the clear implication throughout these texts is that land was passed from fathers to sons and not from fathers to daughters. An understanding of this cultural background issue helps the reader understand the significance of these texts.

The Illustration

While the story of Zelophehad's daughters in Numbers 27:1–11 seems straightforward, some aspects of the story should be emphasized. First, Israelite culture was patriarchal in nature. Men lived and served in the dominate roles. So the request of Zelophehad's daughters was unusual, to say the least.[17] Nevertheless, they presented their petition, and nothing in the text indicates that they were wrong to do so. Clearly, God confirmed that their thoughts and concerns were justified, and He

---

16. *The English Standard Version (ESV) Study Bible* (Wheaton: Crossway Bibles, 2001), 309.

17. T. Cabal, C. O. Brand, E. R. Clendenen, P. Copan, J. Moreland, and D. Powell, eds. *The Apologetics Study Bible: Real Questions, Straight Answers, Stronger Faith* (Nashville: Holman Bible, 2007), 248, and Dennis R. Cole, *Numbers*, vol. 3B of *The New American Commentary* (Nashville: Broadman and Holman, 2000), 464–465.

directed Moses accordingly so that a precedent would be set to take care of similar situations in the future.

The above point concerning precedent actually leads to the second important aspect of this story. While the Lord had obviously provided general principles to guide His people (for example, land should remain within its respective tribe), He continued to lead His people in terms of specifics as they encountered various situations in life. And here is an unforeseen situation from a human perspective. Thus, this story provides an interesting glimpse into how God's general principles took particular shape within the trenches of life.[18] Of course, there is no implication that the Lord was unaware of future unique scenarios; rather, the idea is that God was leading His people into an ever-increasing understanding of His will. He revealed His perfect plan to them in each step of their journey.

Suggestions for Use

This scriptural story is useful for illustrating several biblical truths. First, the account primarily reveals how the general principles of Scripture can be adapted to specific situations. For example, while land typically passed from fathers to sons, the Lord affirmed that exceptions to this standard rule were periodically in order within the perimeters of His Word. For this reason, the title of this chapter is "Decisions Sometime Need Adjustments." And this is a very important point for God's people to remember. Some leaders, for instance, may hold so rigidly to the letter of the law that they miss the heart of God's law in life's trenches. One writer noted, "Moses does not reply immediately [to the request of Zelophehad's daughters] because of a lack of legal precedent

---

18. L. O. Richards, *The Bible Reader's Companion*, electronic ed. (Wheaton: Victor Books, 1991), 109, and Cole, 464.

related to the women's petition. As a quality spiritual leader, he seeks the Lord for an answer to the matter of women and land inheritance."[19] Again, the point here is not that Moses set aside God's Word in the face of this unique situation; rather, he learned how to apply God's principles more accurately within the perimeters of His Word. This aspect of the biblical illustration could serve well as a practical example of how to apply Paul's admonitions in 1 Thessalonians 5:19–22, "Do not quench the Spirit. Do not despise prophecies, but test everything; hold fast what is good. Abstain from every form of evil."

Second, as noted above, a spiritual leader will always remain sensitive to God's leadership. Moses did not prematurely respond to the request of Zelophehad's daughters. Instead, he prayed and sought the Lord's direction. In essence, he responded prayerfully as opposed to presumptuously. This facet of Numbers 27:1–11 also lends itself to illustrate how to apply Paul's charge in 1 Thessalonians 5:17 to "pray without ceasing" in a practical manner.

Third, in perhaps a secondary fashion, the story of Zelophehad's daughters reveals how God has a plan for His people. He has a place for everyone, both men and women, within His plan. While the Lord obviously had a role for men in terms of their leadership within the ranks of His people, He used women within His plan as well.

For example, it was Zelophehad's daughters who approached Moses about this unique situation and not vice versa. However, this very point emphasizes how these women were acknowledging the God-ordained leadership roles of Moses and others.[20] So there is a biblical balance evident in this text: Moses and other men functioned within their roles of spiritual leadership, and Zelophehad's daughters confidently acted as members of God's people to present their request humbly before the

---

19. Cole, 465.
20. Ibid.

Lord and respectfully to His leaders. Again, while this point may be secondary in nature, it is useful in connection with texts like Galatians 3:28, "There is neither Jew nor Greek, there is neither slave nor free, there is neither male nor female, for you are all one in Christ Jesus." As Paul taught on the general equality between men and women in Christ, the story of Zelophehad's daughters shows how the Lord has always related to men and women with equality within their divinely ordained roles.

8

SOME CONSEQUENCES ARE PERMANENT

~ Deuteronomy 3:23–29 ~

The story of a man who regretted jumping from a ten-story building underscores how some consequences are permanent. As he plummeted to his certain death below, he cried out to the Lord at the midpoint of his fall: "God, please forgive me for jumping from this building!" In an instant he heard the Lord respond: "I forgive you. Now, I'll see you in a second!"

While the above story may bring a chuckle to readers, the permanent nature of many consequences are not humorous. God does not typically suspend the laws of nature to prevent the results of foolish decisions, and He also does not usually suspend the consequences that come from violating His moral and spiritual laws. While there is complete forgiveness in Christ (Ephesians 1:7), some consequences are permanent in this life. This biblical principle is clearly evident in Deuteronomy 3:23–29.

Context

The book of Deuteronomy is basically the "second giving of the law" (*deutero*, Greek for "second" and *nomos*, Greek for "law"). However, its first three chapters essentially provide a brief overview of Israel's history from their refusal to believe God to give them the Promised Land (Deuteronomy 1:19–46) to the Lord's power to defeat King Sihon and King Og, respectively (Deuteronomy 2:26–3:11). Then, in Deuteronomy 3:21–23, Moses challenged Joshua to lead the Israelites in fearless faith as they marched forward in the conquest.

Yet, nestled between Moses' charge to Joshua (Deuteronomy 3:21–22) and his formal second giving of the law (Deuteronomy 4:14), Moses pled with God one last time for an opportunity to cross the Jordan with His people as they entered the Promised Land. But the Lord firmly refused Moses' request in Deuteronomy 3:23–29, illustrating how some consequences are permanent.

Of course, the particular sin which Moses committed that led to this permanent consequence is chronicled in Numbers 20:2–13. In this well-known story, the Israelites complained to Moses and Aaron about the lack of food and water in the wilderness (Numbers 20:3–5). So God instructed His leaders to "tell the rock before their eyes to yield its water" (Numbers 20:8). In disobedience to the Lord's clear instructions, however, Moses "struck the rock with his staff twice" (Numbers 20:11). Although God still graciously supplied water from the rock, He rebuked Moses with the following words: "Because you did not believe me, to uphold me as holy in the eyes of the people of Israel, therefore you shall not bring this assembly into the land that I have given them" (Numbers 20:12).

This was the consequence Moses asked the Lord to repeal in Deuteronomy 3:23–29. However, from God's response to Moses' request, it was clear that He would not remove His imposed consequence. The reality Moses learned on this occasion was that some consequences are permanent.

The Illustration

Some scholars note how although the Lord already told Moses that he would not enter the Promised Land (Numbers 20:12), perhaps Moses thought God might adjust His consequence in light of the defeat of King Sihon and King Og.[21] But this was simply not the case. In fact, Deuteronomy 3:26 furnishes God's sharp reply to Moses in the following words: "Enough from you; do not speak to me of this matter again." While the Lord allowed Moses to catch a glimpse of the Promised Land from Pisgah, He held firmly to His previous consequence, forbidding Moses to enter the land of Canaan with the rest of the Israelites (Deuteronomy 3:27–29).

The clear implication from this text is that some consequences are permanent. Of course, this statement signals that others are not. For example, in Numbers 12, the story is recounted how Aaron and Miriam criticized Moses, and the Lord rebuked them (Numbers 12:1–9). Yet, Miriam's consequences went even further; she was inflicted with leprosy (Numbers 12:10). But after Aaron pled with Moses for mercy, Moses interceded with the Lord on Miriam's behalf, and God eventually removed the leprosy (Numbers 12:11–15).

But a temporary consequence was not in view for Moses. God's consequence for him on this particular occasion was permanent in this life. The straightforward flow of thought is that Moses sinned, God disciplined him, and the ultimate ramification of the Lord's chastisement was not negotiable.

Suggestions for Use

The story of how God dealt with Moses in this specific situation is useful as a biblical illustration on several fronts. First, this story should

---

21. Jack S. Deere, "Deuteronomy," in *The Bible Knowledge Commentary: An Exposition of the* Scriptures *by Dallas Seminary Faculty: Old Testament*, ed. by John F. Walvoord and Roy B. Zuck (Wheaton: Victor Books, 1985), 268.

not be misused as an Old Testament example that calls the security of the believer into question. The New Testament is clear that salvation is eternally secure for those who truly receive it in the first place (John 10:27–29; Ephesians 1:13–14; 1 John 2:19). This event does not indicate anything about Moses' eternal relationship with God. Rather, it describes a consequence from God for Moses's earthly life.

Second, this story shows the biblical balance between God's grace and His chastisement in the lives of His people. While some may falsely consider the ideas of discipline and mercy as mutually exclusive, such a view has no biblical support. In fact, the writer of Hebrews actually argued the exact opposite point. Hebrews 12:4–11 quoted from the Old Testament to show how the Lord's discipline demonstrates His love and acceptance for His children. Biblically, God's grace is the greatest call to godliness that exists. This means that the Lord compassionately corrects His sons and daughters when they disobey Him.

Third, this story from the life of Moses (albeit with softer edges) reveals an illustration of more severe New Testament depictions of God's firm discipline. For example, Ananias and Sapphira fall dead because of their dishonesty before the Lord in Acts 5:1–11. In light of this, believers can understand that God's consequences for sins can be severe and permanent, indeed.

While some may argue that Ananias and Sapphira were perhaps not genuine believers, Paul's words in 1 Corinthians 11:20–34 offer another case study for God's discipline. For instance, Paul plainly said in 1 Corinthians 11:29-30, "For anyone who eats and drinks without discerning the body eats and drinks judgment on himself. That is why many of you are weak and ill, and some have died." So, while some consequences are not permanent (*see* the reference to Numbers 12 above, for example), other consequences are permanent.

9

Following God

~ Joshua 3:1–17 ~

A true disciple of Christ follows Him. Jesus used the image of a shepherd and his sheep to picture how His followers need to walk in step with His lead (John 10:27). Of course, this idea of following Jesus is easier said than done. Most believers would confess this common struggle: "I want to follow Christ, but how can I be certain that I'm correctly discerning His leadership?" This is a good question, and the biblical story in Joshua 3:1–17 illustrates important principles of how God's people can follow His guide in life.

Context

At this point, the proverbial sun had set on Moses's life and leadership. So God officially designated Joshua as a new under shepherd for His people (Joshua 1:1–9). But leaders usually have to encounter major tests early in their leadership. These tests are opportunities for them to demonstrate their character and commitments to follow the Lord faithfully. Such is certainly the case with Joshua, and it occurred on the Jordan River's flooded banks.

After Joshua called the Israelites to prepare to enter the Promised Land (Joshua 1:10–18), he sent two spies to Jericho, the first city they would engage on the other side of the Jordan River (Joshua 2:1–24). Just as Moses had to cross the Red Sea after the exodus from Egypt (Exodus 14), Joshua had to cross the flooded river before the conquest of Canaan (Joshua 3). Thus, the story of crossing the Jordan is a powerful illustration of various principles for God's people to live by as they seek to follow Him.

The Illustration

Several facets of this biblical illustration deserve attention. First, the Lord commanded Joshua to place the priests with the ark of the covenant ahead of the rest of the Israelites (Joshua 3:1–4). The reason for this was plain: "Do not come near it, in order that you may know the way you should go, for you have not passed this way before" (Joshua 3:4). God's people needed to trust His sovereign omniscience as they followed Him. They had never been this way before, but the Lord knows all things.

Second, the priests were not merely to move towards the Jordan River in faith; rather, they were to stand in the Jordan River in faith (Joshua 3:7–8). In other words, the priests were to take the lead in demonstrating a trust in the Lord before the rest of the people. As they acted in bold faith by taking their stand in the Jordan ahead of the other Israelites, the Lord was going to demonstrate His power to lead His people according to His supernatural strength.

Third, God's miraculous work to deliver the Israelites through the Jordan River at its flood stage (Joshua 3:15) would encourage people in the future to trust the Lord. Again, just as the previous generation of Israelites recalled God's deliverance through the Red Sea as they faced other struggles (Psalm 106:6–15), Joshua called the next generation of Israelites to remember His deliverance through the Jordan River when they faced their future enemies during their conquest of Canaan (Joshua 3:9–10).

Fourth, the Jordan River did not part until the priests planted their feet in its waters (Joshua 3:14–17). Obviously, the Lord wanted His people to act in faith before He fulfilled His Word to them. The waters did not open before them when they remained a safe distance from the edge of the river. The waters only split when the spiritual leadership of the people proved their faith in obedient action, even before they saw the miraculous work of God displayed in their presence.

Suggestions for Use

The above facets of Joshua 3:1–17 illustrate various principles for all God's people in every age who seek to follow Him. First, even though Joshua sent out spies ahead of the people before they crossed the Jordan River (Joshua 2), the Israelites were not to trust their knowledge in any way. They were to trust in the Lord to lead them into Canaan because they had "not passed this way before" (Joshua 3:4).

This aspect of the scriptural story serves as a great complement to other texts such as Proverbs 3:5–6, "Trust in the Lord with all your heart, and do not lean on your own understanding. In all your ways acknowledge him, and he will make straight your paths." Also, James wrote in James 1:5, "If any of you lacks wisdom, let him ask God, who gives generously to all without reproach, and it will be given him." So, while believers experience life as it unfolds before them, God knows all things in His sovereign omniscience (Isaiah 46:8–11). For this reason, Christians are called to trust the wisdom of God's Word as they follow Him by faith. They do not know all things, but God does.

Second, following the Lord by faith is revealed in both words and works. Just as the priests stood in the river before it parted, believers are to act in faith. Again, James instructed Christians to ask the Lord for wisdom in faith as opposed to being double-minded (James 1:5–8). Clearly, the implication from this text (*see* James 1:21–25; 2:14–26) is that believers are to speak words of faith and live out actions of faith. While works do not save anyone (Ephesians 2:8–9), they are an outward expression of God's salvation (Ephesians 2:10). The story of how the priests stood in the waters of the river illustrates the important biblical principle of acting in faith.

Third, while following God is always about moving forward, it usually involves looking backward for encouragement. Joshua instructed the Israelites to keep this event firmly in mind as they faced future struggles during the conquest. The Lord's work in the past assures believers of His faithfulness as they face present and future challenges. The psalmist repeatedly recounted God's mighty power demonstrated in the past (Psalm 136), and this story from the book of Joshua should encourage Christians as they follow God today (Romans 15:4).

Fourth, not only does the Lord call His people to act in faith, but He is always faithful to fulfill His promises to them. After the priests placed their feet in the waters of the Jordan River, the miracle occurred. An inexplicable wall of water rose on one side of them as the waters of the river drained downstream on the other side of them (Joshua 3:16). Although God calls His people to act in faith without first seeing exactly how He will deliver them, they can rest confidently in their faith that He will fulfill His promises in His perfect ways. This is yet another important truth demonstrated in the trenches of the Lord's supernatural work to deliver His people through the flooded waters of the Jordan River.

10

DEFEAT AND DISOBEDIENCE
~ Joshua 7:2–12 ~

Life's problems are not necessarily tied to disobedience. For example, Jesus described those who obey and disobey His words as both facing troubles (Matthew 7:24–27). Furthermore, Paul wrote that "all who desire to live a godly life in Christ Jesus will be persecuted" (2 Timothy 3:12). Nevertheless, disobedience does lead to difficulties for Christians. While struggles in this life may come for obedient believers, they will certainly come for the disobedient children of God. Joshua 7:2–12 records a brief but vivid narrative of this truth.

Context

Israel's conquest of Canaan began with the fall of Jericho (Joshua 6). Actually, the entering of the Promised Land could be described as God's conquest of Canaan. This is why the story of Achan's sin in Joshua 7:2–12 proves how defeat and disobedience are bound together.

The context for the defeat that followed Achan's sin stretches back into Joshua 6:16–7:1. While Joshua instructed the Israelites to destroy Jericho and all its inhabitants (except Rahab and those in her house, Joshua 6:17), he also commanded them to "keep yourselves from the things devoted to destruction . . . all the silver and gold, and every vessel of bronze and iron, are holy to the Lord; they shall go into the treasury of the Lord" (Joshua 6:18–19). But Joshua 7:1 briefly recounts how "the people of Israel broke faith in regard to the devoted things, for Achan . . . took some of the devoted things. And the anger of the Lord burned against the people of Israel." A more detailed account of Achan's disobedience is found on his own lips in Joshua 7:20–21: "Truly I have sinned against the Lord God of Israel, and this is what I did: when I saw among the spoil a beautiful cloak from Shinar, and 200 shekels of silver, and a bar of gold weighing 50 shekels, then I coveted them and took them. And see, they are hidden in the earth inside my tent, with the silver underneath."

Although Achan's sin brought suffering and death upon himself, his household, and his possessions (Joshua 7:15, 22–26), his disobedience had even more deadly ramifications for the people of Israel (*see* "The Illustration" discussion below). And this is the thrust of the narrative of Achan's sin: Defeat is tied to disobedience. Also, the scope of Joshua's lament revealed all that was at stake in Israel's disobedience and defeat, namely, God's great name among the nations (Joshua 7:9). This is always the ultimate theological context for the overall narrative of Scripture—God's glory among all peoples.

The Illustration

Initially, readers may wonder why the fact that Achan took some of Jericho's spoils was considered sinful on this occasion. Of course, the context of the passage is critical here. It is true that the Lord allowed His people to gather spoils in other settings. For instance, the Israelites plundered the Egyptians when they were delivered from slavery (Exodus 12:33–36). Also, God allowed His people to take the plunder from Ai according to Joshua 8:2. But the key difference between these two occasions and this passage is found in their respective contexts. Because Joshua, the Lord's leader, commanded the Israelites to refrain from taking Jericho's spoils, Achan's actions were disobedient and sinful.

However, the story of Achan is interesting for another reason. As noted above, his sin had a deadly impact beyond himself. After the fall of Jericho, the Israelites continued their march on Canaan, and the next city they engaged was Ai. Unlike Jericho, Ai was small in comparison in every way. When Israel faced Jericho, the Lord directed His people to march around the city and to lift up a shout because He was going to bring down its walls supernaturally without a normal military strategy (Joshua 6:5, 16). But when the Israelite spies returned from scouting Ai, they viewed the enemy as manageable (Joshua 7:2–3). Nevertheless, God's people were routed by the men of Ai and suffered thirty-six casualties (Joshua 7:4–5). Their confidence was shaken to the core as "the hearts of the people melted and became as water" in the wake of their defeat (Joshua 7:5).

So Achan's sin led to his personal demise and to the death of his fellow Israelites. His disobedience was first cast in a corporate light when Joshua 7:1 introduced it in the following words: "The people of Israel broke faith in regard to the devoted things." Also, the last words Joshua spoke to Achan in Joshua 7:25 point to both the corporate consequences of Achan's sin and to his individual responsibility for his disobedience: "Why did you bring trouble on us? The Lord will bring trouble on you today."

But before Joshua even knew the details of the disobedience that led to Israel's defeat at Ai, he cried out to the Lord for answers (Joshua 7:6–9), and God firmly responded to him with a rebuke for His people. In short, rapid-fire statements, the Lord told Joshua, "Get up! Why have you fallen on your face? Israel has sinned. . . . Therefore the people of

Israel cannot stand before their enemies. . . . I will be with you no more, unless you destroy the devoted things from among you" (Joshua 7:10–12). In addition to the corporate nature of Achan's sin (*see* the statement, "Israel has sinned" in Joshua 7:11), another key scriptural truth in this story is that continued disobedience without genuine repentance quenches God's Spirit and brings defeat.

Suggestions for Use

The previous aspects of the story of Achan's disobedience and the defeat Israel suffered in its wake reveal several ways this biblical illustration could be used for preaching and teaching. First, if believers want to walk in ways that please God, they must be sensitive and obedient to His Word. Simply because the Lord allowed the Israelites to plunder the Egyptians and Ai, for instance, does not mean that He allowed His people to spoil their enemies every time. Similarly, believers must carefully follow God's guidance in various situations.

Second, sin always involves consequences that reach beyond the scope of human calculation. Just as the body of Christ is one body with many members, which means that one member's service positively impacts others, even so one person's sin negatively impacts others too (1 Corinthians 12:12–26).

Third, believers are never to rest confidently in their abilities; rather, they are to trust in the Lord's power to work in and through them to accomplish His purposes. Like their trust in God's power to take down the walls of Jericho, Israel was to trust the Lord to conquer every enemy, whether large or small from their human perspective. The simple fact for Christians to keep in focus is that "unless the Lord builds the house, those who build it labor in vain. Unless the Lord watches over the city, the watchman stays awake in vain" (Psalm 127:1). Jesus plainly said, "Apart from me you can do nothing" (John 15:5).

Fourth, progress cannot be made until problems have been resolved. As long as Achan hid his sin, the Lord would not bless His people with His continued presence and power. This story illustrates a general truth in the New Testament as well. For example, Jesus taught His disciples to resolve their conflicts with one another quickly because their relationships with God and their relationships with others were interlinked (Matthew 5:24). Later, in the Sermon on the Mount, Christ taught His followers how to pray, and the one aspect of His model prayer that He elaborated on was forgiveness. Jesus said in Matthew 6:14–15, "For if you forgive others their trespasses, your heavenly Father will also forgive you, but if you do not forgive others their trespasses, neither will your Father forgive your trespasses."

Of course, the issue of forgiveness in this context is not mentioned in terms of salvation. This would mean that salvation is dependent upon human works, which would violate Scripture (Ephesians 1:7; 2:8–9; Colossians 1:13–14). Rather, the issue of forgiveness here relates to Jesus's followers and their fellowship with their heavenly Father. Basically, the point is that when Christ followers are not extending forgiveness to others, they are not walking in line with their heavenly Father who lavished His forgiveness upon them in Christ. And this lack of forgiveness results in broken fellowship with their heavenly Father until they confess and repent of their sin.

The story of Achan generally relates to the above point. Trouble plagued the Lord's people as long as they broke faith with Him because of Achan's sin. In a similar way, as long as believers refuse to deal with their sins, they struggle in their broken fellowship with God.

Lastly, this aspect of the story of Achan could also serve to illustrate Paul's teaching in Ephesians 4:30, "And do not grieve the Holy Spirit of God, by whom you were sealed for the day of redemption." In other words, as long as believers try to hide their sins as Achan did in Joshua 7, they will quench God's Spirit and bring trouble upon themselves and others.

11

THE BATTLE BELONGS
TO THE LORD

~ Joshua 10:9–11 ~

Christians may sometimes be confused about the balance between God's work and their involvement in His work. In other words, believers can do nothing without Christ (John 15:5). Yet, God calls them to action (*see*, for example, Ephesians 6:10–18). Some people wonder if they should sit back and trust God to work, or if they should take action.

The answer to the above dilemma is yes. Believers are called to rest in God's power to accomplish His work because only He can truly fulfill His plans. Nevertheless, they should take action too. The above idea is not an either/or proposition; rather, it is a both/and situation. Paul struck the biblical balance in Colossians 1:28–29 where he outlined his complete commitment to action and acknowledged Christ's strength to empower him. Another example of this scriptural balance is clear in Joshua 10:9–11.

Context

The biblical illustration in Joshua 10:9–11 is a good example of the importance of context. For instance, careful readers will ask an obvious question when they read the word *them* early in Joshua 10:9: To whom does the word *them* refer? Of course, any possible confusion is clarified with a brief review of the story's context.

After the people of Israel executed punishment on Achan for his sinful disobedience (Joshua 7:22–26), they were in a position to see God defeat the city of Ai on their behalf. This is precisely what occurred in Joshua 8:1–29. Next, Joshua reviewed God's covenant with His people as they became more entrenched in the Promised Land (Joshua 8:30–35).

However, the Israelites, like all other believers, were not perfect. They constantly made mistakes, and one of their errors occurred in Joshua 9. As Canaanite rulers gathered their forces against Israel (Joshua 9:1–2), the Gibeonites concocted a deceptive plan, and it initially worked. Basically, the Gibeonites reasoned according to the well-known adage: *If you can't beat them, join them.*

The Gibeonites disguised themselves so that it appeared as if they were from a distant land who had travelled a long way to make a covenant with the Israelites (Joshua 9:3–6). And whenever the Israelites called their story into question, the Gibeonites argued that they had heard about God's great name and powerful work to deliver His people (Joshua 9:8–10). They even produced so-called evidence of the wear and tear of their long journey on their provisions (Joshua 9:11–13).

At this point, the Israelites made their mistake. Joshua 9:14 simply reads, "So the men [of Israel] took some of their provisions, but did not ask counsel from the Lord." Joshua and the leaders made a covenant with the Gibeonites (Joshua 9:15). However, a short time later, the Israelites realized their mistake. But they nevertheless honored their covenant with the Gibeonites (Joshua 9:16–27).

This is the background story that forms the context for Joshua 10:9–11. The opening verses of Joshua 10 describe how five Canaanite kings heard of Israel's military victories over Jericho and Ai, as well as their covenant with the Gibeonites. They grew concerned that Israel's forces were quickly becoming unstoppable (Joshua 10:1–4). So they made war against the Gibeonites (Joshua 10:5), which consequently drew the Israelites into battle because of their covenant commitment (Joshua 10:6–7). The Lord promised to deliver His people (Joshua 10:8), but His deliverance did not hinge on human alliances. He alone had the power to overthrow all of Israel's enemies. As on other occasions, Israel learned once more that the battle belongs to the Lord (*see* also 2 Chronicles 20:1–17).

The Illustration

Although the story in Joshua 10:9–11 is brief, it is powerful. It conveys one central point: God alone has the power to overcome every enemy. This primary thought is repeated in at least three ways in these verses.

First, as Joshua and the Israelites marched to battle, Joshua 10:10 plainly teaches how "the Lord threw them [the Canaanite kings] into a panic before Israel." The obvious emphasis is that God Himself thwarted the plans of Israel's enemies.

Second, as God's people pursued their enemies, "the Lord threw down large stones from heaven on them" (Joshua 10:11). Once again, God is described as the subject of the sentence, directly performing the action of the verb. While Israel did, in fact, chase down her enemies, God's power supernaturally worked beyond the scope of their military capabilities to accomplish victory for them.

Third, the final statement in Joshua 10:11 explicitly reiterated the above point: "There were more who died because of the hailstones than the sons of Israel killed with the sword." These words are the summary statement for the main thrust of the entire biblical illustration.

Although Israel erroneously entered into a covenant with the Gibeonites, their victory over the coalition of Canaanite kings was the result of God's power and nothing else. It is true that the king of Jerusalem feared Israel's alliance with the Gibeonites because "Gibeon was a great city, like one of the royal cities, and because it was greater than Ai, and all its men were warriors" (Joshua 10:2). However, the only One who deserved glory for Israel's victory was the Lord, not Israel and not her alliances with other powerful cities.

Suggestions for Use

The story of God's victory in Joshua 10:9–11 can be used in two primary ways. First, this narrative underscores the scriptural truth that victory belongs to the Lord. David made this point clear in Psalm 20:7 when he sang, "Some trust in chariots and some in horses, but we trust in the name of the Lord our God." Also, Jesus assured His followers in John 16:33, "In the world you will have tribulation. But take heart; I have overcome the world." Just as the Israelites were not to trust in their military alliances, believers are to rest in Christ's power because He alone is their victory over every foe.

Second, while this illustration focuses on God's power, it also paints a picture of the balance between the Lord's supernatural work and the actions of His people. In other words, Joshua and the Israelites were not completely passive in the battle described in Joshua 10:9–11. For example, they apparently launched a surprise attack after an all-night march to Gilgal (Joshua 10:9). Also, the Lord struck panic in the hearts of the enemy forces "before Israel" (Joshua 10:10) who were obviously at the scene of the battle. One commentator emphasized God's power at work while also noting Israel's participation in the following words:

> While Joshua and his force marched all night and took the Amorites by surprise (v. 9), it was Yahweh—and Yahweh alone—who

took the decisive actions against the enemies (v. 10). Every verb in this verse is singular, indicating that he alone *confused, struck, pursued*, and *struck* them. It may have been that the fighting force with Joshua (v. 7) was actually involved in this—indeed, this probably was the case, in light of the reference in verse 11 to the Israelite's swords killing people. But, here, the author has chosen to ignore this fact and to focus instead on Yahweh's direct involvement as Israel's warrior. The land and its people were Yahweh's to give, and he did so here.[22]

The above points clearly demonstrate how God's supernatural work and His invitation for His people to be involved in His work are not mutually exclusive. The Lord can certainly work without any human participation (*see*, for instance, His creation of the world in Genesis 1–2), but He often invites His people to be involved in His work to accomplish His purpose.

In light of this, Joshua 10:9–11 could serve as an excellent illustration for Psalm 127:1, which reads, "Unless the Lord builds the house, those who build it labor in vain. Unless the Lord watches over the city, the watchman stays awake in vain." God's people certainly do *labor* and *watch*, but they also realize that the Lord's power must accomplish every task. Also, as mentioned above, Paul's words in Colossians 1:28–29 point to this biblical principle: "Him we proclaim, warning everyone and teaching everyone with all wisdom, that we may present everyone mature in Christ. For this I toil, struggling with all his energy that he powerfully works within me." Paul apparently applied himself completely to God's work of personal discipleship, but he acknowledged that he did so by Christ's power. Lastly, Paul hinted at this scriptural truth in 1 Corinthians 3:6–7: "I planted, Apollos watered, but God gave the growth. So neither he who plants nor he who waters is anything,

---

22. David M. Howard Jr., *Joshua*, vol. 5 of *The New American Commentary* (Nashville: Broadman and Holman, 1998), 237.

but only God who gives the growth." Once again, the Bible emphasizes both God's power to work and His invitation to His people to participate in His work by His power. All of these passages find an appropriate biblical illustration in the story of Joshua 10:9–11, which shows that every battle belongs to the Lord.

12

FAITH AND A FLEECE

~ Judges 6:33–40 ~

Many believers confess that they want to obey God's will, but they sometimes struggle to know what it is. They cry out in earnest prayer: "Lord, show me Your will, and I will obey."

So how can Christians know God's will? Many aspects of His will are clearly presented in Scripture. There is no question about whether or not the Lord wants believers to do them. For example, Christians do not have to pray about marital fidelity. God's Word plainly commands them to refrain from adultery (Exodus 20:14). These aspects of the Lord's plan may be called universal because they apply to all believers.

However, other aspects of God's will may not be clear initially. For instance, when Christians need to make decisions about housing, should they rent or purchase a house? No verse explicitly commands, "You shall purchase a house." However, the Lord guides His people through His Word (Psalm 119:105).

In these cases, biblical principles are helpful in navigating various scenarios. For example, if believers are struggling financially, they should practice good financial stewardship, live safely within their means, and not pursue greedy ambitions (1 Timothy 6:6–10). This may mean that they purchase a smaller home with a modest mortgage for their income level, or it may mean that they seek a lower rental property in order to save money for a future home purchase. Various options underscore the point in view: Christians need to seek God's direction as supported by sound biblical principles. These aspects of God's plan may be called personal because they are different for each believer and for each circumstance.[23]

Yet, even though Christians seek to follow scriptural guidelines, they may nevertheless struggle to make decisions about determining God's will with confidence. In light of this, they may "put out a fleece" in an effort to confirm a particular course of action. This whole idea of a fleece comes from an episode in the narrative about Gideon in the book of Judges.

Context

The story of Gideon's fleece in Judges 6:33–40 is properly understood against the backdrop of both the book of Judges in general and against the beginning of the Gideon narrative in particular. First, the book of Judges could be described as a series of cycles. For example, the first chapter of Judges chronicles how Israel achieved only a partial measure of the conquest of Canaan (Judges 1:27–36). When this fact was coupled with Israel's unfaithfulness to God's covenant, a recipe for disaster resulted. Although the Lord said, "I will never break my covenant with you [the Israelites]," He continued to rebuke His people for their lack of

---

23. For another discussion of the usefulness of biblical propositions and biblical principles in seeking to discern God's will, see Charpentier, 45–52.

commitment to Him with the following words: "But you have not obeyed my voice. What is this you have done? So now I say, I will not drive them [the Canaanite nations] out before you, but they shall become thorns in your sides, and their gods shall be a snare to you" (Judges 2:2–3). Thus, after Joshua died, "there arose another generation after them [Joshua and his generation] who did not know the Lord or the work that he had done for Israel" (Judges 2:10). The new generation "did what was evil in the sight of the Lord and served the Baals" (Judges 2:11).

This climate of spiritual infidelity led to the cycles of disobedience, discipline, and deliverance described throughout the book of Judges. Basically, when Israel sinned, God used the remaining Canaanite nations to oppress them. In their distress, the Lord's people would cry out for help, and God would raise up a judge[24] to deliver them. However, Israel's obedience in the wake of their deliverance was short-lived, meaning that the previous cycle was repeated in a relatively brief period of time (Judges 2:11–3:6).

In addition to the general background of Judges outlined above, the beginning of the Gideon narrative is crucial for understanding the illustration in Judges 6:33–40. The story of Gideon began with God's

---

24. Because the basic meaning of the word *judge* in contemporary culture is different from the way the word is used in Scripture in the book of Judges, it is important to briefly explain the title's meaning in the context of the book of Judges. One commentator wrote on this point, "The title [Judge] is appropriate as long as the English concept of legal arbitration is expanded to general administrative authority including military deliverance from Israel's enemies. . . . The Hebrew word [translated 'Judge'] has a wider connotation than the English word 'judge.' It was a general term for leadership combining the executive (including military) and judicial aspects of governing. Thus the judges of Israel were primarily military and civil leaders, with strictly judicial functions included as appropriate (cf. [Judges] 4:5)." F. Duane Lindsay, "Judges," in *The Bible Knowledge Commentary: An Exposition of the Scriptures by Dallas Seminary Faculty: Old Testament*, ed. by John F. Walvoord and Roy B. Zuck (Wheaton: Victor Books, 1985), 372, 374.

call on his life to serve as one of Israel's judges. In Judges 6, a new cycle developed in the book. Here the reader finds that "the people of Israel did what was evil in the sight of the Lord, and the Lord gave them into the hand of Midian seven years" (Judges 6:1). The specific way that the Israelites were oppressed during this period is described in Judges 6:2–6. In these verses, the reader learns how God's people retreated to "the mountains and the caves and the strongholds" (Judges 6:2). Every time they planted their crops, "the Midianites and the Amalekites and the people of the East would come up against them" (Judges 6:3) and "devour the produce of the land" (Judges 6:4). For a predominantly agricultural society, such oppression was devastating since the Israelite oppressors "would come like locusts in number—both they and their camels could not be counted—so that they laid waste the land as they came in" (Judges 6:5). However, the oppression by the Midianites ushered in the next phase of the cycle because "Israel was brought very low because of Midian. And the people of Israel cried out for help to the Lord" (Judges 6:6).

After the Lord rebuked His people through a prophet (Judges 6:7–10), He called a judge to deliver them. This judge's name was Gideon, and one of his early encounters with the Lord is the focus of the illustration in Judges 6:33–40.

The Illustration

Gideon is first seen in his narrative as "beating out wheat in the winepress to hide it from the Midianites" (Judges 6:11). Of course, this scene is understandable in light of the background provided above, namely, that the Midianite oppression against Israel primarily centered on the plundering of Israelite produce.

While this scene is somewhat expected because of the backdrop sketched in Judges 6:1–6, the way Gideon is described is surprising in light of the rest of the narrative. For example, although Gideon is referred to as "O mighty man of valor" (Judges 6:12), he does not evidence much valor. First, Gideon was doing what any other average Israelite would do during this period of Midianite oppression—hiding his produce from being plundered as opposed to leading a valiant charge against the enemy (Judges 6:11). His initial response to God's call was a questioning of the reality of the Lord's power among the Israelites of his day (Judges 6:13). Furthermore, his personal assessment of his role in delivering Israel was cloaked in thick doubt: "Please, Lord, how can I save Israel? Behold, my clan is the weakest in Manasseh, and I am the least in my father's house" (Judges 6:15). Basically, Gideon declared that he was the least of the weakest in Israel!

However, Gideon's assessment of himself was simply that—a self-assessment. The Lord was not focused on Gideon's power and ability. God was and always is focused on His own power. For instance, before Gideon was addressed as "O mighty man of valor," the "angel of the Lord" said, "The Lord is with you" (Judges 6:11). And when the Lord gave Gideon the message to "go in this might of yours and save Israel from the hand of Midian," His question was, "Do not I send you?" (Judges 6:14). God's question showed that Gideon's might to save Israel was not in his going but in the Lord's sending. And just as Gideon's call began with a promise of God's presence, the Lord concluded His call to Gideon with the words: "I will be with you, and you shall strike the Midianites as one man" (Judges 6:16). Again, the Lord's emphasis on the power necessary to accomplish His work focused on the promise of His presence.

After Gideon sought to confirm the Lord's call on his life (Judges 6:19–24), he appeared to act with a measure of courageous obedience (Judges 6:25–26). Yet, fear still figured predominantly on the landscape of Gideon's life. For example, his nighttime act of boldness was because "he was too afraid of his family and the men of the town to do it [destroy the altar of Baal and the Asherah] by day, [so] he did it by night" (Judges 6:27). And after he avoided death at the hands of his own people (Judges 6:28–32), the story of Gideon's faith and a fleece took center stage in his narrative.

Once Gideon heard God's call (Judges 6:11–24) and responded in obedience (Judges 6:25–32), he started to serve as an official leader or judge of the Israelites. He gathered people together under his leadership to deal with the Midianite oppression (Judges 6:33–35). Yet, Gideon continued to wrestle with doubt. This is signaled in the opening words of his petition to the Lord: "If you will save Israel by my hand, as you have said, behold, I am laying a fleece of wool on the threshing floor. If there is dew on the fleece alone, and it is dry on all the ground, then I shall know that you will save Israel by my hand, as you have said" (Judges 6:36–37).

A very telling aspect of Gideon's words is the fact that he mentioned twice "as you [God] have said" (Judges 6:36–37) in his petition to the Lord. In other words, the careful reader must wonder why God's word was not sufficient enough for Gideon. Why did he feel he needed a sign in addition to the Lord's clear word on the matter? It seems the obvious reason was Gideon's nagging doubt. This appears to be confirmed when even after God graciously answered Gideon's first request for a sign with the fleece, he asked for another sign involving the fleece (Judges 6:39–40).

Of course, a key question is whether or not Gideon had any faith as indicated by his double petition for a sign even after God had clearly spoken His word. This question reveals how Judges 6:33–40 can be useful for pastors and teachers as a biblical illustration.

Suggestions for Use

The story of Gideon's faith and fleece illustrates three key aspects of how believers can discern God's will. First, the issues of faith and/or doubt are powerfully expressed in this brief narrative. For example, if an expositor or teacher is dealing with how Christians wrestle with faith and doubt, Gideon's story is a vivid picture of this struggle. Like the man who desperately approached Jesus on behalf of his son with the words, "I believe; help my unbelief" (Mark 9:17–27), believers often wrestle with the tug-of-war between faith and doubt too. For this reason, the words of James are particularly relevant and practical: "If any of you lacks wisdom, let him ask God, who gives generously to all without reproach, and it will be given him. But let him ask in faith, with no doubting, for the one who doubts is like a wave of the sea that is driven and tossed by the wind. For that person must not suppose that he will receive anything from the Lord; he is a double-minded man, unstable in all his ways" (James 1:5–8). Here James urged believers to ask God for wisdom and to respond in obedient faith. In other words, Christians who ask the Lord for wisdom are obviously exercising faith in prayer, but they still war against doubt in practical obedience. This is pictured in the story of Gideon, and it is relevant to believers in every age.

Second, the story of Gideon illustrates the important role prayer plays when seeking to overcome doubt's relentless bludgeoning. Simply put: When Gideon came to the crossroads of action, he sought confirmation for the Lord's direction in prayer. While doubt was clearly a part of his motivation to pray, his prayerfulness serves as a good example for believers. Christians are tempted to prayerlessness as they battle with doubts. Paul plainly admonished believers with a call to prayer in the following words: "Do not be anxious about anything, but in everything by prayer and supplication with thanksgiving let your requests be made known to God" (Philippians 4:6). Also, he issued a succinct command for continued prayerfulness in 1 Thessalonians 5:17, "Pray without ceasing." Again, although Gideon's prayerfulness may have been motivated by the less than virtuous reason of doubt, it nevertheless reminds Christians that they should always posture themselves firmly at the feet of Christ's throne in prayerfulness, especially when their hearts are being tossed about by the winds of doubt assailing them.

Third, perhaps the greatest criticism that could be leveled against Gideon in this story is that while he clearly understood God's word on the matter at hand, he still asked for a sign of confirmation. This is precisely where believers must be careful in using his story as an illustration. Obviously, Christians should rest in faith upon the solid foundation of God's Word alone when seeking to follow the Lord's will. The bottom line is that Scripture is sufficient in and of itself to provide all the reasons believers need to obey God's call. Yet, the reality is that Christians desire confirmation that aligns with God's Word in order to affirm whether or not they have correctly discerned the Lord's guidance.

In light of the above point, it is helpful for believers to remember the distinction between the two aspects of the Lord's will mentioned earlier, namely, His universal and personal will. Gideon's story may be considered a negative example in terms of discussing God's universal will. In other words, in matters where God's Word is crystal clear, no fleece or sign of confirmation is needed. God's Word is sufficient in and of itself.

But Gideon's story may simultaneously be a positive example when trying to ascertain God's personal will. In other words, when there is no clear teaching of Scripture related to a particular issue, believers could follow Gideon's pattern of prayerfulness in seeking a sign of confirmation that aligns with biblical principles. Of course, the last phrase of the previous sentence is crucial to keep in focus. Any sign or fleece should be one that squares with the general guidelines of Scripture. God will never lead His children in a way that violates His Word in any shape or form.

13

Victimized by Victory

~ Judges 8:22–27 ~

A nyone familiar with sports understands that many athletes or teams face their greatest challenges after a victory, not after a defeat. Handling success is difficult. The deepest valleys follow the highest mountain peaks.

Of course, the above point does not apply to sports alone. It surfaces in every area of life. The narrative account of how both Gideon and the Israelites struggled with false worship on the heels of God's great victory is evidence of this reality.

Context

The story of Gideon spans three chapters of the book of Judges (Judge 6–8). The Lord's call to Gideon is the primary focus of Judges 6, and Gideon's defeat of Israel's oppressors, the subsequent demise of God's people, and Gideon's death are the primary focuses of Judges 7–8. Thus, the Gideon narrative in Judges 6–8 is similar to the rest of the storyline of the book of Judges. These chapters depict both the peak of spiritual victory as well as the pit of spiritual vice. As the title of this illustration signals, Judges 8:22–27 describes how Israel ironically became victimized by their victory.

After Gideon (also called Jerubbaal at various places in Scripture, *see* Judges 6:32; 7:1; 8:29; 9:1; 1 Samuel 12:11) received confirmation from the Lord by wrestling through the issue of his faith with a fleece (Judges 6:36–40), he set himself and others to be a part of God's plan to deliver Israel from her oppressors. However, the number of men (apparently 32,000, *see* Judges 7:3) Gideon enlisted to fight with him were too many from God's perspective. The Lord's reason for reducing the size of Gideon's army was plain: "The people with you are too many for me to give the Midianites into their hand, lest Israel boast over me, saying, 'My own hand has saved me'" (Judges 7:2).

Yet, even after a mass dismissal of 22,000 of Gideon's 32,000 soldiers, the Lord said, "The people are still too many" (Judges 7:4). So He led Gideon through a process to send even more soldiers away from the front lines of battle (Judges 7:4–7). When God's process was completed, Gideon had 300 soldiers left, and the Lord said, "With the 300 men . . . I will save you and give the Midianites into your hand" (Judges 7:7). Of course, the gradual reduction of Gideon's army from 32,000 to 300 (less than 1 percent of its original size) postured God's people to understand His spiritual point. He alone would deliver Israel from her enemies as opposed to them being delivered by the power of their own hands (Judges 7:2).

In Judges 7:9–18, God gave Gideon confirmation of victory before the battle began. The rest of the narrative prior to the illustration in focus (Judges 8:22–27) chronicles how the Lord accomplished a great victory for His people over their oppressors (Judges 7:19–8:21) and over others who did not show support for them as they engaged in battle (Judges 8:4–9, 13–17).

So the background for Judges 8:22–27 is a story of great spiritual victory. Israel learned to trust God's power to rescue her as opposed to the strength of her own hands. Of course, this is a lesson she had to relearn repeatedly throughout her turbulent history. In fact, the very next aspect of Gideon's story reveals how quickly the Israelites forgot God. They abandoned their devotion to Him alone and became victimized by their victory.

The Illustration

The scriptural story in Judges 8:22–27 occurred in the immediate wake of Israel's victory over their Midianite oppressors. With their deliverance secured by God under Gideon's leadership, "the men of Israel said to Gideon, 'Rule over us, you and your son and your grandson also, for you saved us from the hand of Midian' " (Judges 8:22). The careful reader might already sense how Israel began to waver in their spiritual footing. Their reference to Gideon as the one who saved them from oppression signals an alarm. To his credit, Gideon initially seemed to reject this offer of a more permanent position of leadership when he replied: "I will not rule over you, and my son will not rule over you; the Lord will rule over you" (Judges 8:23). Here Gideon attempted to refocus the Israelites on God since He alone gave them victory over their enemies.

But while Gideon did not become a permanent ruler for the Lord's people, he did make one request. He collected some of the spoils of battle from the Israelites (Judges 8:24–26) and crafted an ephod from the treasures (Judges 8:27). This seemingly benign act spelled the beginning of Israel's next cycle back into sinful disobedience. Judges 8:27 explains that "all Israel whored after it [Gideon's ephod] there, and it became a snare to Gideon and to his family."

Although commentators speculate about the exact nature and use of Gideon's ephod,[25] the Bible is clear that the Israelites engaged in spiritual infidelity in connection with it. In this bizarre way, the spoils of spiritual and military victory became the objects of spiritual vice and covenantal unfaithfulness. Gideon and the Israelites were victimized by their victory.

Suggestions for Use

The story of how Gideon and the Israelites were victimized by their victory could be used to illustrate two primary biblical truths: First, both the Old Testament and the New Testament teach that pride is the precursor to sin. For instance, Proverbs 16:18 reads, "Pride goes before destruction, and a haughty spirit before a fall." While it appears that the Israelites almost immediately moved away from giving God the glory for their deliverance over the Midianites (*see* comments above in relation to Judges 8:22), others seem to think that Gideon too was on the same path of spiritual waywardness.[26] Regardless of Gideon's initial motives in collecting some spoils of battle and his crafting of the ephod, the end result was sin. This story could then serve to illustrate how victory can lead to pride, which oftentimes leads to defeat.

Also, as mentioned above, the New Testament teaches about the dangers of pride. For example, when Paul outlined the qualifications of an overseer in 1 Timothy 3:1–7, he warned that "he must not be a recent convert, or he may become puffed up with conceit and fall into the condemnation of the devil" (1 Timothy 3:6). Pride is the prelude to

---

25. See for example, Lindsey, 396, and Daniel I. Block, *Judges, Ruth*, vol. 6 of *The New American Commentary* (Nashville: Broadman and Holman, 1999), 300.

26. Block, 298–299.

problems for leaders. And, again, the story of Gideon's ephod is a historical example of how victory can lead to victimization if human pride is not kept under the control of God's Spirit. Leaders and all Christians should remember, "God opposes the proud but gives grace to the humble" (1 Peter 5:5).

The second scriptural principle which the story of Gideon's ephod in Judges 8:22–27 illustrates centers on how victory, perhaps even more than defeat, can be difficult to manage in spiritually healthy ways. Once more both the Old and New Testaments speak about this important truth. For instance, after the writer of 2 Chronicles overviews King Uzziah's accomplishments, 2 Chronicles 26:16 reads, "But when he was strong, he grew proud, to his destruction." It is painfully apparent from this text that mishandled success can lead to struggles. Also, Paul came to a deeper understanding of this biblical principle as he wrestled with pride in light of God's great revelations to him (2 Corinthians 12:1–8). The message he embraced from the Lord was straightforward: "'My grace is sufficient for you, for my power is made perfect in weakness.' Therefore, I will boast all the more gladly of my weaknesses, so that the power of Christ may rest upon me. For the sake of Christ, then, I am content with weaknesses, insults, hardships, persecutions, and calamities. For when I am weak, then I am strong" (2 Corinthians 12:9–10). Scripture is clear that weaknesses more than anything else posture believers to depend upon the Lord's all-sufficient grace. Christians often run the risk of delving into pride and encountering its destructive consequences whenever they experience victory but lose sight of the Lord Jesus who ultimately brought about the victory. One writer summarizes how Gideon's ephod and the resulting sin attached to it illustrate a couple of New Testament principles along this line when he writes:

There is no doubting that God had given Gideon direct guidance in the past, but he was not to be an ongoing channel for it. Sadly he seemed to let the people's gratitude affect him so that he thought of himself "more highly than [he] ought" (Rom. 12:3). . . . The end result was that the ephod was put on display and people began to worship it (v. 27). The man who led them out of oppression drew them back into idolatry. . . . We are at our most vulnerable to spiritual defeat when we have seen blessing and success. There is a danger that we can enjoy the attention people give us, and allow pride to creep in so that we put our focus on ourselves rather than on the Lord. The New Testament warns that "if you think you are standing firm, be careful that you don't fall" (1 Cor. 10:12).[27]

As indicated in the previous discussion and in the above quote, the story of Gideon, his ephod, and the sinful actions which swirled around it all point to the fact that believers can unfortunately be victimized by victory if they are not careful to focus on Christ who alone overcame the world (John 16:33).

---

27. Simon J. Robinson, *Opening Up Judges*, in *Opening Up Commentary* (Leominster, United Kingdom: Day One Publications, 2006), 50.

14

Living Better Rather than Bitter

~ Judges 11:1–33 ~

Everyone experiences pain in life (Job 5:7). It has been often said that every Christian is either in a storm, coming out of a storm, or heading into a storm. A saying like this is not an expression of pessimism; rather, it is a statement of reality. So a couple of major questions a believer must ask when he or she faces trials are: *How will I respond when I face inevitable struggles in life? Will I become bitter, or will I become better—more like Christ?* These are questions Jephthah had to answer in Judges 11:1–33.

Context

Since the book of Judges chronicles cycles of disobedience, discipline, and deliverance, the background for the story of Jephthah in Judges 11:1–33 actually begins in Judges 10. After a fairly extensive recounting of the sinfully tragic life of Abimelech, a son of Gideon or Jerubbaal (Judges 9) and a couple of thumbnail sketches of Israel's next two judges, Tola (Judges 10:1–2) and Jair (Judges 10:3–5), another cycle is introduced in Judges 10:6–18.

In typical fashion for the narrative flow of the book, Judges 10:6 reveals, "The people of Israel again did what was evil in the sight of the Lord." In response to the disobedience of His people, the Lord disciplined Israel as described in Judges 10:7–8, "So the anger of the Lord was kindled against Israel, and he sold them into the hand of the Philistines and into the hand of the Ammonites, and they crushed and oppressed the people of Israel that year." But this was only the beginning of God's discipline. Judges 10:9 paints a picture of the Lord's people after eighteen years of oppression: "Israel was severely distressed."

As they writhed in pain at this low point, the Israelites cried out to God for help (Judges 10:10). Although the Lord's initial response was a sharp rebuke to His people for their repeated covenantal infidelity despite His persistent protection (Judges 10:11–14), Israel still begged for mercy and repented (Judges 10:15–16). Nevertheless, the ominous clouds of conflict gathered again on the horizon for God's people (Judges 10:17) as they waited and wondered with the words: "Who is the man who will begin to fight against the Ammonites?" (Judges 10:18).

God is always faithful. Even in the most desperate times, He fulfills His perfect plan for His people. Judges 11:1–33 is yet another confirmation of this truth in the trenches of Israel's history. Actually, the narrative of Jephthah given in Judges 11 is like a story within the story of the book of Judges. It is a subplot that develops in the book's overall storyline. Just as the people of Israel as a whole experienced God's redemption once again, Jephthah personally experienced the Lord's restoration in his personal life. He moved from being an outcast to being a pivotal instrument in God's plan of deliverance, and through this process, he learned how to live better rather than bitter.

The Illustration

When Jephthah is introduced in Judges 11:1–2, his struggles immediately erupt to the surface of his story. While he is called "a mighty warrior," he is also described as "the son of a prostitute" (Judges 11:1). Obviously, a shadow shrouded Jephthah's life from its beginning which almost totally eclipsed any hope of a normal life for him. His half brothers "drove Jephthah out and said to him, 'You shall not have an inheritance in our father's house, for you are the son of another woman'" (Judges 11:2). At this point, Jephthah "fled from his brothers and lived in the land of Tob, and worthless fellows collected around Jephthah and went out with him" (Judges 11:1–3).

To the casual reader of Scripture, Jephthah's story may seem hopeless. He had no past he could be proud of, no family he found comfort in, and no prospects for wholesome companionships in the future. However, a ray of light burst through the dark skies of the stormy beginning of Jephthah's story. For example, the land to which Jephthah fled was called *Tob*—a Hebrew word meaning "good." And the situation he found himself in, although incredibly difficult, was the perfect crucible in which to forge the strength of "a mighty warrior" (*see* Judges 11:1). Thus, from God's perspective, the place to which Jephthah fled was not a bad place but a good place, even though he was driven there because of painful rejection. Furthermore, Jephthah learned to fend for himself because his family certainly did not support him. They were the very ones who rejected him in the first place.

Yet, it is precisely at this junction in his story that Jephthah was confronted with the choice of living bitter or better. An interesting exchange took place in Judges 11:4–12. With the oppression of the Ammonites in full force against the Israelites (Judges 11:4), God's people looked for a leader. And they turned to Jephthah for help.

With a little imagination, the reader could envision Jephthah as he worked through sword drills with one of his worthless fellows when he heard the rumbling of hoofs behind him. As he turned and narrowed his eyes to see who approached his forsaken hideout, he was surprised with a greeting from the elders of his people back home. But their request felt like a dagger thrust in his already wounded soul. Perhaps his heart had been partially deadened over the years by his efforts to forget his painful past. But he could not run away from his past anymore than he could run away from himself. It was who and what Jephthah had become.

Judges 11:6 captured the straightforward request of the elders to Jephthah: "Come and be our leader." One could easily imagine the scowl that must have formed on Jephthah's face as he heard this request. Surely a thousand questions must have rushed through his mind: *You want me to come to your rescue? Where were you when I was driven from my family and my homeland? Where were you when I was trying to survive on my own? Why should I come to help you when you're in trouble, but you never helped me when I was in trouble?* The reality is that all these questions seem embedded in the reply Jephthah fired back at the Israelite leaders: "Did you not hate me and drive me out of my father's house? Why have you come to me now when you are in distress?" (Judges 11:7).

Any reader can feel Jephthah's pain and anger seep through his words. In fact, probably few readers would sympathize with the elders. Their sympathy would fall completely on the side of Jephthah in this situation. Yet, Jephthah still had a choice to make: He could live bitter, or he could live better. He could choose to turn inward, focus on his pain, and shut the door on the opportunity God gave him to be a part of His plan to rescue His people. Or, he could understand that the strength and skills the Lord cultivated in his life, even in the crucible of his rejection and suffering, were placed there for a greater purpose—to be used in God's plan. And after he and the elders further discussed the arrangements for his return and future leadership role among the Lord's people (Judges 11:8–10), "Jephthah went with the elders of Gilead, and the people made him head and leader over them" (Judges 11:11).

Now, although the Lord forged Jephthah into a mighty warrior in the fires of his struggles, the Scripture is clear that Jephthah was not able to deliver God's people by the strength of his own sword. After a failed diplomatic attempt to avoid conflict with the Ammonites (Judges 11:12–28), Jephthah engaged his enemy in battle, but the Scripture emphasizes that "the Spirit of the Lord was upon Jephthah" as he marched forward into conflict (Judges 11:29). God's Spirit strengthened Jephthah in his war efforts, and a great victory was accomplished (Judges 11:32–33) as "the Ammonites were subdued before the people of Israel" (Judges 11:33). Thus, Jephthah moved from being rejected by men to being used by God to rescue His people. He did not allow his pain to paralyze him in bitterness. Instead, he learned to trust the Lord to empower him to move forward into a better life—a life of being used by God for His purposes. He also waged war in the power of the Spirit. Basically, the major lessons from the subplot of Jephthah's life could be summarized in three ways: He let trouble train him; he didn't let pain paralyze him; and he let the Spirit of God strengthen him.

Suggestions for Use

The story of Jephthah is filled with rich insights for believers today. It easily lends itself as an illustration of several biblical truths. First, God uses the pains of life for His purposes. Romans 8:28 teaches that "we know that for those who love God all things work together for good, for those who are called according to his purpose." Just as Jephthah learned to survive on his own as he struggled through the pain of his rejection, he also learned important fighting skills that served a great purpose later in God's plan. This point from Jephthah's story illustrates how the Lord uses even the pains of life to prepare His people for usefulness in His plans.

Second, struggles are good, even when a human perspective cannot make any sense of them. Jesus predicted to Peter before his threefold denial: "Simon, Simon, behold, Satan demanded to have you, that he might sift you like wheat, but I have prayed for you that your faith may not fail. And when you have turned again, strengthen your brothers" (Luke 22:31–32). Of course, after Peter denied Jesus, the Scripture says, "He [Peter] went out and wept bitterly" (Luke 22:62). The period of Peter's weeping was obviously a painful time and one in which he contemplated a complete rejection of following Christ because of his failures (John 21:1–3). But Jesus had a plan for Peter, and the place of Peter's brokenness was a good place, just as the place of Jephthah's painful rejection was a good place from God's perspective because of His plan. So, after Jesus restored Peter to Himself (John 21:4–19), the Lord used him to preach the inaugural message of the church in Acts 2. Christ cultivated humility in Peter's life so that he could move from the boastful, self-reliant Peter of Luke 22 to the Spirit-dependant Peter of Acts 2. The place of bitter weeping between these two points on God's pathway for Peter shows that pain is oftentimes a good place from God's perspective even though human eyes fail to see it. And this is not only true for Jephthah and Peter; it is true for every child of God.

Third, believers can choose to live life bitter or better. Since this world is fallen because of sin (Romans 5:12–21), opportunities always abound for bitterness to take root in human hearts. In this life, people hurt others, and people get hurt themselves. This is why living in forgiveness and the power and fruit of the Spirit are so crucial. For example, Paul wrote in Ephesians 4:31–32, "Let all bitterness and wrath and anger and clamor and slander be put away from you, along with all malice. Be kind to one another, tenderhearted, forgiving one another, as God in Christ forgave you."

The story of Jephthah illustrates what it looks like to live this truth in the trenches of life. From a natural, human perspective, he had every right to seethe in bitterness and to turn a deaf ear to the cries of his people for help. He could have been passive in his bitterness. But Jephthah chose to live better rather than bitter. This is a choice all believers have to make by the power of God's Spirit when they face painful hurts in life.

Fourth, the power of the Holy Spirit is necessary to walk in spiritual victory. While Jephthah did grow in his skills as a mighty warrior and he did engage Israel's enemy in battle, the Scripture is clear that "the Spirit of the Lord was upon Jephthah" (Judges 11:29). The true hero in the story of Jephthah is the true hero in every story of the Bible—God. Apart from the power of God's Spirit at work in and through the lives of His servants, there is no hope for victory on any front. For instance, Jesus spoke to His followers in John 15:5, "I am the vine; you are the branches. Whoever abides in me and I in him, he it is that bears much fruit, for apart from me you can do nothing."

Simply put: There is no victory apart from the power of God's Holy Spirit. As it has been said about other key doctrinal themes, this truth is like a thread woven throughout the entire fabric of Scripture. It is taught and illustrated at numerous points in Scripture, like in the story of Jephthah. While human strength will always have its limits, the power of God's indwelling Spirit in the hearts and lives of believers produces His fruit of love, which enables them to live better rather than bitter.

15

A Test for Boldness

~ 1 Samuel 3:1–21 ~

At some point, usually early in their ministries, leaders will encounter tests of their boldness. These tests often center on whether leaders will live in the fear of man or in the fear of God. Such was the case for young Samuel early in his life.

Context

With the book of 1 Samuel, the storyline of Israel moves from the period of the judges to the period of the monarchy. Samuel was an important seam in this transition. He functioned among God's people as the last judge (1 Samuel 7:3–17).

Although Samuel's sons were technically named judges as well (1 Samuel 8:1–3), they "did not walk in his ways but turned aside after gain" (1 Samuel 8:3). So they should not be viewed as judges over

Israel like the figures so identified in the book of Judges, along with Samuel himself.

Of course, while the biblical illustration in 1 Samuel 3:15–21 focuses on Samuel, a correct understanding of the story must involve details from the lives of both Samuel and Eli, the priest. First, the way in which Samuel came to serve the Lord at Shiloh is the thrust of 1 Samuel 1. Through a miraculous answer to Hannah's prayer, God opened her barren womb and gave her a son, Samuel (1 Samuel 1:1–20). In an act of gratitude for His gift, Hannah dedicated Samuel to the Lord's service after he was weaned (1 Samuel 1:21–28). So it was in this God-ordained fashion that Samuel came to serve the Lord at Shiloh.

After a record of Hannah's prayerful praise to the Lord (1 Samuel 2:1–10), the early narrative of 1 Samuel focuses on the disobedience of Eli, especially in relation to his ungodly sons. Although Eli served as a priest, his priestly sons did not serve faithfully. They mishandled sacrifices according to their greed (1 Samuel 2:12–17), and they acted immorally with the women who served at the Tent of Meeting (1 Samuel 2:22). Even though Eli heard from others about his sons' sins, and he mentioned the danger of their wickedness to them, "they would not listen to the voice of their father, for it was the will of the Lord to put them to death" (1 Samuel 2:25).

After it was established in 1 Samuel that Eli knew of his sons' sinful actions, the Lord's judgment upon the house of Eli was prophesied (1 Samuel 2:27–36). A nameless man of God appeared to Eli (1 Samuel 2:27) and declared, "Behold, the days are coming when I will cut off your strength and the strength of your father's house, so that there will not be an old man in your house" (1 Samuel 2:31).

However, before the Lord removed Eli and his sons, He began to establish Samuel. For example, when Hannah first left Samuel at Shiloh, the reader learns that "he worshiped the Lord there" (1 Samuel 1:28). After the record of Hannah's prayerful praise is given, the reader sees how "the boy ministered to the Lord in the presence of Eli the priest" (1 Samuel 2:11). Then the very next verse presents a sharp contrast between Samuel and the sons of Eli with the following words: "Now the sons of Eli were worthless men. They did not know the Lord" (1 Samuel 2:12), but Samuel is described as "ministering before the Lord, a boy clothed with a linen ephod" (1 Samuel 2:18). Furthermore, after Eli made an attempt to reason with his sons about their sins (1 Samuel 2:22–25), the reader learns that "the young man Samuel continued to grow both in stature and in favor with the Lord and also with man" (1 Samuel 2:26). All of these points indicate how Samuel's spiritual sensitivity heightened, while the spiritual disobedience of Eli and his sons reached a point of irrecoverable judgment.

But the beginning of 1 Samuel 3 brings the contrast between Samuel and Eli, in particular, into the sharpest focus. While "the young man Samuel was ministering to the Lord under Eli," a sad and sweeping commentary on Israel's overall spiritual decline is given: "The word of the Lord was rare in those days; there was no frequent vision" (1 Samuel 3:1). Next, the careful reader learns that although Eli's sight was dim (1 Samuel 3:2), "The lamp of God had not yet gone out, and Samuel was lying down in the temple of the Lord, where the ark of God was" (1 Samuel 3:3). It is clear from these literary clues that Eli and Samuel were moving in the opposite spiritual directions. Eli was already judged, and his spiritual perception had failed. Nevertheless, God was still at work, and He was nurturing the boy Samuel to hear His voice and to walk faithfully according to His ways.

The above general point is also underscored in God's call to Samuel. The reader understands that Samuel was learning to hear the Lord's voice (1 Samuel 3:7), and Eli, who should have had a strong spiritual sensitivity, did not immediately recognize God's call to Samuel (1 Samuel 3:1–10). Yet, once Samuel understood the Lord's voice, he faced a decision: Would he courageously speak God's message of judgment to Eli, or would he compromise the Lord's message? Basically, the biblical illustration in 1 Samuel 3:15–21 was Samuel's first test of boldness as the Lord's spokesman.

The Illustration

When God first issued a call to Samuel, He basically echoed His earlier message to Eli through the nameless man of God in 1 Samuel 2:27–36. The Lord wanted His boy servant to boldly stand before His aged priest with a message of rebuke and judgment. While Samuel's exact age was not told, the background details of the story (*see* previous discussion) indicates that he was relatively young. For instance, twice in the preceding verses Samuel is labeled a "young man" (1 Samuel 3:1, 8). So Samuel's young age could have bred fear in him as God challenged him to confront an older leader, or the hard content of God's message could have been difficult for him to deliver. Of course, Samuel may have struggled with a combination of these two points. Regardless, "Samuel was afraid to tell the vision to Eli" (1 Samuel 3:15).

But Eli was not going to take silence for an answer. He warned Samuel that if he did not disclose the Lord's full message, a severe judgment would come upon his life (1 Samuel 3:16–17). And 1 Samuel 3:18 records the grade of Samuel's first test of boldness: "So Samuel told him [Eli] everything and hid nothing from him." The Lord's boy servant passed the test by God's grace.

Of course, the above test was the first indicator of the bold life Samuel lived as God's prophet to Israel. For example, Samuel was next described in the following words: "Samuel grew, and the Lord was with him, and let none of his words fall to the ground. And all Israel from Dan to Beersheba [south to north] knew that Samuel was established as a prophet of the Lord. And the Lord appeared again at Shiloh, for the Lord revealed himself to Samuel at Shiloh by the word of the Lord" (1 Samuel 3:19–21).

Also, later events in Samuel's life are marked by his God-inspired boldness. For instance, Samuel rebuked King Saul for his disobedience (1 Samuel 15:10–31); he slaughtered the king of the Amalekites, since Saul did not do it himself (1 Samuel 15:32–33); and he anointed David to be Israel's next king even though he knew Saul could have executed him for such an act (1 Samuel 16:1–4). All these events from Samuel's life highlight not only how he passed his first test of boldness but how he continued to live a life of boldness in God's power as well.

Suggestions for Use

The story of how Samuel spoke God's message of judgment to Eli in 1 Samuel 3:15–21 illustrates various biblical principles. For example, God's servants must not live in the fear of man but in the fear of the Lord. Proverbs 29:25 warns that "the fear of man lays a snare, but whoever trusts in the Lord is safe." Paul likewise wrote, "For am I now seeking the approval of man, or of God? Or am I trying to please man? If I were still trying to please man, I would not be a servant of Christ" (Galatians 1:10). The choice between living in cowardice in the fear of man or between living in courage in the fear of the Lord will always be a test for leaders. First Samuel 3:15–21 is a powerful picture of someone who feared the Lord more than man.

Second, young men in particular may struggle with speaking God's message with boldness. Just as Samuel was likely still in his younger years when the Lord called him to rebuke Eli, God's young servants specifically will struggle with boldness as they confront those older than themselves. For instance, Timothy was a young pastor whose age apparently posed potential problems for his leadership (1 Timothy 4:12). Yet, Paul challenged Timothy to rebuke those elders who persist in sin (1 Timothy 5:20) with these solemn words: "In the presence of God and of Christ Jesus and of the elect angels I charge you to keep these rules without prejudging, doing nothing from partiality" (1 Timothy 5:21). Having boldness in rebuke is always challenging, and it is especially difficult for those who are young. But Samuel is an example of one of the Lord's young servants who passed the test for boldness.

Third, along the lines of a more general thought, God's servants should be bold in proclaiming His message even when it's not a popular one. Various aspects of the background for 1 Samuel 3:15-21 reveal how the spiritual climate in Israel was in decline. For example, some of the spiritual leaders were corrupt (1 Samuel 2:12–17). Eli lacked an adequate response to the sins of his sons (1 Samuel 2:22–25, 29). The word of the Lord and His vision were not flourishing (1 Samuel 3:1), and Eli was so spiritually insensitive that he was unable to discern immediately God's call to Samuel (1 Samuel 3:4–9). These context clues indicate that the Lord was not the priority of His people at the time.

Nevertheless, God wanted His servant to speak His Word during this dark season. Of course, Paul challenged Timothy: "I charge you in the presence of God and of Christ Jesus, who is to judge the living and the dead, and by his appearing and his kingdom: preach the word; be ready in season and out of season; reprove, rebuke, and exhort, with complete patience and teaching" (2 Timothy 4:1–2). Pastors are called to speak the truth of God's Word with boldness even in the face of spiritual rebellion. And believers in general are called to live aligned with Scripture even if the currents of corrupt contemporary culture rush against them (Matthew 5:11–16). So the story of Samuel's boldness to speak God's message in a spiritually dark season is a challenge for God's people in every age to speak and live boldly according to His truth whether it is socially acceptable or not.

16

Unfaithful Sons from a Faithful Father

~ 1 Samuel 8:1–3 ~

Parenting is not for the fainthearted. Oftentimes it is incredibly painful. Nothing is as excruciating as loving another person with your whole being, but he or she turns a deaf ear to your counsel and a hard heart to your faith and values. The reality is that while parents have a biblical mandate to teach their children God's ways (Deuteronomy 6:7; Proverbs 22:6; Ephesians 6:4), children are responsible for their choices. Sometimes they embrace the faith of their parents; other times they reject it.

But rebellious children are not always an indication of unfaithful parents. Scripture reveals that faithful fathers at times suffer the pain of having unfaithful children. Such was the case with the prophet Samuel and his sons.

Context

The background for 1 Samuel 8:1–3 is both general and specific. It is general in the sense that the first seven chapters of 1 Samuel present a picture of Samuel as a godly leader. For example, when Hannah, Samuel's mother, dedicated him to the Lord, Scripture simply says that "he worshiped the Lord there [at Shiloh]" (1 Samuel 1:28). When the sinfulness of Eli's sons were first described, Samuel's life was contrasted with their lives with the following words: "Samuel was ministering before the Lord, a boy clothed with a linen ephod" (1 Samuel 2:18). When Eli's sons refused to listen to their father's rebuke, the reader learns that "the young man Samuel," on the other hand, "continued to grow both in stature and in favor with the Lord and also with man" (1 Samuel 2:26). When Eli was described as experiencing poor eyesight in a time when "the word of the Lord was rare," "Samuel was lying down in the temple of the Lord, where the ark of God was" (1 Samuel 3:1–3). So the general context for 1 Samuel 8:1–3 is that Samuel sought to live and lead in faithfulness to the Lord.

The specific backdrop for this passage begins in the early part of 1 Samuel 7. After the Lord allowed Israel to be defeated and the Philistines to capture the ark of the covenant, He worked in a powerful way to bring the ark back among His people (1 Samuel 4:1–7:2). At this point in the narrative, the description of Samuel as an Israelite judge is emphasized. And once again, Samuel's spiritual commitment to God is highlighted in various ways.

First, Samuel called the people to repent of their idolatry (1 Samuel 7:3), and he interceded for the people (1 Samuel 7:5).

Second, Samuel offered a sacrifice to God on behalf of the people (1 Samuel 7:9), and "Samuel cried out to the Lord for Israel, and the Lord answered him" (1 Samuel 7:9). The way God answered Samuel's prayer for Israel demonstrated how he was serving as a legitimate, divinely ordained leader among the people (1 Samuel 7:10).

Third, the basic summary statement of Samuel's tenure as a judge was that "the hand of the Lord was against the Philistines all the days of Samuel" (1 Samuel 7:13). Furthermore, the reader learns in the concluding verses of 1 Samuel 7 that "Samuel judged Israel all the days of his life. And he went on a circuit year by year to Bethel, Gilgal, and Mizpah. And he judged Israel in all these places. Then he would return to Ramah, for his home was there, and there also he judged Israel. And he built there an altar to the Lord" (1 Samuel 7:15–17). Whether he was abroad or home, Samuel lived and served as God's faithful servant, and the Lord obviously used Samuel as His appointed judge for His people.

Simply put: Samuel was faithful. However, the biblical illustration in 1 Samuel 8:1–3 reveals how a faithful father can have unfaithful sons.

The Illustration

The story of Samuel's sons in 1 Samuel 8:1–3 is brief. The reader basically learns that as Samuel aged, "he made his sons judges over Israel" (1 Samuel 8:1). And, after the names of two of Samuel's sons were given (1 Samuel 8:2), a description of their spiritual unfaithfulness followed: "Yet his sons did not walk in his ways but turned aside after gain. They took bribes and perverted justice" (1 Samuel 8:3).

In light of the previous description of Samuel in the first seven chapters of the book, a marked distinction between Samuel and his sons unfortunately erupts in these verses. Although he was a ray of light shining in the darkness, his sons did not walk in the light of their father's faithfulness.

Of course, it must be understood that Samuel was not perfect. The Scripture simply highlights the overall characteristics of his efforts at spiritual faithfulness in order to contrast him with his morally corrupt surroundings. Nevertheless, his sons apparently did not emulate the positive qualities of their father's spiritual integrity. Instead, they made their own decisions to disobey God and to be corrupt in their dealings with others.

Suggestions for Use

First Samuel 8:1–3 is useful as a biblical illustration in at least two key ways. To begin, this story provides a scriptural balance for other passages in the Word of God. For example, Proverbs 22:6 teaches, "Train up a child in the way he should go; even when he is old he will not depart from it." When this proverb is presented in conjunction with the story of Samuel's sons, the reader can struggle with how to interpret these two ideas in the Bible. Surely, it is not a stretch to imagine that Samuel modeled spiritual fidelity in his home life. As indicated above, whether he was at home or away, his faithfulness remained intact (1 Samuel 7:15–17). Although Samuel was an imperfect man, he embraced Joshua's charge to covenantal faithfulness: "As for me and my house, we will serve the Lord" (Joshua 24:15). The only challenge is that Samuel's sons did not serve the Lord. So how is the reader to strike a balance between the story of Samuel's sons and the scriptural teaching about training children to follow God as presented in Proverbs 22:6, for example?

Three points are important to keep in mind. First, Scripture does not contradict itself in any way, shape, or form. Therefore, a biblical balance exists between these passages.

Second, the Bible gives instances where faithful fathers had unfaithful sons, and the story of Samuel in 1 Samuel 8:1–3 is an example of this reality. However, Scripture also gives examples of unfaithful fathers who had faithful sons. The narrative of Josiah in 2 Chronicles, for instance, supports this point. Josiah's father, Amon, "did what was evil in the sight of the Lord. . . . He did not humble himself before the Lord . . . but incurred guilt more and more" (2 Chronicles 33:22–23). Nevertheless,

Josiah, Amon's son, "did was what was right in the eyes of the Lord, and walked in the ways of David his father; and he did not turn aside to the right hand or to the left" (2 Chronicles 34:2).

The above examples show that the issue of faithfulness or unfaithfulness from one generation to another is a two-way street. Sometimes a faithful father wrestles through the pain of having unfaithful sons, and at other times, an unfaithful father sees his son move in the opposite direction of spiritual faithfulness.

Third, a proper approach to the book of Proverbs clarifies that individual proverbs are presented as general truths as opposed to specific promises.[28] For instance, one writer cautioned students of Proverbs with the following words: "As you study [Proverbs], keep in mind that Hebrew proverbs are generalized statements of what is usually true in life, and they must not be treated like promises."[29] This same writer went on to provide examples of this point from the pages of history which chronicle the faithful lives of some of God's most well-known servants:

> The assurance of life for the obedient is given often [in Proverbs] (3:2, 22; 4:10, 22; 8:35; 9:11; 10:27; 12:28; 13:14; 14:27; 19:23; 21:21; 22:4) and generally speaking, this is true. Obedient believers will care for their bodies and minds and avoid substances and practices that destroy, but some godly saints have died very young, while more than one godless rebel has had a long life. David Brainerd, missionary to the American Indians, died at twenty-nine. Robert Murray M'Cheyne died just two months short of his thirtieth birthday. Henry Martyn, missionary to India and Persia, died at thirty-one. William Whiting Borden, who gave his fortune to

---

28. Tremper Longman, III, *How to Read Proverbs* (Downers Grove: InterVarsity Press, 2002), 56.

29. Warren W. Wiersbe, *Be Skillful (Proverbs): God's Guidebook to Wise Living*, The BE Series Commentary (Colorado Springs: David C. Cook, 1995), 27.

God's work, was only twenty-five years old when he died in Egypt on his way to China.[30]

So when readers understand the nature of Proverbs as general truths, they realize there is no contradiction between Proverbs 22:6 and the story of Samuel's sons. God uses the faithful lives of His servants in many ways to impact people both in their homes and abroad. However, the godly lives of some persons do not guarantee that others will follow their examples.

The previous point is actually an appropriate transition to the second way the biblical illustration of 1 Samuel 8:1–3 can be useful in preaching and teaching. This story emphasizes the scriptural principle that all individuals are personally responsible for their lifestyle choices. In other words, they must make personal decisions about their spiritual lives by God's grace. No one can choose to follow God for other persons, regardless of how much they might wish to do so. Just as Joshua called the generation after the wilderness wanderings to choose whom they would serve (Joshua 24:15), every generation must make the same choices. Just like Jesus called His disciples to either follow Him or turn back because His message was challenging (John 6:24–71), believers must make personal decisions about their commitment to discipleship. Parents are clearly called to bring their children "up in the discipline and instruction of the Lord" (Ephesians 6:4); yet, they cannot choose Christ's salvation and faithfulness to Him for their children. These are personal decisions all persons in every home must make. While it is incredibly joyous when everyone in a home lives a life of spiritual devotion to God, it is still a painful reality that sometimes children choose lives of unfaithfulness even though their parents have modeled faithfulness before them.

---

30. Ibid.

17

THREE STRIKES BUT NOT OUT

~ 1 Samuel 26:1–30:6 ~

Believers can feel down-and-out many times in life. However, although Christians can be knocked down temporarily, they cannot be knocked out for good. Proverbs 24:16 says, "For the righteous falls seven times and rises again, but the wicked stumble in times of calamity." Of course, the resiliency of the righteous is not rooted in their personal resolves; it is rooted in their God. He has promised to be with them always (Hebrews 13:5–6), and His grace is sufficient to meet their every need (2 Corinthians 12:7–10). This is the truth revealed in David's life in 1 Samuel 26:1–30:6.

Context

Although David had already been anointed king of Israel, he did not assume the throne for quite some time. Samuel anointed David to be king before he killed Goliath when he was only a youth (1 Samuel 17:33), yet he did not begin to reign over all of Israel until he was thirty years old (2 Samuel 5:4). So David's ascent to the throne was not a brief journey. It was a long road—a hard road.

Saul, Israel's first king, hounded David for a considerable amount of time (1 Samuel 19–26). His murderous envy drove him to hunt for David like an animal in the wilderness. David could have taken Saul's life on more than one occasion, but he did not (1 Samuel 24; 26). Instead, he entrusted himself to God's perfect plan and timing. David's trust in the Lord sustained him through all the difficulties he encountered.

In fact, this is where David found himself yet again in the stretch of narrative between 1 Samuel 26:1–30:6. Over the course of these verses, David experienced rejection systematically on three fronts. But he never lost hope completely. In the realm of baseball, the saying, "Three strikes, and you're out" may be true. However, in the lives of God's servants, even three strikes doesn't equal being out because the Lord's grace is sufficient for every need.

The Illustration

David experienced the first strike against him in 1 Samuel 26. In this chapter, Saul was on the prowl to take David's life again (1 Samuel 26:1–2), and although David had an opportunity to kill Saul, he refrained from doing so (1 Samuel 26:6–12). But Saul's admission of David's innocence and future success was not enough to assure David of his long-term safety (1 Samuel 27:1). So the first strike against David in 1 Samuel 26:1–27:1 was the rejection of his own king.

Another strike came against David later in 1 Samuel 29. Sometime after he sought asylum in Philistine territory (1 Samuel 27:1), a battle brewed between the Philistines and Israelites (1 Samuel 29:1). Of course, since David lived in Philistine territory at the time, he and his men planned to march to war with the Philistines (1 Samuel 29:2). But the Philistine commanders voiced their lack of trust in David to Achish, the Philistine king. They basically tried to convince Achish that David could not be trusted to fight against Saul and the Israelites (1 Samuel 29:3–5). Although Achish vouched for David's reliability, he could not allay the suspicions of his commanders, and he sent David and his men home with these stinging words: "The lords do not approve of you" (1 Samuel 29:6). In this turn of events, David experienced a second strike against him. Even his foreign enemies rejected him.

The final strike against David came in 1 Samuel 30. As David and his men approached their homes in Philistine territory, they saw smoke rising from the charred ruins. While they were away, the Amalekites swept through on a raid and captured their wives, children, and possessions (1 Samuel 30:1–3). Obviously, David and his men were distraught, but the men fell to an even lower point than their leader. First Samuel 30:6 reveals that "David was greatly distressed, for the people spoke of stoning him, because all the people were bitter in soul, each for his sons and daughters." Here was strike three against David. Even his own soldiers blamed him for the tragedy they faced, and they rejected him to the point of death.

Yet, with three strikes against him, David was not out. The final words of 1 Samuel 30:6 provide a window into David's soul, revealing that God's strength was the rock solid, abiding foundation of David's life: "But David strengthened himself in the Lord his God." This is how David, even with three strikes against him, did not remain knocked down. The Lord's strength sustained him in the face of rejection on every possible human front.

Suggestions for Use

The story of how "David strengthened himself in the Lord his God" is a powerfully versatile biblical illustration. For instance, any exposition dealing with how early Christians faced struggles in the book of Acts (for example, Acts 4) or the New Testament epistles (for example, 2 Corinthians 4:6–10) could make use of this story. Its message emphasizes God's power to sustain His people through every test and trial.

Also, a New Testament parallel to David's story in 1 Samuel 26:1–30:6 can be found in 2 Timothy 4:9–18. In the last letter Paul penned, he recounted how various people had abandoned him for different reasons when he was in prison (2 Timothy 4:10). In fact, Paul eventually says, "At my first defense no one came to stand by me, but all deserted me. May it not be charged against them! But the Lord stood by me and strengthened me, so that through me the message might be fully proclaimed and all the Gentiles might hear it" (2 Timothy 4:16–17). Paul's testimony of God's presence and power to strengthen him connects well with David's story.

Lastly, the general truth of God's sustaining work in David's life can also be used to illustrate other key texts. For example, Jesus's Great Commission commences with a declaration of His absolute authority and culminates with a promise of His unending presence (Matthew 28:16–20). Also, as Paul dealt with the pain of a "thorn in his flesh," he realized the all-sufficiency of the Lord's grace in his life. Like David, he learned that in the depths of relentless struggles (John 16:33), Christ's strength is perfected in human weakness (2 Corinthians 12:7–10). Once again, Scripture is clear that even when believers have three or more strikes against them, they are still not out (Proverbs 24:15–16).

18

LEADERSHIP TRANSITIONS
~ 2 Samuel 1-9 ~

Some transitions in life are smooth. Others are not. Instead of being described as seamless in nature, many transitions, especially in areas of leadership, are turbulent. Power struggles and the politics of pride can produce violent upheavals during seasons of transition. David experienced many difficult dynamics related to leadership transitions over the course of 2 Samuel 1–9.

Context

Certain biblical illustrations are brief. For example, the scriptural story focusing on Samuel's unfaithful sons centers on just three verses (1 Samuel 8:1–3). However, other biblical illustrations span much larger sections of Scripture. This is certainly the case in the present discussion of "Leadership Transitions" from 2 Samuel 1–9.

When preachers or teachers handle a small portion of Scripture, they can afford to be more thorough in their analysis. But when a large section of the Bible is in focus, only the major contours of the text can be highlighted in a sermon or a lesson. And just as the biblical illustration itself may cover a large area of Scripture, the context for the story may also be broad in its scope. This naturally necessitates a general overview as well.

In light of the above points, the context for 2 Samuel 1–9 begins in the biblical book that precedes it, 1 Samuel. A proper understanding of how David transitioned into effective leadership requires an accurate grasp of Saul's reign, the first king of Israel.

God sent the prophet Samuel to anoint Saul to be king over Israel in 1 Samuel 9. And although the people readily accepted his monarchy (1 Samuel 10), the Lord quickly rejected him. Simply put: Saul was sinfully presumptuous in his leadership decisions. He lived in the fear of men rather than in the fear of the Lord (1 Samuel 13:8–15). Furthermore, Saul did not commit himself to obey the Lord's instructions completely, and for this reason as well, God rejected him as king over His people (1 Samuel 15). In fact, 1 Samuel 15:35 provides a chilling summary of Saul's reign before God turned His attention to David: "The Lord regretted that he had made Saul king over Israel."

After David was anointed king, the Scripture describes how "the Spirit of the Lord rushed upon David from that day forward" (1 Samuel 16:13). Simultaneously, the Bible declares how "the Spirit of the Lord departed from Saul" (1 Samuel 16:14). In the short span of two verses, the reader realizes that God shifted the blessing and power of His Spirit to David and from Saul.

Then, in the very next chapter, 1 Samuel 17, David killed the Philistine giant named Goliath by God's power, and Saul officially brought David into his service (1 Samuel 18:1–5). However, Saul was soon consumed with jealousy over David's military successes that received higher praise than his own feats in war (1 Samuel 18:6–9). From this point forward, Saul's envy escalated to murderous proportions (1 Samuel 18:10–11).

Yet, the reader understands that the transfer of God's blessing from Saul to David was the underlying spiritual dynamic at work during this tumultuous time. For instance, the following statements in 1 Samuel 18:12, 14–16 make this point clear: "Saul was afraid of David because the Lord was with him but had departed from Saul . . . David had success in all his undertakings, for the Lord was with him. And when Saul saw that he had great success, he stood in fearful awe of him. But all Israel and Judah loved David, for he went out and came in before them." Since Saul knew God's blessing had left him and moved to David, Saul was determined to kill David.

Saul's assaults on David were not confined to 1 Samuel 18:10–11. Rather, those attacks were the first in a long line of similar efforts, spanning from 1 Samuel 19–24, 26. While David had more than one opportunity to kill Saul during this turbulent time (1 Samuel 24; 26), he nevertheless refused to attack Saul. Instead, he sought to honor God's anointed king. On the first occasion, David refrained from taking Saul's life with the words: "The Lord forbid that I should do this thing to my lord, the Lord's anointed, to put out my hand against him, seeing he is the Lord's anointed" (1 Samuel 24:6). And on the second occasion, David's reason for not killing Saul was more detailed as he explained his actions to one of his men: "Do not destroy him, for who can put out his hand against the Lord's anointed and be guiltless? . . . As the Lord lives, the Lord will strike him, or his day will come to die, or he will go down into battle and perish. The Lord forbid that I should put out my hand against the Lord's anointed" (1 Samuel 26:9–11). David's words in these verses reveal that he trusted the Lord to deal with Saul either through supernatural means, natural causes, or death in military conflict. And one of these options for death eventually occurred as 1 Samuel closed with Saul and his sons slain in battle (1 Samuel 31).

The Illustration

The biblical illustration in 2 Samuel 1–9 obviously opens where its background in 1 Samuel closes—the death of Saul. Again, a detailed examination of 2 Samuel 1–9 is beyond the scope of this discussion, but five major contours of David's transition to leadership are apparent at various points in this stretch of narrative. First, David sought to honor his enemies and in turn to deal justly with their enemies. For example, David had the messenger who told him about Saul's death executed (2 Samuel 1:1–16), but he prayed a blessing for those who treated Saul's slain body with dignity (2 Samuel 2:4–7). Also, David (along with his men) personally expressed his grief over the death of Saul and his sons (2 Samuel 1:11–12). In fact, he even offered a song of lament for Israel's fallen king and his sons (2 Samuel 1:17–27).

In a similar light, David was greatly displeased when his servant Joab killed Abner, the servant of Saul's surviving and reigning son Ish-bosheth (2 Samuel 3:31–39). It was because of David's mourning over the death of Abner that "all the people and all Israel understood that day that it had not been the king's will to put to death Abner the son of Ner" (2 Samuel 3:37). Furthermore, David was outraged when Ish-bosheth's two servants murdered him (2 Samuel 4). David voiced his disgust with these men when he said, "As the Lord lives, who has redeemed my life out of every adversity, when one told me, 'Behold, Saul is dead,' and thought he was bringing good news, I seized him and killed him at Ziklag, which was the reward I gave him for his news. How much more, when wicked men have killed a righteous man in his own house on his bed, shall I not now require his blood at your hand and destroy you from the earth?" (2 Samuel 4:9–11). Lastly, David initiated a plan to continue to show kindness to anyone remaining from the house of Saul, namely, Mephibosheth (2 Samuel 9; 16:1–4; 19:24–30). All of these events demonstrate how David sought to honor his enemies and deal justly with their enemies.

Second, David sought God's direction. Once David heard of and wept over Saul's death, he asked the Lord for guidance about what his plans should be (2 Samuel 2:1–4). David did not act presumptuously; he acted prayerfully. Also, after David officially became king over all God's people, both Israel and Judah (2 Samuel 5:1–5), he led the whole nation in military conflicts in order to establish his kingdom (2 Samuel 5:6–10). One of his early battles was with the Philistines (2 Samuel 5:17–25). As David led the entire nation in battle, he did so with a keen sensitivity to God's direction. For instance, as the Philistines positioned themselves to engage David in conflict, 2 Samuel 5:19 records the prayerful exchange between David and the Lord: "And David inquired of the Lord, 'Shall I go up against the Philistines? Will you give them into my hand?' And the Lord said to David, 'Go up, for I will certainly give the Philistines into your hand.'" But just a few verses later, Israel and the Philistines engaged one another in battle again, and the following prayerful interchange between David and God occurred: "And when David inquired of the Lord, he said, 'You shall not go up; go around to their rear, and come against them opposite the balsam trees. And when you hear the sound of marching in the tops of the balsam trees, then rouse yourself, for then the Lord has gone out before you to strike down the army of the Philistines.' And David did as the Lord commanded him" (2 Samuel 5:23–25).

So David did not trust his own thoughts, military strength, or war strategies. Instead, he relied completely on God's guidance and power to overcome his enemies. In fact, the "sound of marching in the tops of the balsam trees" mentioned above may be an indication that God sent angelic forces ahead to overthrow David's enemies.

Third, David was patient with God's timing to establish him as king over all Israel. This observation is supported at various points in the narrative where the issue of chronology surfaces. For example, after David initially inquired of the Lord for direction, he only went to Hebron where he was anointed king over Judah alone (2 Samuel 2:1–4).

Of course, although Ish-bosheth, Saul's son, ruled over Israel at the same time David ruled over Judah (2 Samuel 4:8–11), David did not initiate a coup to overtake the house of Saul through a murderous plot. In fact, the conflict between Judah and Israel during this time is described with the following words: "There was a long war between the house of Saul and the house of David. And David grew stronger and stronger, while the house of Saul became weaker and weaker" (2 Samuel 3:1).

David's patience is also implied in the text when Ish-bosheth accused Abner of being involved with one of Saul's concubines (2 Samuel 3:6–7). Such an accusation insinuated that Abner was trying to supplant Ish-bosheth as leader. This obviously infuriated Abner, even to the point of transferring his allegiance from the house of Saul to David (2 Samuel 3:8–10). It is evident here that the house of Saul, while in conflict with David and Judah, was crumbling from within. Then, after Ish-bosheth's own men murdered him, the Lord gave David full access to govern all of His people as their rightful king. Along this line, 2 Samuel 5:3–5 describes God's timing in establishing David as the leader of the whole nation: "So all the elders of Israel come to the king at Hebron, and King David made a covenant with them at Hebron before the Lord, and they anointed David king over Israel. David was thirty years old when he began to reign, and he reigned forty years. At Hebron he reigned over Judah seven years and six months, and at Jerusalem he reigned over all Israel and Judah thirty-three years." While these verses are brief to read, they were very long to live! Furthermore, the chronological information in these verses do not include the time David spent fleeing from Saul's murderous attempts on his life in the wilderness, although he had already been anointed king by Samuel the prophet (1 Samuel 16–26).

All of this underscores David's patience with God's process. He did not take revenge on Saul or Ish-bosheth according to his timing and ways. He trusted the Lord's direction and waited for God to establish him as king.

Fourth, David acknowledged the Lord's presence and power at work in his life and reign. When the king mentioned to the prophet Nathan that "the ark of God dwells in a tent" (2 Samuel 7:2), Nathan had to adjust his initial response to David (2 Samuel 7:3). While God promised to bless David and his lineage as rulers over the house of Israel, He also declared how David's son as opposed to David himself would "build a house for my [God's] name" (2 Samuel 7:5–16).

David's response to the Lord's message through the prophet Nathan revealed what was in his heart. In these words, David acknowledged God's presence and powerful work in his life. For example, he expressed his humility in his opening rhetorical question: "Who am I, O Lord God, and what is my house, that you have brought me thus far?" (2 Samuel 7:18). David revealed that he understood the Lord's blessings were the result of God's might and majesty and not his merit: "Because of your promise, and according to your own heart, you have brought about all this greatness, to make your servant know it" (2 Samuel 7:21). David understood that all of God's work in the past, the present, and in the future was for the Lord's glory and not his own when he said, "You established for yourself your people Israel to be your people forever. And you, O Lord, became their God. And now, O Lord God, confirm forever the word that you have spoken concerning your servant and concerning his house, and do as you have spoken. And your name will be magnified forever, saying, 'The Lord of hosts is God over Israel,' and the house of your servant David will be established before you" (2 Samuel 7:24–26). The final words of David's prayer summarized his acknowledgment of the fact that every blessing he received was from God: "Now therefore may it please you to bless the house of your servant, so that it may continue forever before you. For you, O Lord God, have spoken, and with your blessing shall the house of your servant be blessed forever" (2 Samuel 7:29). David's response to God's message through the prophet Nathan was a declaration that he knew he was nothing without the Lord's presence and powerful work in his life.

Fifth, David was confident in God's call. Although David was kind to those whom others likely considered to be his enemies (such as Abner, Ish-bosheth, and Mephibosheth), he still knew that he was God's anointed king for Israel. For example, when the men of Judah anointed David as their king, he did not resist such action (2 Samuel 2:4). While David was sensitive to God's direction and timing for his life, he was convinced that the Lord was working to establish him as the ruler of His people. For instance, when Abner covenanted with David to bring all of Israel under his authority, even though Ish-bosheth was ruling as a rival king at the time, David did not reject Abner's offer of assistance (2 Samuel 3:12–21). As with the men of Judah earlier, David did not resist when the elders of Israel anointed him as their ruler (2 Samuel 5:3), and after David took some initial actions as the leader over all Israel, the Scripture says, "David became greater and greater, for the Lord, the God of hosts, was with him" (2 Samuel 5:10). Also, "David knew that the Lord had established him king over Israel, and that he had exalted his kingdom for the sake of his people Israel" (2 Samuel 5:12). All of these texts underscore the fact that David rested and led God's people with an appropriate level of confidence in knowing that he was serving as the Lord's leader over Israel. So a biblical balance is evident here: David waited on God to work, and he moved forward confidently when God established his leadership.

Suggestions for Use

Leadership transitions take place in a host of places and for many reasons. As mentioned above, some transitions are seamless; others are incredibly difficult. The five aspects of David's leadership transition from being a renegade to being a royal figure are helpful as a biblical illustration. First, David's story shows how leaders should seek to honor their predecessors and/or others who may be inclined to oppose them for whatever reason. For example, Paul instructed Timothy, a young pastor in a turbulent ministry setting: "Have nothing to do with foolish, ignorant controversies; you know that they breed quarrels. And the Lord's servant must not be quarrelsome but kind to everyone, able to teach, patiently enduring evil, correcting his opponents with gentleness. God may perhaps grant them repentance leading to a knowledge of the truth, and they may escape from the snare of the devil, after being captured by him to do his will" (2 Timothy 2:23–26). David's acts of kindness are practical demonstrations of how leaders can work gently with others as they trust God to deal with their enemies. On this front, Jesus's call for His followers to love their enemies (Matthew 5:43–48) as well as Paul's admonitions for believers to bless their enemies and refrain from taking vengeance on them (Romans 12:14, 16–21) can both find illustrations in the story of David's leadership transition.

Second, David's sensitivity to God's direction is a useful example of what persistent prayerfulness looks like in the lives of believers in general and leaders in particular. Texts such as Philippians 4:6–7 and 1 Thessalonians 5:17 which call Christians to constant dependence upon the Lord in prayer find an excellent illustration in the story of David.

Third, David's patience with the Lord's timing is another great point of emphasis for believers. Just as David did not try to advance himself presumptuously nor prematurely, the Scripture exhorts God's people to wait for His perfect timing (Isaiah 40:25–31). Also, it does not take much imagination to figure that David doubtlessly wrestled with God's timing when the reader considers all the years which transpired between David's initial anointing by Samuel (1 Samuel 16) and his final anointing as ruler over all Israel (2 Samuel 5). For example, during those years, David fled from Saul's murderous attempts on his life, even though he had more than one opportunity to take Saul's life. Others surely did not understand God's plan during these incredibly trying times, but David showed through his leadership transition what it looks like for a leader to "trust in the Lord with all your heart, and do not lean on your own understanding. In all your ways acknowledge him, and he will make straight your paths. Be not wise in your own eyes; fear the Lord, and turn away from evil" (Proverbs 3:5–7).

Fourth, David's acknowledgment of God's presence and powerful work in his life is a vivid portrait of a humble trust in the Lord. When Scripture urges believers to realize that God alone calls and enables them to do His work (1 Thessalonians 5:24), David's leadership transition is a picturesque example of this principle. When Scripture beckons Christians to give God the glory for all He has accomplished in and through the lives of His leaders and people (Psalm 115; 150), the story of David's transition reveals what this biblical truth looks like in living color.

Fifth, David's healthy confidence in the Lord's work to establish his rule is an excellent balance for the previous point. Some may falsely understand humility as never stepping into a position of leadership and honor. However, David demonstrated that true humility is to acknowledge God's supreme authority over all, while simultaneously embracing his God-ordained role of leadership. In light of this, Paul urged Timothy to see that the church honored those leaders who served well, especially in preaching and teaching (1 Timothy 5:17).

Also, Peter wrote about leadership roles in the church in the following words:

> So I exhort the elders among you, as a fellow elder and a witness of the sufferings of Christ, as well as a partaker in the glory that is going to be revealed: shepherd the flock of God that is among you, exercising oversight, not under compulsion, but willingly, as God would have you; not for shameful gain, but eagerly; not domineering over those in your charge, but being examples to the flock. And when the chief Shepherd appears, you will receive

the unfading crown of glory. Likewise, you who are younger, be subject to the elders. Clothe yourselves, all of you, with humility toward one another, for "God opposes the proud but gives grace to the humble." Humble yourselves, therefore, under the mighty hand of God so that at the proper time he may exalt you, casting all your anxieties on him, because he cares for you (1 Peter 5:1–7).

In these instructions to leaders and those who submit to their authority, Peter emphasized how some men are called to lead, and they need to rest confidently in their calling from the Lord. However, Peter also urged these leaders to lead with humility, understanding that they serve under the Lord's ultimate authority. Furthermore, Peter called humble leaders to trust God with their anxieties as opposed to trying to take matters into their own hands. All of these aspects of leadership that Peter emphasized are illustrated in the story of David's leadership transition in 2 Samuel 1–9 as well. David served as God's leader because he knew the Lord established him, but he also served with humility as he trusted the Lord to work according to His perfect timing and plan.

19

A Portrait of Grace

~ 2 Samuel 9:1–13 ~

As the old hymn proclaims, God's grace is truly amazing. Many have sought to convey this truth in various ways. For example, the well-known acronym for *grace:* G. R. A. C. E.—G (God's) R (Riches) A (At) C (Christ's) E (Expense)—emphasizes Jesus's substitutionary atonement for sin. Peter framed this scriptural truth succinctly in 1 Peter 3:18, "For Christ also suffered once for sins, the righteous for the unrighteous, that he might bring us to God." Paul also declared God's amazing grace when he wrote, "For our sake he [God] made him [Jesus] to be sin who knew no sin, so that in him we might become the righteousness of God" (2 Corinthians 5:21). While these verses encapsulate God's grace in light of Christ's substitutionary atonement, other passages paint pictures of His unconditional love. The story of Mephibosheth is one such powerful portrait of grace.

Context

Mephibosheth basically appears four times throughout the narrative of 2 Samuel. He is introduced in 2 Samuel 4:4 as the crippled but surviving son of Jonathan. Mephibosheth next appears in 2 Samuel 9 as David chose to demonstrate kindness to a member of the house of Saul. Then his name surfaces in 2 Samuel 16:1–4. However, the focus of this passage is more on Ziba, Mephibosheth's servant, rather than on Mephibosheth himself. Finally, Mephibosheth factors back into the storyline in 2 Samuel 19:24–30. This last text essentially resumes the mention of Mephibosheth in 2 Samuel 9.

The background for the biblical illustration in 2 Samuel 9:1–13 is the establishment of David's rule over Israel. After the death of Ishbosheth, Saul's son who ruled Israel while David ruled Judah (2 Samuel 2:10), David reigned as king over all Israel (2 Samuel 5:1–5).

Second Samuel 5–9 essentially chronicles David's initial acts as Israel's new ruler. He fought for and came to reside in the city of David (2 Samuel 5:6–10), and from the very beginning of his reign, "David became greater and greater, for the Lord, the God of hosts, was with him" (2 Samuel 5:10). Next, he defeated the Philistines on two occasions (2 Samuel 5:17–25). Then he set a plan in motion to bring the ark of the covenant to the city of David (2 Samuel 6:1–15). After David heard from the prophet Nathan of the Lord's covenant with him and his descendants (2 Samuel 7:1–17), he offered praise to God for His blessings and promises (2 Samuel 7:18–29). Lastly, several of David's victories are briefly described in 2 Samuel 8:1–14. A recurring theme in the description of these military exploits, however, focuses on the Lord rather than David. For example, the following words appear twice in the above stretch of text: "And the Lord gave victory to David wherever he went" (2 Samuel 8:6, 14). Then the opening verse of the final summary passage of David's rule to this point says: "So David reigned over all Israel. And David administered justice and equity to all his people" (2 Samuel 8:15).

Of course, the above declaration that David's reign was firmly established makes the biblical illustration concerning Mephibosheth in 2 Samuel 9:1–13 a powerful portrait of grace. David did not need anyone or anything to bolster his position among the Lord's people. From a human perspective, Mephibosheth was a threat as a surviving member of the house of Saul. Yet, he was a weak threat because of his physical handicap. So, why would David give Mephibosheth any thought? Much less, why would David dispense compassion on him? The average monarch in the time of David would have likely executed Mephibosheth. He certainly would not have extended an indefinite invitation to him to live and dine like royalty. All of this points to the fact that the story of David and Mephibosheth is a portrait of grace, indeed.

The Illustration

The biblical illustration in 2 Samuel 9:1–13 easily divides into three basic parts. First, David initiated a demonstration of kindness to Mephibosheth. Since grace is typically defined as "unmerited favor," this aspect of the narrative is crucial. Furthermore, the particular kindness that David lavished on Mephibosheth is important. When David first asked about whom he could show kindness to from the house of Saul, he said, "Is there still anyone left of the house of Saul, that I may show him kindness for Jonathan's sake?" (2 Samuel 9:1). But when David later repeated his question to Ziba, a former servant of Saul, he asked, "Is there not still someone of the house of Saul, that I may show the kindness of God to him?" (2 Samuel 9:3). Obviously, the specific type of kindness David wished to bestow was beyond a mere token of human benevolence. He wanted to demonstrate the Lord's deep love, mercy, and grace.

Second, Mephibosheth's response to David's act of grace is insightful. It reveals Mephibosheth's gratitude for David's unbelievable compassion. When Mephibosheth entered David's presence, the Scripture says, "And Mephibosheth the son of Jonathan, son of Saul, came to David and fell on his face and paid homage." After David called his name, "he [Mephibosheth] answered, 'Behold, I am your servant'" (2 Samuel 9:6). Mephibosheth's initial posture and response to David communicated more than mere protocol. The reader must remember the context of the story: David is established as king, and Mephibosheth is a surviving member of the previous ruling house. The typical transition of power from one ruling house to another was not marked with benevolence shared but with blood spilled! This is doubtless why David's first words to Mephibosheth were: "Do not fear" (2 Samuel 9:7). Of course, after David conveyed that his intentions were for blessing and not for harm, 2 Samuel 9:8 further describes Mephibosheth's response in the presence of such grace: "And he paid homage and said, 'What is your servant, that you should show regard for a dead dog such as I?'"

Third, David's final words concerning how Mephibosheth was to be cared for and treated along with the closing picture of how Mephibosheth lived in light of God's kindness as demonstrated through David's kind actions is a fitting conclusion to this portrait of grace. For example, while David commanded Ziba and his family to work the land for Mephibosheth's benefit, Mephibosheth was not to live outside of David's presence. Rather, David declared to Ziba, "But Mephibosheth your master's grandson shall always eat at my table" (2 Samuel 9:10). Thus, the illustration in 2 Samuel 9:1–13 ends with the following two descriptions of how Mephibosheth continued to live in light of the grace that was so richly offered to him: "So Mephibosheth ate at David's table, like one of the king's sons . . . So Mephibosheth lived in Jerusalem, for he ate always at the king's table. Now he was lame in both his feet" (2 Samuel 9:11, 13). The closing comment about Mephibosheth's handicap only serves to further reiterate the portrait of grace so beautifully presented in this story. Not only was Mephibosheth a surviving member of an enemy household, but his disability also rendered him basically helpless to either defend or tend to his own needs effectively. Yet, in his completely undeserving and vulnerable state, he experienced a continual outpouring of grace.

Suggestions for Use

The portrait of grace in 2 Samuel 9:1–13 is useful as an illustration of God's unconditional love presented in other passages of Scripture. For example, if a pastor or teacher is explaining the scriptural truth that God initiates His relationship with sinners (John 15:16; 1 John 4:19), the first aspect of Mephibosheth's story is a powerful demonstration of what this looks like as it was played out on the stage of Israel's history. Paul made the clear case that sinners do not seek God on their own initiative when he wrote: "We have already charged that all, both Jews and Greeks, are under sin, as it is written: 'None is righteous, no, not one; no one understands; no one seeks for God. All have turned aside; together they have become worthless; no one does good, not even one' " (Romans 3:9–12).

Later, Paul drew the obvious conclusion that if sinners do not seek God on their own initiative, God has to be the One to demonstrate His unconditional love to them. This is precisely what the Lord did in the person and work of Jesus Christ: "For while we were still weak, at the right time Christ died for the ungodly. For one will scarcely die for a righteous person—though perhaps for a good person one would dare even to die—but God shows his love for us in that while we were still sinners, Christ died for us" (Romans 5:6–8). In a similar way to Mephibosheth, the crippled souls of sinners lie dead at the feet of the King who is just to banish them forever from His holy presence (Ephesians 2:1–3).

Yet, God, the King of grace, initiates and demonstrates His unmerited favor upon repentant and believing sinners so that they experience His redemption and the forgiveness of sins freely in and through Christ alone (Ephesians 1:3–8; 2:4–9).

Also, Mephibosheth's response to grace is an excellent picture of what the proper reaction to grace looks like—humble gratitude. If an expositor was handling Romans 12:1, for instance, where Paul wrote, "I appeal to you therefore, brothers, by the mercies of God, to present your bodies as a living sacrifice, holy and acceptable to God, which is your spiritual worship," he could easily refer to Mephibosheth's humility in David's presence as an example of Paul's exhortation to complete surrender to God in light of His mercies. The simple point is that an appropriate response to grace is an appreciation of grace as opposed to an abuse of grace. This is what is evident in the story of Mephibosheth, and it is what is taught in other passages of Scripture as well (Romans 6:1–4).

Lastly, the closing scene of crippled Mephibosheth dining with David for the rest of his days is a powerful illustration of what it looks like for the believer to live daily in the light of God's grace. David did not dispense a single drop of grace that merely refreshed Mephibosheth's parched life for an isolated moment in time. Rather, David's grace was like a continual flow of pristine water that never ceased to provide for Mephibosheth's daily needs.

And so it is for the believer in Christ. Paul penned this marvelous truth in Romans 5:1–2: "Therefore, since we have been justified by faith, we have peace with God through our Lord Jesus Christ. Through him we have also obtained access by faith into this grace in which we stand, and we rejoice in hope of the glory of God." Believers are not simply saved by grace in the sense that this is an isolated event confined to their past. Instead, they continually live in the grace of God. Even through every trial of life, believers rest assured that "if God is for us, who can be against us? He who did not spare his own Son but gave him up for us all, how will he not also with him graciously give us all things? . . . Who shall separate us from the love of Christ? Shall tribulation, or distress, or persecution, or famine, or nakedness, or danger, or sword? . . . No, in all these things we are more than conquerors through him who loved us" (Romans 8:31–37). According to Paul, Christians are not to begin in the Spirit but then try to sustain their freedom through their own efforts (Galatians 3:3). Rather, Paul argued that "if we live by the Spirit, let us also walk by the Spirit" (Galatians 5:25).

The writer of Hebrews also emphasized how believers are to live constantly in light of God's grace, which supplies everything they need in their daily lives. For example, Hebrews 4:15–16 assures God's children: "For we do not have a high priest who is unable to sympathize with our weaknesses, but one who in every respect has been tempted as we are, yet without sin. Let us then with confidence draw near to the throne of grace, that we may receive mercy and find grace to help in time of need." Just as Mephibosheth found David's throne to be a throne of grace for him in his time of desperate need, believers find the ultimate throne of grace in the Lord Jesus. His grace is all-sufficient not only to offer salvation for all eternity but also to sustain His followers through every season of life (2 Corinthians 12:7–10). In this way, a crippled soul robed in Christ's righteousness as an heir of God and a joint-heir with Jesus and feasting now and forever at the table of the King of kings is the supreme portrait of grace (Romans 8:16–17; 2 Corinthians 5:21).

20

Festering and Fatal Resentment

~ 2 Samuel 13:19–37 ~

Someone has described the ironic bondage of unforgiveness like this: "Unforgiveness is like drinking poison and then waiting for the other person to die." When Christians harbor hurts and withhold forgiveness from others, they open their lives to the work of the enemy. Paul admonished believers in Ephesians 4:26–27, "Be angry and do not sin; do not let the sun go down on your anger, and give no opportunity to the devil." The story of Absalom is a tragic example of how resentment can fester in the heart of a person until it becomes fatal.

Context

Since 2 Samuel 13:19 begins with a description of Tamar, the sister of David's son Absalom, the reader may suppose that the proper context for this narrative begins with the description of Tamar's rape by her brother Amnon (2 Samuel 13:1–17). And while this would be correct insofar as it goes, it nevertheless does not go far enough. In actuality, the background for the story of Absalom's festering and fatal resentment extends to the consequences David received from God through the prophet Nathan because of his infidelity with Bathsheba and subsequent murder of Uriah (2 Samuel 11:1–12:12).

After David committed adultery with Bathsheba and tried to conceal his sin by having her husband Uriah killed (2 Samuel 11), "the Lord sent Nathan to David" (2 Samuel 12:1). God knew of David's sins of immorality and murder because He knows all things. So He rebuked David and outlined the consequences for his disobedience (2 Samuel 12:7–14). An immediate ramification for his sins was that the child of his immorality with Bathsheba would die (2 Samuel 12:14), and this occurred within a short time (2 Samuel 12:15–23). However, a more distant consequence for David's sins was that "the sword shall never depart from your house . . . I [the Lord] will raise up evil against you out of your own house. And I will take your wives before your eyes and give them to your neighbor, and he shall lie with your wives in the sight of this sun. For you did it secretly, but I will do this thing before all Israel and before the sun" (2 Samuel 12:10–12). Because the stories of Tamar's rape, of Absalom's murder of Amnon, of Absalom's plot to usurp his father's throne, and of Absalom's death at the hands of David's men all occur after God's rebuke through Nathan (2 Samuel 13:20–18:33), the narrative of Absalom's festering and fatal resentment is, in a broad sense, the fulfillment of God's prediction of David's struggles as a consequence of his sins.

Of course, the immediate context of Amnon's rape of Tamar (2 Samuel 13:1–17) serves as the dark backdrop to this tragic story. Both Absalom and Amnon were David's sons, and Tamar was Absalom's sister (2 Samuel 13:1). Amnon was dazzled by Tamar's beauty and drunk on his lust for her (2 Samuel 13:1–2). Amnon's friend, Jonadab, concocted a deceptive plan so that Amnon could lure Tamar into a trap (2 Samuel 13:3–5).

While Jonadab's plan basically worked from a sinfully human perspective (2 Samuel 13:6-14), sin never really satisfies. In fact, sin only takes what it promises to give. So after Amnon raped Tamar, "Amnon hated her with a very great hatred, so that the hatred with which he hated her was greater than the love with which he had loved her" (2 Samuel 13:15). At this point, Absalom's festering and fatal resentment began.

The Illustration

Second Samuel 13:19–37 opens with Tamar rushing out of Amnon's presence overcome with shame (2 Samuel 13:19). Then the focus of the narrative shifts to Absalom. Once he determined that Amnon violated Tamar, hatred flooded his heart, and murderous resentment took root in his life (2 Samuel 13:22, 32). It is not hard to imagine that since "Tamar lived, a desolate woman, in her brother Absalom's house" (2 Samuel 13:20), Absalom's rage over his brother's sin gradually rose in intensity as he watched his violated sister suffer in shame.

However, Absalom did not act on his anger immediately. He held his tongue while his resentment festered until it reached a fatal point (2 Samuel 13:22). The period of maturation for Absalom's bitterness to grow from seething hatred to full-blown murder took two full years according to 2 Samuel 13:23. At this time, he hatched a scheme to end Amnon's life because of his sinful actions (2 Samuel 13:23–29). Still, however, the reader learns in 2 Samuel 13:32 that Absalom's plan to murder Amnon was linked to the moment he learned of Amnon's rape of Tamar: "For by the command of Absalom this has been determined from the day he violated his sister Tamar." The link between these two events, Tamar's rape and Amnon's murder, was Absalom's festering and fatal resentment. It grew for two years, but it was an unbroken chain. It first wrapped its deadly hold around Amnon's neck, and then it indirectly but ultimately resulted in Absalom's very own death.

Suggestions for Use

Resentment is never good, and it can even be fatal. The above illustration makes this point abundantly clear. This is why Scripture warns believers against allowing bitterness to take root and fester in their hearts. For instance, one of the first sinful attitudes of the heart Jesus dealt with in the Sermon on the Mount was the attitude of anger—the seedbed for murder (Matthew 5:21–26). Also, as noted in the introductory" section above, Paul warned Christians about the sin of resentment in Ephesians 4:26–27. Obviously, Paul acknowledged that there is a level of anger that is not sinful. But there is a fine line between righteous indignation and sinful anger. Surely, Jesus expressed holy anger over the way money changers corrupted His Father's house (John 2:14–17). On another occasion, when people watched to see if Christ would heal a man "with a withered hand . . . on the Sabbath," the Scripture says that Jesus "looked around at them with anger, grieved at their hardness of heart" (Mark 3:1–5).

Yet, while there is an anger that is pure before God, another type of wrath is ungodly. And Absalom's anger was more than a justified, godly reaction to Amnon's sin. This is why he plotted to murder Amnon from the very day that Amnon violated his sister Tamar (2 Samuel 13:32). The story of Absalom's anger is an example of what could happen when anger is not kept in check.

Furthermore, the story of Absalom's resentment paints a picture of what extreme forms revenge can take. Scripture teaches that God's people are not to take vengeance on their enemies. Instead, they are to allow Him to execute justice in His perfect timing and ways (Romans 12:19; Hebrews 10:30). Instead of entrusting Amnon into God's just hands, Absalom took matters into his own hands and acted out his hatred for his brother. Of course, when the Lord executes His justice against sin, His plan from start to finish is perfect and brings Him glory, but when people react in their unbridled sinful anger, the result is always more sin because "the anger of man does not produce the righteousness that God requires" (James 1:20). This was the case for Absalom, and it will always be the case for the Lord's people in every generation.

Lastly, the story of Absalom is also a chronicle of costly consequences. For example, since the general background for 2 Samuel 13:19–37 reaches back to David's sins of adultery and murder, this is where the chain of consequences really began. The consequences of David's sins surfaced in the suffering of his house. One expression of this was the death of his son Amnon at the hands of his son Absalom (2 Samuel 13:28–29). Also, the death of Absalom himself could ultimately be linked to both David's and Absalom's sins. David mishandled the events following the murder of Amnon, which only led to more problems on an even broader scale (2 Samuel 13:34–18:33). So David's sins of adultery and murder left a trail of collateral damage that littered the landscape of his house. In this way, the biblical illustration in 2 Samuel 13:19–37 is a powerful example of the words of James: "Let no one say when he is tempted, 'I am being tempted by God,' for God cannot be tempted with evil, and he himself tempts no one. But each person is tempted when he is lured and enticed by his own desire. Then desire when it has conceived gives birth to sin, and sin when it is fully grown brings forth death" (James 1:13–15). Simply put: Sin leads ultimately to death. David sinned with Bathsheba, and both Uriah and the child in her womb died (2 Samuel 11:17; 12:18). Amnon sinned, and he died at the hands of Absalom (2 Samuel 13:29). Absalom sinned, and he died at the hands of David's men (2 Samuel 18:14–15). Again, sin leads to death, and this biblical principle is presented graphically in the broader context and specific details of the story of Absalom's festering and fatal resentment.

Before this chapter closes, one additional comment is beneficial. While the above discussion emphasizes the negative consequences of sin, it should also be noted that God's grace is still at work even in the midst of sin's bitter impact. For example, although one of the first casualties in the entire chronicle of costly consequences outlined above is the death of David and Bathsheba's first child (2 Samuel 12:18), God blessed them with a second child. In fact, the Scripture says, "Then David comforted his wife, Bathsheba, and went in to her and lay with her, and she bore a son, and he called his name Solomon. And the Lord loved him" (2 Samuel 12:24). The house of David continued after his death through the reign of Solomon (1 Kings 1:28–40), and both Solomon and Bathsheba surface in Jesus's genealogy. Solomon is named directly, and Bathsheba is named indirectly as "the wife of Uriah" (Matthew 1:6). Here is a powerful reminder that God's grace is greater than sin, and His sovereign purposes script the story of history as opposed to sin's worse attempts to do so (Revelation 20–22).

21

CONFRONTING LEADERSHIP WITH THE TRUTH

~ 2 Samuel 19:1–8 ~

Confrontation is never easy. It is especially difficult when someone under authority needs to confront someone in authority. However, this is necessary at times. While such cases should always be handled with the greatest of care, they should not be avoided. Even leaders are not above rebuke. All believers are accountable to God and to one another for His glory and for the greater good of the church. For example, Paul instructed Timothy, "Do not admit a charge against an elder except on the evidence of two or three witnesses. As for those who persist in sin, rebuke them in the presence of all, so that the rest may stand in fear" (1 Timothy 5:19–20). It is clear that everyone, including leaders, need to be confronted with the truth, and such was the reality for David in 2 Samuel 19:1–8.

Context

The background for the story of 2 Samuel 19:1–8 has both cultural and textual facets to it. First, the cultural backdrop for the narrative centers around the absolute authority with which a king ruled in a monarchial society. While this may be a strange concept to contemporary democratic nations, it was a daily reality for those who lived in biblical times. Simply put: No one ever confronted the king. At least, no one who valued his or her life ever confronted the king (*see*, for example, Esther 4:10–16). Yet, this is precisely what Joab did in 2 Samuel 19:1–8. He fearlessly entered David's presence and confronted him with the truth. In fact, his words even carried the tone of a sharp rebuke.

Second, the textual background for this story began with the introduction of Absalom into the story of Amnon's rape of Tamar (2 Samuel 13:1–22). After Absalom plotted and carried out Amnon's murder (2 Samuel 13:23–33), Absalom fled (2 Samuel 13:34–39). Later, Absalom returned to Jerusalem (2 Samuel 14:1–27), but things were not normal. For instance, "Absalom lived two full years in Jerusalem, without coming into the king's presence" (2 Samuel 14:28).

During this time of tension, Absalom schemed to overthrow his own father's throne (2 Samuel 15:1–12). His plot partially worked because David had to flee from Jerusalem, at least for a period of time (2 Samuel 15:13–16:23). However, Absalom's reign was short-lived. The Lord restored David to his throne (2 Samuel 17), and, consequently, Absalom fled, only to meet a bitter and deadly end (2 Samuel 18:1–18).

When the news of Absalom's death reached David, a highly unusual scene occurred. Typically, the report of an enemy's death erupted into joyful celebration. However, when the king's enemy was also his son, a joyful celebration was replaced with deep mourning. David's response to the news of Absalom's death dripped with the deep sorrow only a father could express: "O my son Absalom, my son, my son Absalom!

Would I had died instead of you, O Absalom, my son, my son!" (2 Samuel 18:33). In this valley of emotional turmoil, Joab entered the picture and confronted David with the truth.

The Illustration

While David's grief over Absalom's death is surely understandable to any reader, his lament over the death of his enemy caused confusion for his soldiers and his city. For example, 2 Samuel 19:2–3 says, "So the victory that day was turned into mourning for all the people, for the people heard that day, 'The king is grieving for his son.' And the people stole into the city that day as people steal in who are ashamed when they flee in battle." Basically, David's weeping turned the atmosphere of the city into a sense of defeat rather than victory.

As David continued his chorus of mourning with the words: "O my son Absalom, O Absalom, my son, my son" (2 Samuel 19:4), Joab emerged boldly in the story. His confrontation with David and sharp rebuke for his actions followed several points of emphasis. First, Joab launched his challenge to David with a powerful ironic twist. While David covered his face because of his grief (2 Samuel 19:4), Joab issued a charge to the king: "You have today covered with shame the faces of all your servants" (2 Samuel 19:5).

Second, Joab helped David see that not only was his life spared by the valiant efforts of his soldiers who fought to overthrow Absalom's coup, but "all your servants . . . this day saved your life and the lives of your sons and your daughters and the lives of your wives and your concubines" (2 Samuel 19:5).

Third, Joab continued his rebuke as he argued that the reason David's sorrow covered his servant's faces with shame was because the king's actions demonstrated this sad truth: "You love those who hate you and hate those who love you" (2 Samuel 19:6).

Fourth, Joab confronted his king with the harsh reality that his behavior conveyed this unfortunate message: "For you have made it clear today that commanders and servants are nothing to you, for today I know that if Absalom were alive and all of us were dead today, then you would be pleased" (2 Samuel 19:6). To the careful reader, the previous words indicate a subtle but strong shift. Joab literally painted himself into the message by using the words *commanders* and *us* in his rebuke.

Second Samuel 19:7 marks a change in Joab's confrontation with David. He moved from confronting David to commanding him. Joab urgently pressed David: "Go out and speak kindly to your servants, for I swear by the Lord, if you do not go, not a man will stay with you this night, and this will be worse for you than all the evil that has come upon you from your youth until now" (2 Samuel 19:7). To his credit, David listened to Joab's words (2 Samuel 19:8).

Suggestions for Use

The biblical illustration of how Joab confronted David with the truth is important for at least three reasons. First, this story demonstrates how rebuke is sometimes necessary. Proverbs 27:5 admonishes that "better is open rebuke than hidden love." Of course, the book of Proverbs emphasizes how wisdom sometimes calls for being silent and sometimes calls for being outspoken (*see*, for example, Proverbs 26:4–5). In the New Testament as well, Paul argued that a rebuke is not always appropriate, and other times a rebuke is necessary (1 Timothy 5:17–20). Scripturally, bold confrontation is simply not an either/or proposition. The Bible teaches that there are both times for speaking out and times for being silent.

Obviously, the above point raises the question about how to discern when confrontation is required and when it is not. This highlights the second way 2 Samuel 19:1–8 is useful as a biblical illustration:

Confrontation is necessary when the truth is at stake. Joab rebuked David because his actions were plainly wrong. Yes, everyone in David's kingdom could understand that his heart was grieved for his son, but the hard reality still remained that Absalom led an assault on the city, his father's throne, and the entire nation of Israel. In light of this, the difficult but correct course of action was to put a courageous end to Absalom's threat, and this is exactly what David's soldiers did. They fought to protect their king and his kingdom. So David had to somehow balance his personal sorrow with what was best for the safety and well being of the rest of his house and for the entire nation. Since he clearly lost his balance in this regard, Joab confronted him with the truth.

As mentioned above, Paul also made this point to young Timothy in 1 Timothy 5:17–20. Paul instructed Timothy, a young pastor, to refrain from entertaining every criticism that flew at an elder. Since elders were leaders, they would always have their critics, whether justified or not. However, if elders were living in sin, they were to be rebuked. Simply put: Their position did not set them above God's guidelines for purity. They were not to receive preferential treatment. In fact, their positions of leadership required them to live by a higher standard of account-ability. Therefore, Timothy had to boldly confront others who may have intimidated him (1 Timothy 5:21) because the issue at stake was God's truth. When the Lord's truth is on the table in a situation, boldness is the appropriate response.

Third, while confrontation is sometimes necessary, it must flow from a heart of compassion. Just as Joab courageously challenged David because the king needed to think about what was best for others, believers understand that Scripture calls them to speak "the truth in love" as the church grows and matures (Ephesians 4:15). Also, Paul urged Timothy to confront false doctrines (1 Timothy 1:3–4) and to understand that "the aim of our charge is love that issues from a pure heart and a good conscience and a sincere faith" (1 Timothy 1:5).

As noted previously, the issues of compassion and confrontation are not either/or propositions. They are both/and propositions. Christians must engage in confrontation at appropriate times, and they must always be motivated by love in their efforts. Peter's words are a helpful reminder: "In your hearts regard Christ the Lord as holy, always being prepared to make a defense to anyone who asks you for a reason for the hope that is in you; yet do it with gentleness and respect, having a good conscience, so that, when you are slandered, those who revile your good behavior in Christ may be put to shame" (1 Peter 3:15–16). Jude, who challenged believers "to contend for the faith that was once for all delivered to the saints" (Jude 3), also exhorted them to "have mercy on those who doubt; save others by snatching them out of the fire; to others show mercy with fear, hating even the garment stained by the flesh" (Jude 22–23). Scripture is clear in both biblical narratives like Joab's rebuke of David and in other teaching passages like Proverbs 27:5 and 1 Timothy 5:17–20 that sometimes even leaders need to be confronted with the truth.

22

HUMAN CONFLICTS AND SPIRITUAL CHASTISEMENT
~ 1 Kings 11:14–25 ~

The reality that God chastises His children is a clear principle taught in both the Old and New Testaments (Psalm 119:67–68; Hebrews 12:3–11). But the exact ways that God disciplines believers is more nebulous. For instance, when the Lord gave Paul "a thorn in his flesh," the purpose for Paul's painful trial was explicitly stated: "To keep me from being too elated by the surpassing greatness of the revelations" (2 Corinthians 12:7). The precise nature of the struggle remains unknown today. Yet, there are other places in Scripture where the reader plainly understands how and why God disciplined His people. The biblical illustration of human conflicts and spiritual chastisement in 1 Kings 11:14–25 is an example of this scriptural truth.

Context

The background for the Lord's discipline in the life of Solomon actually extends back into the reign of David, even before Solomon was born. God established His covenant with David in the following words in 2 Samuel 7:8–16:

> Thus says the Lord of hosts, I took you from the pasture, from following the sheep, that you should be prince over my people Israel. And I have been with you wherever you went and have cut off all your enemies from before you. And I will make for you a great name, like the name of the great ones of the earth. And I will appoint a place for my people Israel and will plant them, so that they may dwell in their own place and be disturbed no more. And violent men shall afflict them no more, as formerly, from the time that I appointed judges over my people Israel. And I will give you rest from all your enemies. Moreover, the Lord declares to you that the Lord will make you a house. When your days are fulfilled and you lie down with your fathers, I will raise up your offspring after you, who shall come from your body, and I will establish his kingdom. He shall build a house for my name, and I will establish the throne of his kingdom forever. I will be to him a father, and he shall be to me a son. When he commits iniquity, I will discipline him with the rod of men, with the stripes of the sons of men, but my steadfast love will not depart from him, as I took it from Saul, whom I put away from before you. And your house and your kingdom shall be made sure forever before me. Your throne shall be established forever.

In the Davidic covenant, God promised to put a descendant of David on his throne (2 Samuel 7:12), and He also promised to discipline him when he sinned (2 Samuel 7:14).

These core truths are implied and/or repeated at various points in passages leading to 1 Kings 11:14–25. For example, in David's last words to Solomon, he quoted the Lord's promise: "If your sons pay close attention to their way, to walk before me in faithfulness with all their heart and with all their soul, you shall not lack a man on the throne of Israel" (1 Kings 2:4). Also, the Lord's words in 1 Kings 3:14 imply the conditional aspects of His blessings for Solomon: "If you will walk in my ways, keeping my statutes and my commandments, as your father David walked, then I will lengthen your days." Furthermore, Solomon reiterated God's promise to David in 1 Kings 8:25 when he prayed, "O Lord, God of Israel, keep for your servant David my father what you have promised him, saying, 'You shall not lack a man to sit before me on the throne of Israel, if only your sons pay close attention to their way, to walk before me as you have walked before me.'" Of course, throughout the rest of Solomon's prayer in 1 Kings 8, he mentioned the various ways God chastises His people: Military defeat because of sin (1 Kings 8:33), turmoil in the natural realm because of sin (1 Kings 8:35), and even national captivity or exile because of sin (1 Kings 8:46).

Finally, God appeared to Solomon and underscored His promises to him in 1 Kings 9:4–9. Both His promises of blessing for obedience and discipline for disobedience were mentioned:

And as for you, if you will walk before me, as David your father walked, with integrity of heart and uprightness, doing according to all that I have commanded you, and keeping my statutes and my rules, then I will establish your royal throne over Israel forever, as I promised David your father, saying, "You shall not lack a man on the throne of Israel." But if you turn aside from following me, you or your children, and do not keep my commandments and my statutes that I have set before you, but go and serve other gods and worship them, then I will cut off Israel from the land that I have given them, and the house that I have consecrated for my name I will cast out of my sight, and Israel will become a proverb and a byword among all peoples. And this house will become a heap of ruins. Everyone passing by it will be astonished and will hiss, and they will say, "Why has the Lord done thus to this land and to this house?" Then they will say, "Because they abandoned the Lord their God who brought their fathers out of the land of Egypt and laid hold on other gods and worshiped them and served them. Therefore the Lord has brought all this disaster on them."

So God was abundantly clear in His covenant with David and with David's descendant, Solomon. His blessing and discipline upon their reigns hinged on either their obedience or disobedience. Therefore, when 1 Kings 11:1–8 outlines Solomon's clear violations of God's commandments, there is no surprise that the Lord rebuked him in the following language: "Since this has been your practice [Solomon's disobedience to God's commands, *see* 1 Kings 11:1–2, for instance] and you have not kept my covenant and my statutes that I have commanded you, I will surely tear the kingdom from you and will give it to your servant" (1 Kings 11:11). And the exact ways the Lord executed His discipline is found in the verses that follow God's sober rebuke. They reveal the truth about how God sometimes uses human conflicts as instruments of spiritual chastisement.

The Illustration

The illustration in 1 Kings 11:14–25 is fairly straightforward in its content. God used human conflict in order to chastise Solomon for his spiritual unfaithfulness. This is clear from the opening words of 1 Kings 11:14, "And the Lord raised up an adversary against Solomon, Hadad the Edomite." It is plain from these words that the military clash between Solomon and Hadad was not a chance event. Rather, God worked to get the attention of Solomon's wayward heart. Literally, spiritual disobedience resulted in a physical consequence. In fact, all the details regarding how this national conflict came to pass from a historical perspective in 1 Kings 11:7–22 underscores how the Lord used past events to orchestrate His present and future purposes for His people.

Next, 1 Kings 11:23–25 presents a second example of how human conflicts and spiritual chastisement were linked together at this point in Solomon's reign. For instance, 1 Kings 11:23 begins with words similar to the opening of the previous passage (*see* 1 Kings 11:14): "God also raised up as an adversary to him, Rezon the son of Eliada." Again, the historical roots for Solomon's conflict with Rezon reveal how the Lord used the events of the past for His ongoing purposes in the lives of His people.

Suggestions for Use

While the nature of the biblical illustration above is straightforward, a cautionary word is appropriate concerning how to use scriptural examples like these. In other words, the introductory thoughts to this chapter about how God's methods of chastisement are sometimes plain to see and other times nebulous should be kept in mind. The military conflicts Solomon faced in 1 Kings 11:14–25 were obviously an expression of the Lord's discipline because Scripture itself is clear on this point. This is akin to the cycles of disobedience, discipline, and deliverance Israel faced throughout the storyline of the book of Judges (*see* "Context" sections for chapters 12–14). However, human conflicts occur at other times, and there is no indication that such struggles are the execution of spiritual discipline (for example, *see* the early battles and victories of David in 2 Samuel 8:1–14).

Therefore, expositors and teachers should use caution when appealing to biblical illustrations such as those found in 1 Kings 11:14–25 for the simple reason that not every human conflict is an expression of God's discipline. Unless Scripture makes this connection either explicitly or implicitly, the interpreter should not make such a link. Human conflicts could occur for various reasons.

Nevertheless, when it is obvious in the biblical text that an example of human conflict is an expression of spiritual discipline (as is the case in 1 Kings 11:14–25), the story could be useful in several ways. First, the events of history are not the result of chance. Instead, they serve God's purposes in the lives of His people. The opening words in 1 Kings 11:14 and 23 reveal how the Lord worked in and through these historical events. And this should give believers great encouragement when they face the pain of chastisement. The writer of Hebrews taught, "For the moment all discipline seems painful rather than pleasant, but later it yields the peaceful fruit of righteousness to those who have been trained by it" (Hebrews 12:11). While Solomon was facing an expression of discipline with some long-term consequences, many times Christians experience God's chastisements, learn their lessons, and move forward in spiritual growth.

Second, spiritual discipline is rooted in God's love for His people. Although the Lord's chastisement is painful, it is an expression of His compassionate correction. Again, this aspect of discipline is evident from both the Old Testament and the New Testament as the writer of Hebrews noted in Hebrews 12:5–6: "And have you forgotten the exhortation that addresses you as sons? 'My son, do not regard lightly the discipline of the Lord, nor be weary when reproved by him. For the Lord disciplines the one he loves, and chastises every son whom he receives.'" Interestingly, many believers may falsely conclude as they struggle through the pain of God's discipline that the Lord does not love them or has rejected them. But Scripture emphasizes the exact opposite points when it mentions God's chastisement. According to God's Word, His discipline is actually evidence that He loves His children and accepts them as His legitimate sons and daughters.

Although Solomon's discipline was intensely difficult and had long-term consequences, God's compassion was still evident. For example, when the Lord told Solomon that His discipline would come, He spoke of both His chastisement and His compassion: "Therefore the LORD said to Solomon, 'Since this has been your practice and you have not kept my covenant and my statutes that I have commanded you, I will surely tear the kingdom from you and will give it to your servant. Yet for the sake of David your father I will not do it in your days, but I will tear it out of the hand of your son. However, I will not tear away all the kingdom, but I will give one tribe to your son, for the sake of David my servant and for the sake of Jerusalem that I have chosen'" (1 Kings 11:11–13). This is a powerful expression of God's compassionate correction in the lives of His people.

Third, God's discipline of His leaders oftentimes has an impact on His people. While Solomon is the specific individual in focus in terms of both the breaking of God's commandments and the subsequent consequences for his sin (1 Kings 11:1–25), the people of Israel as a whole also experienced the pain of the Lord's chastisement for Solomon. Obviously, the nation was engaged in the military clashes with Hadad and Rezon. This aspect of the biblical illustration in 1 Kings 11:14–25 is useful to demonstrate how one believer's sin and the consequences for it impacts others (Romans 5:12–14).

Fourth, spiritual chastisement can be expressed in physical ways. At times Christians may think that God's spiritual discipline will not take any type of natural expression. However, the biblical illustration in 1 Kings 11:14–25 reveals that physical circumstances could be a manifestation of the Lord's chastisement in the lives of His people. In other words, a traceable link may exist between some physical circumstances and spiritual causes. For example, Solomon committed spiritual adultery, and he faced the pain of military adversity. In a similar way, Ananias and Sapphira who lied to the Holy Spirit experienced physical death (Acts 5:1–11).

Of course, the final point here is a good opportunity to reiterate the first thought which began this discussion concerning "Suggestions for Use." Human conflicts are not always the result of spiritual discipline. For instance, Jesus experienced relentless human conflict throughout

His ministry, and He never sinned (Hebrews 4:15). In fact, sometimes struggles may signal that a person is not out of God's will but rather in God's will (Matthew 5:10–12; 2 Timothy 3:12). Interpreters must always remember that the explicit or implicit details of the text indicate how a scriptural story should be used to illustrate God's truth in the trenches of life.

23

THE POWER OF COUNSEL

~ 1 Kings 12:1–20 ~

All Christians should seek counsel from time to time. Scripture emphasizes this principle of wisdom almost with the force of a command in Proverbs 15:22, "Without counsel plans fail, but with many advisers they succeed." The obvious thrust of this passage is to gather advice from others so that your plans will be as successful as possible.

Of course, Scripture is not indiscriminate regarding the type of counsel believers should seek. Wise guidance is powerfully beneficial, but foolish advice is woefully detrimental. God's Word makes this point clear in texts such as Proverbs 13:20: "Whoever walks with the wise becomes wise, but the companion of fools will suffer harm." Ultimately, biblical teaching is the standard by which counsel should be judged. Scripture challenges the Lord's people to "trust in the Lord with all your heart, and do not lean on your own understanding. In all your ways acknowledge him, and he will make straight your paths. Be not wise in your own eyes; fear the Lord, and turn away from evil"

(Proverbs 3:5–7). Also, James 1:5 urges believers to look to God for wisdom: "If any of you lacks wisdom, let him ask God, who gives generously to all without reproach, and it will be given him."

Context

While the above counsel is true for all Christians, it is particularly true for leaders. For this reason, the scriptural story in 1 Kings 12:1–20 illustrates the power of counsel. The backdrop for this narrative begins with the previous chapter, 1 Kings 11. Since Solomon chose to disobey God's commands (1 Kings 11:1–8), the Lord disciplined him (1 Kings 11:9–13). The first two expressions of God's chastisement in Solomon's life appeared in the form of military conflicts with Hadad and Rezon, respectively (1 Kings 11:14–22, 23–25).

However, the Lord's third (and more long-term) form of discipline is expressed in 1 Kings 11:26–40. In these verses, God sent His prophet, Ahijah, to deliver a message to one of Solomon's capable servants, Jeroboam, the son of Nebat (1 Kings 11:26–29). Ahijah used his new robe and his words to convey the Lord's clear message. Basically, God was going to tear ten tribes away from the rule of David's house because of Solomon's sin, and He was going to establish the reign of Jeroboam over these tribes. Although a descendant of David would remain on the throne in Judah (the southern kingdom), Jeroboam would rule the ten tribes of Israel (the northern kingdom) (1 Kings 11:29–37). Of course, the Lord challenged Jeroboam to spiritual faithfulness and revealed that His blessings hinged on Jeroboam's obedience to God's commandments (1 Kings 11:38–39).

When Solomon heard of Jeroboam's meeting with Ahijah, he tried to kill Jeroboam. But Jeroboam took refuge in Egypt until Solomon died, and his son, Rehoboam, began to reign (1 Kings 11:40–12:2). This is the storyline that brings the reader to the beginning of 1 Kings 12, to the narrative about Rehoboam, and to the biblical illustration of the power of counsel.

The Illustration

As Rehoboam began to rule, Jeroboam and other Israelites sought to petition him for a much-needed reprieve from their hard labor. Solomon's reign was a prosperous and peaceful period, but it was also an incredibly busy time for various building projects. And such projects required both money and manpower to complete.[31] In light of this, Jeroboam and others issued this reasonable request to Rehoboam: "Your father made our yoke heavy. Now therefore lighten the hard service of your father and his heavy yoke on us, and we will serve you" (1 Kings 12:4). Rehoboam initially appeared wise to ask his people for time to consider their request (1 Kings 12:5). However, all semblance of wisdom quickly vanished as 1 Kings 12:1–20 unfolds.

The king first "took counsel with the old men, who had stood before Solomon his father while he was yet alive" (1 Kings 12:6). Although Solomon drifted astray in the fields of folly at a point in his life, he is still remembered as one of the wisest kings of Israel. Certainly, the men who stood before him would have gleaned wisdom from him and shared their wisdom with him. And their counsel to Rehoboam was wise, indeed. They gave the following instruction to their young ruler: "If you will be a servant to this people today and serve them, and speak good words to them when you answer them, then they will be your servants forever" (1 Kings 12:7).

Rehoboam should have heeded the wise counsel of his elderly advisers. However, their appeal for him to dispense generosity, humility, and

---

31. Paul R. House, *1, 2 Kings*, vol. 8 of *The New American Commentary* (Nashville: Broadman and Holman, 1995), 181.

patience to his subjects fell on deaf ears, a closed mind, and a prideful, hardened heart. This is evident because Rehoboam clearly did not take the advice of his father's counselors. First Kings 12:8 indicates that "he abandoned the counsel that the old men gave him." Instead, he sought guidance from his younger counselors.

The fact that Rehoboam asked all his counselors, old and young, for advice is not foolish. Actually, Scripture teaches that "where there is no guidance, a people falls, but in an abundance of counselors there is safety" (Proverbs 11:14). Yet, wisdom is not found in simply counting noses when it comes to seeking advice. In this instance, quality was certainly more important than quantity. And this is obvious because the counsel of Rehoboam's young advisers could not have been more diametrically opposed to the words of their elderly counterparts. The young men "who had grown up with him" (1 Kings 12:8) told the king to chastise the people with the following words: "My little finger is thicker than my father's thighs. And now, whereas my father laid on you a heavy yoke, I will add to your yoke. My father disciplined you with whips, but I will discipline you with scorpions" (1 Kings 12:10–11). And to Rehoboam's own harm, he followed the foolish counsel of his younger counselors. So when Jeroboam and the others returned to hear their king's response to their petition, Rehoboam "answered the people harshly, and forsaking the counsel that the old men had given him, he spoke to them according to the counsel of the young men" (1 Kings 12:13–14).

Due to Rehoboam's lack of sympathy for his own people's struggles and needs, his kingdom immediately became unstable (1 Kings 12:16–17). Next, one of his servants who represented his harsh and heavy-handed approach to leadership was stoned to death (1 Kings 12:18). At that very point, it became clear that the northern kingdom of Israel began a rebellion against the southern kingdom of Judah. The ten tribes in the north rallied behind Jeroboam's leadership because they obviously felt that he would listen to and address their needs (1 Kings 12:19–20). Although this story focuses on Rehoboam's ultimate decision as a leader, it emphasizes the power of counsel to influence life-changing decisions.

Suggestions for Use

The above biblical illustration is useful in preaching and teaching in three ways. One way is plainly evident, and two other ways are more subtle. To begin with, it is apparent from this story that a person's companions exert a major influence on his or her life. This can have either positive or negative results. For example, Psalm 1:1–2 teaches, "Blessed is the man who walks not in the counsel of the wicked, nor stands in the way of sinners, nor sits in the seat of scoffers; but his delight is in the law of the Lord, and on his law he meditates day and night." Also, Paul warned believers in 1 Corinthians 15:33 to be careful about who they listened to: "Do not be deceived: 'Bad company ruins good morals.'"

So both Psalm 1 and Paul's words in 1 Corinthians 15 indicate two general types of companions who exist in this world, namely, the godly and the ungodly. Rehoboam faced these two types of counselors. Sadly, he chose to listen to the advice of the ungodly. Believers face this same choice daily. They are surrounded by those who seek to follow the Lord and His ways, and they also rub shoulders with others who do not have a desire to serve Christ. Depending on whose advice they follow, Christians will be either helped or harmed.

Concerning the two subtle ways that 1 Kings 12:1–20 can be useful in preaching and teaching, the following suggestions may be considered. First, young people, especially leaders, should avail themselves of the wisdom of their elders. Rehoboam's initial action to seek guidance from his older counselors who once served his father was admirable. Proverbs 20:29 teaches, "The glory of young men is their strength, but the splendor of old men is their gray hair." Of course, simply living a long life does not guarantee wisdom. Proverbs 16:31 says, "Gray hair is a crown of glory; it is gained in a righteous life." Thus, young people would be wise to seek guidance from those who have sought the Lord. Wisdom is gained over the course of sustained godly living.

Second, an important point when seeking counsel is to be open to God's truth rather than to focus only on personal preferences. The truth is oftentimes hard to hear because it challenges believers to the core. This is why Paul called Christians to "let the word of Christ dwell in you richly, teaching and admonishing one another in all wisdom, singing psalms and hymns and spiritual songs, with thankfulness in your hearts to God" (Colossians 3:16). Also, Paul challenged Timothy to "preach the word; be ready in season and out of season; reprove, rebuke, and exhort, with complete patience and teaching" (2 Timothy 4:2). Lastly, Paul taught that "all Scripture is breathed out by God and profitable for teaching, for reproof, for correction, and for training in righteousness, that the man of God may be complete, equipped for every good work" (2 Timothy 3:16–17). Words like *admonishing* (Colossians 3:16), *reprove, rebuke, exhort* (2 Timothy 4:2), and *reproof* and *correction* (2 Timothy 3:16) all signal that God's truth is challenging to sinful hearts. It's been well said that "God's Word comforts the afflicted and afflicts the comfortable."

All this relates to the story of Rehoboam in 1 Kings 12:1–20 and to the power of counsel in the lives of believers in the following subtle but sober way. When Christians seek advice, they need to ask God for grace to hear what they need to hear rather than what they want to hear. Rehoboam obviously heard the words of his older counselors who challenged him to demonstrate generosity, humility, and patience before his people, but this was not the message he wanted to hear. Therefore, he kept seeking guidance until he heard the message that dovetailed with his sinful desires and selfish ambitions. Obviously, Christians must not follow Rehoboam's negative example.

24

VALLEYS USUALLY FOLLOW PEAKS

~ 1 Kings 19:1–18 ~

I n an almost unexplainable way, valleys usually follow peaks in life. The greatest successes are often preludes to the most devastating failures. Put another way: Defeats often rear their ugly heads in the wake of victories.

Context

The above thought is true in every realm of life—even in the spiritual realm. The story of the prophet Elijah in 1 Kings 19:1–18 is a good example of this common phenomenon. While some narratives require a fair amount of background material by way of review, other stories need hardly any comment on their backdrop because they are so well-known. The account of Elijah in 1 Kings 19 fits the category of a familiar biblical story.

Soon after Rehoboam succeeded Solomon as the king of Israel, the nation divided (1 Kings 12:19–20). In fulfillment of the prophet Ahijah's message to Jeroboam even during the reign of Solomon, the house of David ruled the southern part of the divided nation known as Judah, while Jeroboam ruled the northern part known as Israel (1 Kings 11:26–40).

For the most part, the kings of both Judah and Israel did not faithfully follow the Lord. While occasional bright spots of spiritual fervency took place (*see*, for example, the revival under Josiah in 2 Chronicles 34:1–35:19), the more frequent summary of the kings was that they did not lead in covenant loyalty before God (*see*, for instance, 1 Kings 14:21–24; 15:25–26). These comments were unfortunately true for both Judah and Israel.

However, the northern kingdom of Israel forms the specific background for the biblical illustration in 1 Kings 19:1–18. The rule of Ahab, the king of Israel during the events recorded in 1 Kings 19, was introduced into the narrative of 1 Kings 16:29–34 with the following words:

> In the thirty-eighth year of Asa king of Judah, Ahab the son of Omri began to reign over Israel, and Ahab the son of Omri reigned over Israel in Samaria twenty-two years. And Ahab the son of Omri did evil in the sight of the Lord, more than all who were before him. And as if it had been a light thing for him to walk in the sins of Jeroboam the son of Nebat, he took for his wife Jezebel the daughter of Ethbaal king of the Sidonians, and went and served Baal and worshiped him. He erected an altar for Baal in the house of Baal, which he built in Samaria. And Ahab made an Asherah. Ahab did more to provoke the Lord, the God of Israel, to anger than all the kings of Israel who were before him. In his days Hiel of Bethel built Jericho. He laid its foundation at the cost of Abiram his firstborn, and set up its gates at the cost of his youngest son Segub, according to the word of the Lord, which he spoke by Joshua the son of Nun.

It is painfully clear from these verses that Ahab was not only wicked, but he was the vilest king Israel had known to this point in history.

Of course, 1 Kings 16 leads into chapter 17, which then introduces the prophet Elijah (1 Kings 17:1). Elijah surfaced on the national scene during an incredibly dark night of spiritual corruption, and his first words, the prediction of an impending drought, conveyed a message of judgment upon both Ahab and his wayward kingdom. After he delivered his prophetic proclamation, he disappeared from the scene. The Lord took care of him in the midst of the drought (1 Kings 17:2–24), and Ahab and his people languished under the dire conditions of an agricultural nation caught in the merciless lashing of three-and-a-half rainless years (1 Kings 18:1; James 5:17).

But the drought came to an end in 1 Kings 18 when Elijah resurfaced on Israel's public stage and called for a meeting between himself and the false prophets of the land (1 Kings 18:1–19). When they gathered on Mount Carmel, Elijah gave his opponents the first opportunity to see if their false god could send fire from heaven. But not a single ember fell from the cloudless sky. Their idol did not exist. He was only a figment erected in the chambers of their dark, dead, and depraved minds and hearts (1 Kings 18:20–29).

However, after Elijah repaired the altar of the Lord, he called out to God in prayer, and fire bolted down from the skies to engulf the sacrifice he had prepared because God is God (1 Kings 18:30–39). Next, Elijah had the false prophets executed for their spiritual lawlessness, and he sent Ahab on his way ahead of the torrential downpour that God unleashed upon His parched people and land (1 Kings 18:40–46).

The reader might initially think that Elijah's supernatural transport to heaven (2 Kings 2:1–12) would take place immediately after this account of a massive spiritual victory. But such is not the case. In fact, the next story about Elijah in 1 Kings 19:1–18 shows how he even wanted his life to end on the heels of his mountaintop experience. All this shows how valleys usually follow peaks.

The Illustration

After God demonstrated His power and glory over all other false gods as the one and only Lord of Israel (1 Kings 18:30–39), Elijah sent Ahab home (1 Kings 18:41). When Ahab returned home, he told his wife, wicked Jezebel, all that Elijah had done to her false prophets, and she become murderously angry (1 Kings 19:1–2). So when Elijah heard that Jezebel swore to have him put to death because of the executions of her prophets, "he was afraid, and he arose and ran for his life" (1 Kings 19:3). He rushed south approximately one hundred miles from Mount Carmel to Beersheba, then he "went a day's journey into the wilderness" (1 Kings 19:3–4) and "sat down under a broom tree. And he asked that he might die, saying, 'It is enough; now, O Lord, take away my life, for I am no better than my fathers" (1 Kings 19:4). But the Lord would not take His prophet's life. Instead, He sent His angel to give Elijah instructions and resources for some much-needed physical rest and food before He gave him another ministry assignment (1 Kings 19:5–8).

After Elijah was refreshed, God heard his cries of desperation as Elijah lamented: "I have been very jealous for the Lord, the God of hosts. For the people of Israel have forsaken your covenant, thrown down your altars, and killed your prophets with the sword, and I, even I only, am left, and they seek my life, to take it away" (1 Kings 19:10, 14). However, after listening to His prophet's cries, the Lord revealed Himself to Elijah in such a special way that "when Elijah heard [the sound of God's reassuring presence], he wrapped his face in his cloak" (1 Kings 19:11–13). At this point, the Lord commissioned Elijah for more prophetic work, and He comforted His prophet with the knowledge that he was not alone in his spiritual dedication (1 Kings 19:15–18).

Suggestions for Use

While it may initially appear that the biblical illustration in 1 Kings 19:1–18 might be best suited to demonstrate the sober principle of a verse like 1 Corinthians 10:12: "Therefore let anyone who thinks that he stands take heed lest he fall," a more careful understanding of the story leads to a different conclusion. Paul's words above deal more specifically with instances of spiritual arrogance. And although Scripture teaches that pride leads to failures (Proverbs 16:18), Elijah did not appear to battle pride. Rather, he struggled with the emotional letdown that often burdens those involved in an all-consuming ministry. For this reason, a more positive approach to Elijah's struggles is likely the best understanding of his story.

No less than four aspects of the biblical illustration in 1 Kings 19:1–18 should prove helpful to expositors and teachers. First, fear leads to failure. The fear of man always leads to failure, while the fear of the Lord always leads to victory. Proverbs is clear on both these fronts: "The fear of the Lord prolongs life, but the years of the wicked will be short" (Proverbs 10:27), and "The fear of man lays a snare, but whoever trusts in the Lord is safe" (Proverbs 29:25).

In 1 Kings 19:3, Elijah reacted in fear of Jezebel's threatening message, and he ran away in desperation. It may be difficult to imagine how a prophet, who just witnessed fire fall from heaven, could run for his life at the words of a mere mortal. Nevertheless, "the fear of man lays a snare," indeed. This first aspect of 1 Kings 19:1–18 clearly illustrates how valleys usually follow peaks.

Second, physical rest is an important part of being spiritually refreshed. The first need the Lord addressed in the life of His struggling prophet was a physical one. Not only did Elijah travel the one hundred miles from Mount Carmel to Beersheba, but he also went a day's journey into the wilderness (1 Kings 19:3–4). Simply put: Elijah was physically depleted, and his drained body doubtlessly had a major impact on his spiritual focus. So God provided opportunities for His prophet to rest and recuperate his physical strength in order to regain his spiritual equilibrium.

Jesus taught the above principles by His interaction with His disciples. For example, after they had returned from a mission venture (Luke 9:1–6), Jesus took them to a town called Bethsaida (Luke 9:10). Valleys often follow peaks because believers who are physically worn are spiritually susceptible to temptation. But if Christians tend to their physical needs and rest, they will avoid pitfalls that come to those who are drained from their work.

Third, the Lord listened to Elijah's desperate cries and reminded him of His reassuring presence. God not only tended to Elijah's physical needs, but He also revealed Himself to His prophet in a personal and powerful way. Of course, this point along with the previous one should not give the impression that life is made up of physical and spiritual compartments that have no influence on one another. In fact, the opposite is true. As is clear from the case of Elijah, the physical and spiritual dimensions of life are intertwined.

Nevertheless, the Lord worked in a certain order: After He rested His prophet physically, He reassured His prophet spiritually. As with the first aspect of God's work discussed above, the second facet of the Lord's work is equally significant. Even Elijah, the noted prophet of Israel, had to focus on God's power to gain reassurance during his struggles.

Of course, Scripture is clear that believers need to "be transformed by the renewal" of their minds (Romans 12:2), "take every thought captive to obey Christ" (2 Corinthians 10:5), "take the helmet of salvation" (Ephesians 6:17), and "think about whatever is true, whatever is honorable, whatever is just, whatever is pure, whatever is lovely, whatever is commendable" (Philippians 4:8). The Lord reassures His people with the promises of His presence, power, and purposes in the difficult and draining trenches of life. This is not to be confused with positive thinking, which falsely calls people to have confidence in their ability to change their reality with their thoughts. Rather, this is biblical thinking, which challenges Christians to rest in God and the truth of His Word. As believers remain focused by God's grace on the message of Scripture, they will walk and work in God's strength through the peaks and valleys of ministry.

Fourth, the Lord often uses new assignments to move His people through ministry valleys. Elijah had recently experienced a major victory, which was the culmination of years of struggle (1 Kings 17–18), but the peak Elijah experienced was not the end of his prophetic ministry. Instead, it was a transition point to a new assignment from God (1 Kings 19:15–18). In fact, one aspect of Elijah's new ministry task, the anointing of Elisha to serve as a prophet in Israel (1 Kings 19:16, 19–21), actually implied that Elijah would be moving off the stage of human history in the near future. Some may view this point as a negative indication that Elijah was facing the end of his ministry. However, God's word on this occasion emphasized the following positive message: The Lord is always greater than His human instruments because His work is ultimately about His power and for His glory.

The above thoughts about the biblical illustration in 1 Kings 19:1–18 might be useful in illustrating a scriptural principle, such as the one found in 2 Timothy 2:1–2. In these verses, Paul admonished Timothy to steadfast faithfulness even through his struggles. He also urged Timothy to pass on his teachings to other faithful servants who would then teach others. Just like Elijah, believers may get the false sense after major spiritual victories that their work is finished. And this feeling of having nothing left to do because the work is done could create a deep valley following a mountaintop experience. Yet, the story of Elijah demonstrates that God does have more for His servants to do. Furthermore, it illustrates that even when their time on earth is fulfilled, the Lord's work continues. All of this should encourage Christians who find themselves in valleys. It should give them something to set their focus on beyond their most recent spiritual victories. Valleys do not spell the end of God's story since He alone writes it. He continues to use His people for His purposes. Even when their time on earth is completed, His plans are sustained through others. This truth should assist believers as they walk over the peaks and through the valleys of ministry.

25

A SIMPLE MEDICINE AND A SUPERNATURAL CURE

~ 2 Kings 20:1–7 ~

God is sovereign, and He is good. Therefore, all His ways are perfect. Although believers often struggle during times of pain with how the Lord works in their lives, they can rest upon His sovereignty and goodness (Psalm 119:67–68). Nestled in the story of Hezekiah's illness and healing in 2 Kings 20:1–7 is an example of how the Lord works mysteriously in the lives of His people according to His power and goodness.

Context

As mentioned in the previous chapter (*see* "Valleys Usually Follow Peaks"), many of the kings of both Judah and Israel did not follow the Lord's commandments. This eventually led to their exile in foreign lands. The first to fall in captivity was Israel, the northern kingdom.

161

While 2 Kings 18:9–12 summarizes this event, a longer description of it is found in 2 Kings 17:1–23.

Interestingly, at the very point in the storyline of 2 Kings that chronicles the fall of Israel (2 Kings 17:7–18), Hezekiah, king of Judah, is introduced (2 Kings 18:1–8). His biographical sketch outlined that "he did what was right in the eyes of the Lord . . . He trusted in the Lord, the God of Israel, so that there was none like him among all the kings of Judah after him, nor among those who were before him. For he held fast to the Lord. He did not depart from following him, but kept the commandments that the Lord commanded Moses. And the Lord was with him; wherever he went out, he prospered" (2 Kings 18:3, 5–7). So Hezekiah was one of the few bright spots on the spiritual landscape of Judah's historical horizons.

One way 2 Kings reveals Hezekiah's desire to follow God is by the repeated observation that he "trusted in the Lord" whenever he faced struggles. For example, when Assyria sent emissaries to mock and threaten Judah (2 Kings 18:13–37), Hezekiah's immediate response was that "he tore his clothes and covered himself with sackcloth and went into the house of the Lord" (2 Kings 19:1). He also sent some of his servants to the prophet Isaiah to ask him to intercede for the nation (2 Kings 19:2–4). Isaiah then delivered God's message of reassurance for Hezekiah and Judah (2 Kings 19:5–7).

Also, even when Assyria continued to send their message of an impending attack on God's people, Hezekiah did not waver in his trust in the Lord. Second Kings 19:14 reveals, "Hezekiah received the letter from the hand of the messengers and read it; and Hezekiah went up to the house of the Lord and spread it before the Lord." The content of the king's prayer is presented in 2 Kings 19:15–19. It affirmed Hezekiah's confidence in God's power to glorify His name among all nations. And, as with the previous example of Hezekiah's trust in the Lord, the prophet Isaiah once again proclaimed how God would establish victory for His people over Assyria (2 Kings 19:20–34). This is exactly what supernaturally took place (2 Kings 19:35–37). Thus, the background for the story of Hezekiah's illness and supernatural healing in 2 Kings 20:1–7 is how God worked for His glory in and through Hezekiah's reign as he sought to trust the Lord in all circumstances.

The Illustration

At some point after God saved the kingdom of Judah from devastation (2 Kings 19:35–37), He miraculously saved Hezekiah from death (2 Kings 20:1). However, the Lord's initial message was that his time on earth was finished (2 Kings 20:1). But when he heard the news of his impending death, "Hezekiah turned his face to the wall and prayed to the Lord, saying, 'Now, O Lord, please remember how I have walked before you in faithfulness and with a whole heart, and have done what is good in your sight.' And Hezekiah wept bitterly" (2 Kings 20:2–3).

At this poignant moment of the story, everything changed. Literally, "before Isaiah had gone out of the middle court" (2 Kings 20:4), the Lord turned His messenger on his heels and sent him back to Hezekiah with the following words of hope: "Thus says the Lord, the God of David your father: I have heard your prayer; I have seen your tears. Behold, I will heal you. On the third day you shall go up to the house of the Lord, and I will add fifteen years to your life. I will deliver you and this city out of the hand of the king of Assyria, and I will defend this city for my own sake and for my servant David's sake" (2 Kings 20:5–6).

Next, a very brief but interesting verse concludes this story of Hezekiah's illness and healing. Second Kings 20:7 provides the final words of Isaiah to the king's servant: "Bring a cake of figs. And let them take and lay it on the boil, that he may recover." Clearly, although God had already pronounced His promise to heal Hezekiah, He nevertheless chose to use simple medicinal means to accomplish His supernatural healing.

Suggestions for Use

The brief story of Hezekiah's illness and miraculous healing in 2 Kings 20:1–7 could be useful for preaching or teaching in a number of ways. First, this narrative illustrates the mystery of both God's providence and prayer. Scripture is clear that the Lord and His ways are perfect. Moses sang, "The Rock, his work is perfect, for all his ways are justice" (Deuteronomy 32:4). David worshiped the Lord with this declaration: "This God—his way is perfect; the word of the Lord proves true; he is a shield for all those who take refuge in him" (2 Samuel 22:31; Psalm 18:30). Therefore, prayer does not change God, since His ways never need to adjust according to the suggestions of His people. Instead, prayer is the believer's opportunity to praise the Lord for His perfect will and to surrender to it (Matthew 6:9–10).

Nevertheless, Jesus calls His followers to pray and to bring their petitions before their heavenly Father who knows what they need even before they ask (Matthew 6:7–8; 7:7–11). And it is at this precise point a mystery emerges. While prayer does not change God, He still calls Christians to pray. The Lord often reveals His perfect will through persistent intercession as His peace saturates the lives of His people who prayerfully trust Him (Philippians 4:6–7). Apparently, God's plan was always to extend the king's life, but the Lord used Hezekiah's earnest intercession to bring him to this realization. And the Lord continues to work in this way in the lives of His people today.

Second, trusting prayerfulness is the response God desires from His people regardless of the size of the problems they face. For instance, Hezekiah's expression of trust in God through prayer at the news of his impending death was not an isolated event. On the contrary, the king's faith and prayerfulness in this story is simply another expression of his faith in God. He prayed in faith when he was confronted with the threats of an enemy king, and he also prayerfully trusted God when he heard the news of a deadly infection in his body. Hezekiah's response was the same in both cases: He sought God in prayer and trust to accomplish His will for His glory (2 Kings 19:1–4, 14–19; 20:2–3). Once more, regardless of the size of his struggle, Hezekiah's faith remained intact.

Of course, this aspect of the story could be used as a historical example of trusting God in prayer in general. Scripture is clear in its call for believers to remain in a constant attitude of prayer (Philippians 4:6; 1 Thessalonians 5:17). And although Hezekiah is a good example of prayerfulness in the face of trials, Jesus is the only perfect example for the believer to follow since He bathed every event (Luke 3:21–22; 9:28–29), decision (Luke 6:12–16), and struggle (Matthew 26:36–46) in prayer.

Third, as the title of this chapter indicates, the story of Hezekiah's illness and healing also illustrates how God can work not only through His supernatural power but also through a simple channel. Regardless of what means the Lord chooses to use, His plans are only accomplished by His power. In this way, He alone is worthy to receive all glory, honor, and praise in this life and forever. Thus, the psalmist declared, "Some trust in chariots and some in horses, but we trust in the name of the Lord our God" (Psalm 20:7). The point here is clear: While God may use chariots and horses in His plan to deliver His people in military conflicts, for example, the ultimate power for victory is in the Lord.

This Old Testament narrative may actually serve as a parallel for an interesting point that emerged during the ministry of Jesus in the Gospel accounts. For example, Christ healed people in various ways. Sometimes He touched an ailing person (Mark 1:40–42); others times He simply spoke a word from a distance (Matthew 8:5–13); on another occasion He made spittle with mud, applied it, and told the person to go and wash (John 9:1–7); and still in another fascinating instance, He seemed to heal a person in stages (Mark 8:22–26).

In light of these events in Jesus's ministry, natural questions arise: Why did Christ heal in these different ways during His ministry? Why did He not simply heal everyone in the same manner? Furthermore, if Jesus could merely speak a word from a distance and procure healing for someone, surely He did not need to use any intermediate means of healing, did He?

The answer to these questions is that Christ performed healings according to His supernatural power alone. Furthermore, He either healed with or without intermediate means according to His sovereign prerogative. This answer is a helpful link between the parallel ideas which surface in the story of Hezekiah in 2 Kings 20:1–7 and in the healing ministry of Jesus. For instance, twice in the overall narrative of Hezekiah, God acted in miraculous power to deliver His people: He sent an angel to kill 185,000 Assyrian soldiers in one night (2 Kings 19:35), and He made the sun's shadow move in reverse ten steps to assure Hezekiah of His promise to heal (2 Kings 20:8–11).

In light of these facts, God had the supernatural power to heal Hezekiah's illness in any way He chose, and He chose to do it through a simple medicinal process (2 Kings 20:7). But the reader should understand that the king's healing was the result of God's supernatural work, even though it came through a simple medicinal means. This is also true in the ministry of Jesus.

So this point is helpful for believers today. They are free to trust the Lord to use various medical resources and procedures for His healing purposes in their lives. However, they should always understand that their healing comes from their heavenly Father's hand. He created the human body, and He knows exactly how it is supposed to function. Also, the above thoughts should comfort Christians as they trust the Lord, whether they or their loved ones experience healing or not. In other words, God can heal according to whatever means He chooses because of His sovereign prerogative, but sometimes He chooses not to heal. Even in these painful times, He works for His ultimate purposes and glory. Simply put: God is not obligated to heal every person, nor does He heal every person in this life. Still, believers can trust their heavenly Father even in these painful times because of His sovereignty and goodness.

Fourth, God's healing purposes are for His glory. When the Lord responded to Hezekiah's prayer, He said, "I will add fifteen years to your life. I will deliver you and this city out of the hand of the king of Assyria, and I will defend this city for my own sake and for my servant David's sake" (2 Kings 20:6). Clearly, Hezekiah's healing was not for the king alone; it was for God's glory. In fact, on one occasion when Hezekiah prayed to God for deliverance from the Assyrians, he asked the Lord to act for the following reason: "So now, O Lord our God, save us, please, from his hand, that all the kingdoms of the earth may know that you, O Lord, are God alone" (2 Kings 19:19). The focus in both passages from the narrative of Hezekiah is God's glory.

This final emphasis from 2 Kings 20:1–7 illustrates Jesus's teaching about prayer in His model prayer in Matthew 6:9–13. Before Jesus taught His followers to bring their petitions to the Lord, He taught them to focus on God's sovereign will and to surrender to His perfect purposes.[32] Of course, both Jesus (Matthew 6:11; 7:7–11) and Paul (Philippians 4:6) urged believers to bring their petitions to the Lord. The emphasis here is simply that God's glory should remain the ultimate focus in prayer above all other requests. This is how Jesus prayed while He struggled in agony in the garden of Gethsemane (Matthew 26:39–43), and His life is the perfect example for His followers to emulate by the power of God's Spirit. Regardless of what pain enters the lives of believers and how God chooses to deal with it, Christians can rest in the sovereign power and goodness of their heavenly Father.

---

32. Charpentier, 77–80.

26

Leading One Step at a Time

~ 2 Chronicles 30:1–20 ~

Trying to do everything perfectly in this life is impossible. Those who pursue perfection place themselves under a crushing weight. They will never measure up to their self-imposed standards. God says to believers, "You shall be holy, for I am holy" (1 Peter 1:16). However, the Lord knows better than anyone else how imperfect His people are in their daily lives. And He is gracious and merciful to lead His people one step at a time as they seek to follow Him, albeit with their lack of perfection as an ever-present reality.

Context

This point is vividly illustrated in 2 Chronicles 30:1–20 with a story from the life and reign of Hezekiah. Although many leaders of the southern kingdom of Judah did not serve the Lord, Hezekiah was one of the few rulers who "did what was right in the eyes of the Lord, according to all that David his father had done" (2 Chronicles 29:2). In fact, his first act as king was that "he opened the doors of the house of the Lord and repaired them" (2 Chronicles 29:3). Hezekiah purified the temple and its worship from the corruption of idolatry that had contaminated the land and provoked God's judgment (2 Chronicles 29:4–9). Hezekiah articulated his motivation for his actions in a simple and straightforward manner: "It is in my heart to make a covenant with the Lord, the God of Israel, in order that his fierce anger may turn away from us" (2 Chronicles 29:10).

Of course, an entire system of worship that had been derailed by years of unfaithfulness did not rectify itself in a single act of purification. Hezekiah had to work with the priests and Levites to take all the necessary steps to set God's house in order. This was necessary so God's people could worship Him according to His prescribed commands (2 Chronicles 29:11–36). But as the priests labored to lead in purity, they fell short of God's ideal. For example, 2 Chronicles 29:34 says, "The priests were too few and could not flay all the burnt offerings, so until other priests had consecrated themselves, their brothers the Levites helped them, until the work was finished—for the Levites were more upright in heart than the priests in consecrating themselves." The people were so far off God's path that they had to take a series of steps to get back on course. And in the process of returning to the Lord's ideal, they were doing the best they could in light of their circumstances. Basically, they were trying to lead one step at a time.

The Illustration

Second Chronicles 29:34 hints at the fact that the priests were doing the best they could while not fulfilling the ideal details of God's law. However, 2 Chronicles 30:1–20 removes all doubt and reveals that this was the exact situation for Hezekiah, the priests, and the people. For instance, 2 Chronicles 30:2 reports that "the king and his princes and all the assembly in Jerusalem had taken counsel to keep the Passover in the second month." Now this time reference is important. Exodus 12:2 stipulated that the Passover should be observed in the first month of the year. But Hezekiah, his leaders, and the people evidently discussed their situation and made a decision. They choose to celebrate the Passover on this alternative date as opposed to not celebrating it at all because the prescribed date was not a possibility. Perhaps the king and others made this decision because God's law provided for alternate celebration dates for different circumstances.[33]

Also, once the Passover celebration was underway, some aspects of the festivities were not conducted according to the letter of the law. Second Chronicles 30:17–18 indicates, "For there were many in the assembly who had not consecrated themselves. Therefore the Levites had to slaughter the Passover lamb for everyone who was not clean, to consecrate it to the Lord. For a majority of the people, many of them from Ephraim, Manasseh, Issachar, and Zebulun, had not cleansed themselves, yet they ate the Passover otherwise than as prescribed."

The potential seriousness of this act is highlighted in Hezekiah's prayer: "May the good Lord pardon everyone who sets his heart to seek God, the Lord, the God of his fathers, even though not according to the sanctuary's rules of cleanness" (2 Chronicles 30:18–19). Of course, the fact that God accepted the worship of His people even though it was not presented perfectly is clear from His response to Hezekiah's prayer: "And the Lord heard Hezekiah and healed the people" (2 Chronicles 30:20).

Thus, the story of Hezekiah and the celebration of the Passover in 2 Chronicles 30:1–20 indicates how God mercifully worked among His

---

33. Eugene H. Merrill, "2 Chronicles," in *The Bible Knowledge Commentary: An Exposition of the Scriptures by Dallas Seminary Faculty: Old Testament*, ed. by John F. Walvoord and Roy B. Zuck (Wheaton: Victor Books, 1985), 642.

people even when their efforts were imperfect. Obviously, this statement indicates what is true in every occasion because the efforts of the Lord's people are never perfect in this life. God's acceptance of His people is based on the finished work of His Son and not on their efforts. They are always in the process of being conformed to the image of Christ in their daily walk (Romans 8:28–30; Philippians 1:6).

Suggestions for Use

The story of Hezekiah and how he led the people of Judah in celebrating the Passover in 2 Chronicles 30:1–20 is a powerful biblical illustration on several fronts. First, this narrative provides a historical example of how leaders must begin somewhere in the process of helping others seek after God. In other words, when pastors, for example, read the Scripture's call to follow God's Word so that believers know how "one ought to behave in the household of God, which is the church of the living God, a pillar and buttress of the truth" (1 Timothy 3:15), they could become overwhelmed. All honest church leaders know that every ministry is not what it should be in terms of meeting the Lord's ideal standards in Scripture. And this could breed leadership paralysis for pastors who seek perfectionism. They could convince themselves: If it can't be done right, then it shouldn't be done at all.

But it is clear that Hezekiah did not follow this type of flawed thinking. While he tried to do the best he could, Hezekiah knew he would not get everything right the first time. Yet, he also knew that he had to start somewhere and move forward from there. His story is an example of how God is cultivating greater Christlikeness in His people, although they stumble in many ways (Colossians 1:28–29; James 3:2).

Second, the previous point should be balanced with the fact that Hezekiah, his leaders, and his people sought to do the best they could in light of their situation. While the Lord accepted their less than perfect efforts, this does not mean that Hezekiah and his people did not pay attention to details with a desire to get them right. Every aspect of this story shows that they worked to celebrate the Passover in a way that honored God. In fact, Hezekiah's prayer revealed that both he and Judah were aware of what the law required. They sought to comply with its details at every point with precision. This is the reason Hezekiah prayed for mercy. He wanted to do what was right and honorable before the Lord (2 Chronicles 30:18–19). Hezekiah was not careless. The reality was that he was honest with his shortcomings as he led God's people in covenant faithfulness.

This facet of Hezekiah's story shows a practical example of the balance all believers should seek to exhibit in every aspect of their lives. Just as Paul described his consuming desire to be all that God desired for him to be while he also acknowledged his imperfections (Philippians 3:12–14), most believers struggle in the same way. They realize that God calls them to practical holiness, but they also understand that they have not arrived. While they throw themselves completely into a desire to pursue personal holiness (1 Timothy 4:7–8), they also realize that God is sanctifying them daily (1 Thessalonians 5:23–24).

Third, God sees the hearts of His people and responds accordingly out of His great love and mercy. While it is true that Hezekiah and his people were not able to fulfill every requirement of the Passover regulations perfectly, they nevertheless had pure heart attitudes. Hezekiah's prayer emphasized this point: "May the good Lord pardon everyone who sets his heart to seek God, the Lord, the God of his fathers, even though not according to the sanctuary's rules of cleanness" (2 Chronicles 30:18–19). In other words, even though their actions were imperfect, God knew their hearts and extended His mercy to them.

Of course, God always looks at the heart. For example, some people may approach a time of worship with every external indicator appearing to be in order. However, if their hearts are harboring anger against others, Jesus said to "leave your gift there before the altar and go. First be reconciled to your brother, and then come and offer your gift" (Matthew 5:24). Also, the prophet Isaiah declared that even though God's people entered into His courts with outward fanfare in worship, His eyes gazed into the depths of their hearts where He looked for purity and justice (Isaiah 1:10–17).

Some believers enter a place of worship, and while the outward indictors scream that they should not be in God's presence, the Lord actually declares their worship to be acceptable to Him. For example, when Jesus told the story of the Pharisee and the tax collector in the temple (Luke 18:9–14), He clearly indicated that God responded favorably to the tax collector's humility and brokenness. But He rejected the worship of those "who trusted in themselves that they were righteous, and treated others with contempt" (Luke 18:9).

So it is clear that God looks at the hearts of worshippers, and He wants them to worship Him in spirit and truth (John 4:23–24). Obviously, believers are clean before God only because of Christ's righteousness imputed to them; they do not engage in any self-reliant boasting (1 Corinthians 1:30–31; 2 Corinthians 5:21). And just as Hezekiah and his people evidenced humility as they entered God's presence, even so Christians can come confidently before the throne of grace because of the merit of Christ's finished work and not because of their inferior, inadequate, and imperfect attempts at legalistic righteousness (Hebrews 4:14–16).

27

WORK AND RESISTANCE

~ Nehemiah 4–6 ~

Any time God calls His people to a particular work, they face resistance. This has been true throughout history. Jesus told His followers, "In the world you will have tribulation. But take heart; I have overcome the world" (John 16:33). Paul wrote that "all who desire to live a godly life in Christ Jesus will be persecuted" (2 Timothy 3:12). James also said, "Count it all joy, my brothers, when you meet trials of various kinds" (James 1:2). It has been well-noted that James did not say "if you meet trials" but "when you meet trials." Everyone who seeks to walk in obedience to God's call faces opposition. This was clearly the case with Nehemiah.

Context

The historical context for the book of Nehemiah is simple: God's people have been captured and sent into exile. The northern kingdom of Israel fell first to the Assyrians (2 Kings 17:6–23), and the southern kingdom of Judah fell next to the Babylonians (2 Kings 25:1–21). But God was not finished with His people. While they had been unfaithful to His covenant, He had always been faithful. So, just as He promised to restore His people (Jeremiah 29:10–14), the book of Nehemiah chronicles an important aspect of their restoration—a return to Jerusalem to rebuild the walls of the city.

In relation to the textual background of the story of Nehemiah and the resistance he faced as he labored in God's work, Nehemiah 1–3 is the primary focus. The book of Nehemiah begins with a report from Hanani, Nehemiah's brother, concerning the horrid conditions in Judah during the time of the exile (Nehemiah 1:1–3). In response to this sad news, Nehemiah offered a prayer of confession, contrition, and petition to the Lord. He expressed his desire to work and to help his people and their fallen city (Nehemiah 1:4–11).

Then, in Nehemiah 2:1–8, God opened a door through Nehemiah's dialogue with King Artaxerxes to give His servant authority to rebuild Jerusalem's walls. After Nehemiah arrived in Judah, he took time one evening to assess the work before him (Nehemiah 2:9–18). But when he and others put their hands to the proverbial plow to rebuild the wall, their enemies, Sanballat, Tobiah, and Geshem, emerged in the story (Nehemiah 2:19). Yet, with the threats of his enemies ringing in his ears, Nehemiah sought the Lord for strength to accomplish His work (Nehemiah 2:20).

Nehemiah 3 provides an overview of how God's work was distributed among Nehemiah and his coworkers. But as the reader could imagine, he and the others had not heard nor seen the last of their enemies. The reason why is because God's work is always coupled with resistance in this world.

The Illustration

In Nehemiah 4–6, various aspects of resistance confront Nehemiah as he rallies God's people to rebuild the walls of Jerusalem. And, like a quilt,

Nehemiah stitched together each patchwork piece of struggle with a prayer. Prayer pulsates through the flow of this story as it moves forward with every twist and turn of resistance. This reveals how the Lord accomplished the task He put before His people.

For example, after the overview of how Nehemiah and the others positioned themselves for God's work in chapter three, Sanballat and Tobiah lashed out against God's servants. They mocked and demeaned the efforts of the Lord's people (Nehemiah 4:1–3). But Nehemiah's response to this ridicule was intercession. He looked to God to deal justly with the sinfulness of his enemies (Nehemiah 4:4–5).

Next, when sections of the reconstruction were completed (Nehemiah 4:6), Sanballat, Tobiah, and others increased their level of opposition. Nehemiah 4:8 says that "they all plotted together to come and fight against Jerusalem and to cause confusion in it." And what was Nehemiah's response to his enemies' intensified resistance? Nehemiah 4:9 reads, "We prayed to our God and set a guard as a protection against them day and night." As indicated in this verse, Nehemiah not only prayed; he also acted with practical wisdom. He trusted the Lord for protection and made preparations to guard himself, his people, and their city by God's power.

As Nehemiah's enemies continued to pursue their plots against him and his people, perseverance and further planning were necessary (Nehemiah 4:10–12). He adjusted his plan (Nehemiah 4:13), and he encouraged his people with the following words: "Do not be afraid of them. Remember the Lord, who is great and awesome, and fight for your brothers, your sons, your daughters, your wives, and your homes" (Nehemiah 4:14). Once again, it is clear that Nehemiah's persistent focus on God and His power was the fuel that kept both him and his people moving forward with the Lord's work even in the face of relentless resistance. In fact, the rest of Nehemiah 4 describes how the work to rebuild the wall continued amidst hostilities.

Even when Nehemiah had to deal with complaints that some of his own people were taking advantage of others (Nehemiah 5:1–5), he dealt with this internal problem with a challenge that each person should, among other things, "walk in the fear of God" (Nehemiah 5:6–11). Through Nehemiah's leadership, the Lord resolved this conflict from within which threatened to stifle His work (Nehemiah 5:12–13). Also, Nehemiah 5:14–19 reveals that Nehemiah did not simply challenge others to treat their fellow laborers well, but he practiced what he preached. For instance, he refrained from taking Artaxerxes's luxurious provisions for himself (Nehemiah 5:14–16), and he also gave generously out of his own resources to others (Nehemiah 5:17–18). As noted above, Nehemiah lived differently from those who had governed before him "because of the fear of God" (Nehemiah 5:17). He trusted that the Lord took inventory of his living faithfully before God and generously toward others (Nehemiah 5:19).

Just when the reader might think that the resistance against Nehemiah vanished, Sanballat, Tobiah, Geshem, and others surfaced again. They once more came against God's people with resistance. On this occasion, they tried to distract Nehemiah and the others from their tasks (Nehemiah 6:1–2). But Nehemiah saw through their schemes and refused to be taken away from the Lord's work (Nehemiah 6:2–3). Nehemiah's enemies made multiple attempts to pull him away from his work, and they leveled false accusations against him (Nehemiah 6:4–7). Nevertheless, Nehemiah maintained his focus on the truth, and he prayed, "Now, O God, strengthen my hands" (Nehemiah 6:8–9).

One final attempt to derail God's work occurred in Nehemiah 6:10–14. But Nehemiah saw through his enemies' plan to convince him through a prophet that the Lord did not want him to finish rebuilding Jerusalem's wall (Nehemiah 6:10–13). As any careful reader would expect, Nehemiah closed this scene with an appeal to God to deal justly with Tobiah and Sanballat and their false prophets (Nehemiah 6:14).

The biblical illustration in Nehemiah 4–6 concludes with the completion of God's work to rebuild the wall of Jerusalem (Nehemiah 6:15). All the plots of Nehemiah's enemies to strike fear in the hearts of God's people failed, and Nehemiah 6:16 says that "when all our enemies heard of it [the completion of the wall], all the nations around us were afraid and fell greatly in their own esteem." Of course, Nehemiah points out that all the surrounding people "perceived that this work had been accomplished with the help of our God" (Nehemiah 6:16).

While the story of the resistance Nehemiah faced as he labored in God's work came to a close, the resistance did not end! Like an ominous "To Be Continued . . ." announcement scrolling across the book of Nehemiah at this point, the reader learns of more attempts from Nehemiah's enemies to make him fearful (Nehemiah 6:17–19). This only serves to prove that all who engage in God's work face resistance.

Suggestions for Use

The story of how Nehemiah and his people faced resistance while engaged in God's work to rebuild the walls of Jerusalem lends itself well to illustrate various truths from Scripture. For instance, any teaching message dealing with the reality of trials such as John 16:33, 2 Timothy 3:12, or James 1:2 could find a narrative parallel in Nehemiah 4–6. Woven throughout the flow of these chapters in Nehemiah is the repetitive theme of opposition and struggle that accompanies God's call to obedience.

Also, Nehemiah's faithfulness in prayer, even with resistance constantly bludgeoning against him, is a powerful illustration for passages focused on diligence in prayer. Both Jesus's instructions to His disciples to pray "lead us not into temptation, but deliver us from evil" (Matthew 6:13) and Paul's admonitions to "not be anxious about anything, but in everything by prayer and supplication with thanksgiving let your requests be made known to God" (Philippians 4:6) and to "pray without ceasing" (1 Thessalonians 5:17) all find a practical illustration in Nehemiah 4–6.

Another helpful aspect of the story is how Nehemiah did not take personal vengeance on his enemies. Instead, he always asked the Lord to deal with them justly (see Nehemiah 4:4–5; 6:14). This point could illustrate teachings from several passages such as Psalm 3 and Romans 12:19–21 which begins with the following words: "Beloved, never avenge yourselves, but leave it to the wrath of God, for it is written, 'Vengeance is mine, I will repay, says the Lord.'"

Nehemiah's faithfulness even when he encountered temptations to turn from God's work (Nehemiah 6:1–14) is another way this story could be used as a biblical illustration. For instance, Jesus called people to follow Him with a singular focus: "No one who puts his hand to the plow and looks back is fit for the kingdom of God" (Luke 9:62). Also, Paul urged Christians, "Do not be conformed to this world, but be transformed by the renewal of your mind, that by testing you may discern what is the will of God, what is good and acceptable and perfect" (Romans 12:2). He also exhorted believers to "set your minds on things above, not on things that are on earth. For you have died, and your life is hidden with Christ in God" (Colossians 3:2–3).

Clearly, God's people will always have ample opportunities to be distracted from His work, but they must learn a lesson from the story of Nehemiah and remain focused on God's work by His strength (Nehemiah 6:1–9). They should always remember that their labor for the Lord is never in vain (1 Corinthians 15:58).

28

God's Fingerprints

~ Esther 1-10 ~

The book of Esther is the only book of the Bible that does not include a direct mention of God's name. While certain passages (such as Esther's call to others to fast) imply the Lord's presence in the book (Esther 4:15–16), the words *God* or *Lord* do not surface anywhere on its pages.

However, although God's name does not appear in the book of Esther, His fingerprints are on every page. Esther's storyline contains many interesting and ironic twists and turns that point unmistakably to the Lord's providential sovereignty. An anonymous proverb says, "A coincidence is a small miracle when God chooses to remain anonymous." Such is the case with the story of Esther: God clearly worked at every point in the narrative, but He simply chose to remain anonymous.

Context

Since this chapter deals with an overview of the entire book of Esther (Esther 1–10), a brief summary of the historical background of the book is in order. (*See* the next chapter entitled "Staying Focused" for a discussion of the textual background for Esther 1–3.) The historical context for Esther is similar to the book of Nehemiah (*see* previous chapter) since both books describe events that took place while God's people were exiled in foreign lands. Specifically, the book of Esther describes a particular struggle the Jews faced while they lived under Persian rule. After the Assyrians conquered the northern kingdom of Israel (2 Kings 17:6–23) and the Babylonians vanquished the southern kingdom of Judah (2 Kings 25:1–21), the Persians came into power (2 Chronicles 36:17–21).

The period of the Persians was the final phase of Israel's exile in the Old Testament. God used Cyrus, king of Persia, to make an official decree to allow the Lord's people to return to their homeland (2 Chronicles 36:22–23). However, simply because the Persian period marked the last stage of Israel's exile, this did not mean that the Israelites had clear sailing during this time. The book of Esther focuses on how the wicked schemes of an enemy named Haman threatened the very existence of the Jews in Persia. But God, who kept His covenant and preserved His people prior to their captivity, continued to sustain His people by His sovereign power. This is exactly why His fingerprints appear on every page of the book of Esther.

The Illustration

The major contours of Esther reveal God's providential workings to protect the survival of His people even in the face of a genocidal threat. The first chapter of the book reveals how Vashti, the queen of Persia, was removed from her royal position because of her insubordination. This may be an interesting foreshadowing within the book. Later in the story, Esther herself will risk her life and defy Persian law in order to thwart Haman's deadly plot to kill the Jews (Esther 4). However, while

God used Persian customs to remove one queen and to establish another, He set aside the consequences of Persian rules to save His people.

Once the queen of Persia had been removed from her post, another queen was needed. So God arranged for Esther to assume this position of influence (Esther 2:1–18). Interestingly, the Lord accomplished His perfect purpose by using the king of Persia's unsavory practice of assembling a harem. In fact, when Esther is first introduced into the storyline of the book, the Scripture says that Mordecai, Esther's relative, had raised "Hadassah, that is Esther, the daughter of his uncle, for she had neither father nor mother. The young woman had a beautiful figure and was lovely to look at, and when her father and her mother died, Mordecai took her as his own daughter" (Esther 2:7). Surely God alone could place an orphaned exile in one of the most prestigious positions of an empire, even while a pagan king acted on immoral impulses.

While much of the first two chapters of Esther cover rather large scale events, Esther 2:19–23 focuses on what may initially appear as an insignificant detail. This is the brief account of how Mordecai acted to save the Persian king from a plot against him. But this event proves significant later in the story. It surfaces again to show how God providentially worked to spoil Haman's plot against the Jews (Esther 6:1–11).

Once again, the reader encounters an interesting foreshadowing in the book of Esther. While God used Mordecai, a Jew, to save the Persian king, the Lord later used the Persian king to save the Jews. He set up a plan for Mordecai and the other Jews to save themselves. This sequence of events magnifies God's sovereign fingerprints on the story.

After Esther and Mordecai, the two human heroes, have been introduced into the narrative, their arch rival Haman is introduced in Esther 3. After Haman secured permission from the Persian king to have the Jews killed on a particular day, Mordecai learned about Haman's sinister scheme. He then asked Esther to use her influential position to help save her people. Again, while God's name is not found in the book of

Esther, the truth of His providential sovereignty bleeds through Mordecai's words to Esther. He urged her with these now-famous words: "Do not think to yourself that in the king's palace you will escape any more than all the other Jews. For if you keep silent at this time, relief and deliverance will rise for the Jews from another place, but you and your father's house will perish. And who knows whether you have not come to the kingdom for such a time as this?" (Esther 4:13–14). Mordecai's closing words form a powerful rhetorical question. It beckoned Esther in her day, and it beckons every reader to acknowledge that God positions His people to be a part of His plan for His glory. All of this book's details and all of life's struggles are not happenstance. Rather, they are opportunities for God's people to be a part of His holy strategy to accomplish His will.

Esther 5:1–8 begins to chronicle how Esther courageously acted to do whatever she could to uncover Haman's murderous plot. Even Esther 5:9–14 factors into God's sovereign plan because no detail escapes His providential orchestration of events to fulfill His grand design. Rather than immediately unleashing his lethal jealousy against Mordecai, Haman agreed to have gallows built for Mordecai's future execution. But Haman did not design this delay to give him greater satisfaction in watching Mordecai die. God actually used it for His purposes. It created the necessary time to reveal to the Persian king a reason to honor Mordecai for his past act of loyalty in saving the king from a plot against him (Esther 6:1–13). At this point in the story, the irony of the unfolding events is explicitly revealed. Those close to Haman tell him: "If Mordecai, before whom you have begun to fall, is of the Jewish people, you will not overcome him but will surely fall before him" (Esther 6:13).

And this is precisely what happens in Esther 7. The climax of the story occurs in Esther 7:1–6 as Esther uncovered Haman's plot to the Persian king. And then all the tension of the story is resolved in the rest of the book. For example, Haman was hung on the very gallows he had prepared for Mordecai (Esther 7:7–10). In addition to this ironic reality, the careful reader also recalls how others who plotted against the Persian king died on gallows earlier in the narrative (Esther 2:23). And so the Lord used gallows twice in this story to spoil deadly plots. But this time it was not a plot against a pagan king; it was a plot against God's chosen people. Furthermore, while one man, Haman, died on the gallows, an entire nation living in exile was saved. And all this occurred because of God's sovereign power to preserve His covenant people.

The literary tension in the story of Esther continued to be resolved in the rest of the book. In chapter eight, Esther and Mordecai worked with the Persian king to establish a plan for the Jewish people to protect themselves against their attackers, and Esther 9:1–19 chronicles how the Jews successfully defended themselves. The remainder of the book describes how the Feast of Purim was established to commemorate the Jewish victory over their enemies (Esther 9:20–32) and how Mordecai served well in his positions of leadership during the exile (Esther 10). Although God's name does not appear in these closing verses, His providential sovereignty is evident in the military conflicts, the joyful celebrations, and the noble lives His people lived for His glory while abroad in a foreign land.

Suggestions for Use

The general thrust and theme of how God worked according to His sovereign power in and through the events of the book of Esther serve to illustrate a variety of biblical truths. For instance, Proverbs 21:1 says, "The king's heart is a stream of water in the hand of the Lord; he turns it wherever he will." This scriptural principle is clearly presented in the story of Esther. Not only does God use the Persian king's decisions and activities for His purposes, but every other leader, even wicked Haman, is not successful in his plots and schemes. The Lord's will is ultimately accomplished throughout every human circumstance because every ruler or leader is ultimately subject to His sovereign power.

Also, God uses those in authority to execute His justice in this life. While human hearts are corrupt and are always tempted to compromise justice for the sake of their own purposes, the Lord nevertheless uses earthly authorities at times to exact His judgment on earth. Paul taught in Romans 13:1–4:

> Let every person be subject to the governing authorities. For there is no authority except from God, and those that exist have been instituted by God. Therefore whoever resists the authorities resists what God has appointed, and those who resist will incur judgment. For rulers are not a terror to good conduct, but to bad. Would you have no fear of the one who is in authority? Then do what is good, and you will receive his approval, for he is God's servant for your good. But if you do wrong, be afraid, for he does not bear the sword in vain. For he is the servant of God, an avenger who carries out God's wrath on the wrongdoer. Therefore one must be in subjection, not only to avoid God's wrath but also for the sake of conscience.

Both of the above points are illustrated in Esther. Haman serves as an example of how people sometimes use their positions of power for sinful purposes, but the king of Persia could serve as a picture of how the Lord uses authority figures to execute justice.

In addition to the two broad points above, another basic biblical teaching is illustrated in the book of Esther, namely, persons' sins find them out. Just as Haman died on the gallows he prepared for Mordecai, people who plot against God will eventually suffer punishment. Sometimes the penalty for their sins surfaces both in this life and the next. Other times it surfaces only in the next life. But the reader should make no mistake about it: The wicked definitely face the consequences of their sins.

This insight could be used as an example for passages such as Psalm 37:12–13: "The wicked plots against the righteous and gnashes his teeth at him, but the Lord laughs at the wicked, for he sees that his day is coming." The more general idea that the wicked will face judgment at some point in time, either in this life or the next, is in view here. However, the more specific thought that the sinful actions of the wicked could be turned upon themselves for their own downfall factors into the next verses in Psalm 37: "The wicked draw the sword and bend their bows to bring down the poor and needy, to slay those whose way is upright; their sword shall enter their own heart, and their bows shall be broken" (Psalm 37:14–15). These verses could easily serve as a powerful picture of what happened to wicked Haman in the story of Esther. Haman drew his proverbial sword against Mordecai when he had gallows built for his execution, but his blade pierced his own heart as his corpse dangled publicly in God's judgment for all to see.

29

STAYING FOCUSED

~ Esther 4:1–17 ~

A proverbial Rubicon River signals a point of no return. All believers face their Rubicon Rivers at some pivotal crossroads. Christians will always have to confront decisive moments in life with God's courage. In the midst of life's challenges, they will have to stay focused on Christ. This was certainly the case for both Mordecai and Esther in Esther 4:1–17.

Context

Three essential events from Esther 1–3 form a proper background and orientation for Esther 4:1–17. (For an overview of the entire flow of the book of Esther, see the previous chapter, "God's Fingerprints.") First, the setting for this narrative is the Persian Empire where the Jews were living in exile (Esther 1:1–2). Second, the Lord positioned Esther in the palace of the Persian king as queen (Esther 2:5–18). Esther's relative,

Mordecai, raised her as an orphaned Jewish girl. Third, Haman devised a plot to slaughter all the Jews (Esther 3:1–15). He served as a high-ranking Persian official, but he was consumed with hatred for Mordecai because the Jew refused to bow before him. These three events set the stage for the curtain to open on Esther 4:1–17. Here Mordecai challenged Esther in a pivotal moment to stay focused.

The Illustration

Esther 4:1 opens with a very moving scene. Mordecai had learned of Haman's murderous scheme, and he publicly cried out in desperation for the deliverance of his people. While God's name is not explicitly mentioned, His presence is strongly implied. The mention of "sackcloth and ashes" and "fasting and weeping, and lamenting" signal fervent prayer to God (Esther 4:1–3).

At this juncture, Esther entered the scene. She was deeply distressed at the news of Mordecai's bitter weeping (Esther 4:4). However, when she heard his command to go before the king on behalf of their people, she explained that such an action could be lethal. The law forbade going into the king's inner court without a summons. Anyone (including the queen) risked his or her life for such a bold stand (Esther 4:10–11). Nevertheless, the classic axiom held true: Desperate times call for desperate measures.

The dialogue between Mordecai and Esther in Esther 4:12–17 captures the main thrust of this biblical illustration. It highlights the importance of staying focused in the midst of extraordinary challenges. To begin with, Mordecai explained to Esther that silence was simply not an option. If she spoke up, she might die at the hand of the king, but if she did not break her silence, she would surely die at the hand of Haman (Esther 4:12–14). Furthermore, Mordecai assured Esther that God would act to save His people. The Lord's name is not explicitly mentioned here, but He is surely the ultimate subject of the verbal ideas embedded in the words "relief and deliverance" in Esther 4:14.

In light of Mordecai's two challenging insights, he made two additional points before he ended his dialogue with Esther. First, he essentially told Esther that she could be a part of God's plan to deliver His people. Or she could step aside while the Lord used someone else to accomplish His purpose (Esther 4:14). Second, Mordecai asked Esther to ponder the reason why God made her queen. It was not for herself but for the Lord's glory (Esther 4:14). He wanted to use her (and others) to save His people (Esther 4:14).

Esther ended her side of the dialogue with Mordecai in dramatic fashion. She first called all the Jews to fast on her behalf for three days, thus implying they ask God to move in power (Esther 4:16). She did not trust in her own power to change the dreadful circumstances confronting her and the Jews. Also, she stepped across the line of commitment completely. Esther knew that her stand could result in her death, and she was willing to pay this ultimate price.

Suggestions for Use

Preachers and teachers can easily appeal to Esther 4:1–17 in order to illustrate six points in relation to how believers can stay focused in dangerously difficult circumstances. First, silence is not always good or safe. Sometimes Christians need to speak up even if human laws command them to be silent. While it is true that believers should submit to authority (Romans 13:1–7), honor leaders (1 Peter 2:17), and seek to live at peace with everyone (Romans 12:18; 1 Timothy 2:1–2), they are also called to live godly in Christ Jesus and to face the inevitable persecutions which result (Acts 14:19–22; 2 Timothy 3:12). Esther is an example of someone who obeyed God and defied human authority when these became mutually exclusive. (For other scriptural examples of this, *see* the midwives in Exodus 1:15–22, the three Hebrew young men in Daniel 3, Daniel himself in Daniel 6, and Peter in Acts 5:27–32.)

Second, God accomplishes His plan. Mordecai's words in Esther 4:14 assured Esther that the Lord would deliver His people whether she chose to risk her safety or not. This truth surfaces repeatedly in Scripture. For instance, Proverbs 19:21 teaches, "Many are the plans in the mind of a man, but it is the purpose of the Lord that will stand."

This second point makes the following third point even more powerful. A believer can be a part of God's plan or step aside while the Lord uses others for His purposes. This is basically what Mordecai explained to Esther when he said, "For if you keep silent at this time, relief and deliverance will rise for the Jews from another place, but you and your father's house will perish" (Esther 4:14). Mordecai's words were not so much a threat as they were simply the truth. Esther had to realize that God was not required to use her. He chose to use her. This point illustrates texts emphasizing the Lord's call to difficult service (Isaiah 6:8–13; Jeremiah 1:4–10).

Fourth, focusing on God's sovereignty helps believers stay focused when confronting challenging circumstances. Mordecai's words, "And who knows whether you have not come to the kingdom for such a time as this?" (Esther 4:14), reveal how God is in control in all situations. For example, Proverbs 16:33 says, "The lot is cast into the lap, but its every decision is from the Lord." For the Christian, there is no such thing as luck in life. While God calls people to act as responsible moral agents, He works in and through their activities by His sovereign power to accomplish His plans. Believers can learn from the story of Esther that God's plan is always bigger than they are. It is about accomplishing His purposes for His glory. So when Christians focus on God's sovereignty, they can remain focused in the midst of difficult challenges.

Fifth, hope is found in God alone. Esther's call for all Jews to fast with her was a clear indication that she realized the need for the Lord to act in power. No one else could accomplish deliverance for God's people but He Himself. This point illustrates various texts that call Christians to put their confidence only in the Lord. For instance, two passages from the Psalter present this principle: Psalm 20:7, "Some trust in chariots and some in horses, but we trust in the name of the Lord our God," and Psalm 127:1, "Unless the Lord builds the house, those who build it labor in vain. Unless the Lord watches over the city, the watchman stays awake in vain." The New Testament as well draws attention to this key biblical truth (John 15:5; 1 Corinthians 3:5–9; Colossians 1:28–29; 1 Thessalonians 5:24).

Finally, staying focused requires believers to count the cost of their commitment to Christ. Esther entered the king's presence with her eyes wide open. She acknowledged the most costly consequence for her action, but she declared her willingness to face it by God's power when she uttered: "I will go to the king, though it is against the law, and if I perish, I perish" (Esther 4:16). Her bold declaration of complete commitment regardless of the cost serves as a powerful illustration of Jesus's call to count the cost of discipleship as well (*see*, for example, Luke 14:25–33). If believers set out to follow Christ in their own strength and without counting the cost, they will surely lose heart and focus (*see* the story of Peter in Luke 22:31–34). But when they count the cost and rely on God's power to sustain them through every trial, they can stay focused and endure any struggle faithfully to the end (John 21:15–23).

30

Sovereignty, Satan, and Suffering

~ Job 1:1–2:10 ~

The poet William Cowper wrote a beautiful hymn in 1773:

God works in a mysterious way | His wonders to perform; | He plants His footsteps in the sea | And rides upon the storm.

Believers do not always understand how the Lord works and may feel that His ways are mysterious. Yet, they know that He accomplishes His perfect purposes. This seems to be most obvious when Christians face suffering. Pain has a way of bringing pointed questions to the surface of the human heart and mind. In the struggles of life, believers wrestle with the issues of God's sovereignty, Satan's sinister schemes, and their suffering. They also strive to understand how all these issues fit together.

Context

Job certainly dealt with all of these biblical truths. The book of Job is perhaps the most well-known story of suffering in Scripture. Since Job's suffering is recounted in Job 1–2, the following two sections fulfill a couple of purposes: They set the stage for the whole book of Job, and they show how sovereignty, Satan, and suffering are involved in the mysterious ways God works.

However, before Job 1:1–2:10 is discussed, a brief explanation should be offered for the order of the words in the title of this chapter. First, the words appear in this order because of the way the narrative of Job 1:1–2:10 unfolds. The title begins with *Sovereignty* because God alone reigns supreme over all. He does not react; He acts. The word *Satan* appears next since he enters the scene early in the book of Job to tempt Job to blasphemy. But even he is subject to God's sovereign plan. The word *Suffering* appears last in the title because this is what follows in the wake of Satan's sinful schemes. It is also what God uses to bring Job to a greater understanding of Himself and His character.

In summary, God reigns over all in His sovereignty, even over Satan and suffering. Satan still tries to rob God of His glory. Although suffering may be the result of Satan's assaults, the Lord uses even Satan and suffering for His good purposes and glory. In this way, His people grow in their understanding of Him.

The Illustration

The book of Job opens with a thumbnail biographical sketch of Job. It highlights two important aspects of his life. First, Job sought to live a righteous life that honored the Lord. This is clear from Job 1:1, 4–5. In addition to being described as devout, Job performed priestly functions on behalf of his children in case they sinned against God during their feasts.[34]

Second, Job was a wealthy man. The amount of livestock and servants outlined in Job 1:3 makes this clear. Also, the final words of this verse remove any doubts: "This man was the greatest of all the people of the east" (Job 1:3).

It was precisely Job's uprightness and blessings that became the focal point of the rest of Job 1:1–2:10. Satan approached God one day, and the Lord brought Job into their dialogue. While the reader can be confident Job probably would not have appreciated this, God's reasons for doing so are clear: "There is none like him on the earth, a blameless and upright man, who fears God and turns away from evil" (Job1:8). But Satan accused Job of shallow and selfish motives for his allegiance to the Lord when he retorted, "Stretch out your hand and touch all that he has, and he will curse you to your face" (Job 1:11). At this point, God's sovereignty took center stage. He permitted Satan to tempt Job to the sin of blasphemy with any type of suffering except physical pain (Job 1:12). Even though a torrential flood of agony crashed into Job's life, nothing took place except what God allowed in His sovereignty.

At this point, the reader anxiously awaits what types of suffering Satan will unleash on Job and how Job will respond to it. Job 1:13–19 outlines in rapid succession Satan's horrific plan to inflict suffering on Job. First, some of Job's livestock and servants were killed by Sabean raiders (Job 1:14–15). Second, the fire of God consumed his sheep and more of his servants (Job 1:16). Third, another raiding party of Chaldeans plundered Job's camels and killed more of his servants (Job 1:17). Fourth, a fierce wind destroyed the home of Job's firstborn son where

---

34. Robert L. Alden, *Job*, vol. 11 of *The New American Commentary* (Nashville: Broadman and Holman, 1993), 51–52.

all of his children were gathered, crushing all ten of them in one fatal moment (Job 1:18–19).

What is Job's response to all this suffering? Does Job prove Satan right, or does he prove God right? Job 1:20–22 leaves no doubt that Satan was wrong, and the Lord was right. First, Job worshiped God even in the midst of his suffering (Job 1:20). Second, Job confessed the Lord's sovereign power over all things and the fact that He is always worthy to be praised: "The Lord gave, and the Lord has taken away; blessed be the name of the Lord" (Job 1:21). Third, the closing verse of Job 1 plainly states, "in all this Job did not sin or charge God with wrong."

If the first chapter of Job alone chronicled his suffering, the book would still be a powerful message regarding God's sovereignty and human pain. However, Job 2 also describes more of his suffering, but this time His physical body was afflicted with severe pain. When Satan dialogued with God further about Job in Job 2:1–6, God spoke of His servant's spiritual fidelity: "He still holds fast his integrity, although you incited me against him to destroy him without reason" (Job 2:3). Of course, Satan persisted in his false accusations that Job still only served God because of his shallow and selfish motives: "Stretch out your hand and touch his bone and flesh, and he will curse you to your face" (Job 2:5). Satan claimed that if Job's suffering became severe enough, he would forsake his commitment to God. Once again, the Lord's sovereignty is highlighted as He allowed Satan to wreak havoc within prescribed limits (Job 2:6).

The next description of Job's suffering is much shorter than the previous one, but it is still graphic in terms of revealing Job's agony. On this second occasion, "Satan . . . struck Job with loathsome sores from the sole of his foot to the crown of his head. And he took a piece of broken pottery with which to scrape himself while he sat in the ashes" (Job 2:7–8). Next, like pouring salt into open wounds, Satan apparently borrowed the vocal chords of Job's wife. Through her words he spewed in Job's face his wicked temptation to blaspheme God: "Then his wife said to him, 'Do you still hold fast your integrity? Curse God and die'" (Job 2:9). She was the only family member who commented about Job's sufferings, and she urged him to blaspheme the Lord and die. But Job posed a rhetorical question to his wife: "Shall we receive good from God, and shall we not receive evil?" (Job 2:10). The obvious answer Job expected was clear from his actions—God is worthy of praise in every circumstance of life, in both seasons of pleasure and plenty as well as in seasons of pain. Then, as with the conclusion of Job 1, the second chapter of Job assures the reader of Job's continual commitment to spiritual faithfulness. The final words of Job 2:10 summarize his God-honoring response in the midst of suffering: "In all this Job did not sin with his lips."

Suggestions for Use

The message of sovereignty, Satan, and suffering in Job 1:1–2:10 could be used in several ways to illustrate all three of these themes. First, both the declarations (1 Timothy 6:15) and descriptions of God's sovereignty (Proverbs 19:21) find a powerful picture here. Although Satan inflicted his painful plan in Job's life, he could do nothing without God's permission.

The above observation brings the next point into view: Satan's plan is to destroy God's people because he hates God's glory. However, God even uses the enemy to accomplish His perfect plans. First, Jesus plainly taught, "The thief comes only to steal and kill and destroy" (John 10:10). While this verse occurs in the context of false shepherds (*see* John 9:1–10:18), Scripture is clear that Satan is the ultimate false teacher who "prowls around like a roaring lion, seeking someone to devour" (1 Peter 5:8). Every time Satan is mentioned in Scripture without exception, he is acting in deception and for destruction.

While Satan tempts humanity, his hatred for God's glory is his ultimate motivation. The suffering he brought into Job's life was merely a step towards the goal of seeing Job curse God. Job was a means to an end, as far as Satan was concerned. This point could be used to illustrate various texts that teach about Satan's wicked ways. For example, the first time he tempted humanity, he sought to make deity itself the coveted prize for Adam and Eve. He lied to them with the following words: "God knows that when you eat of it [the forbidden fruit] your eyes will be opened, and you will be like God, knowing good and evil" (Genesis 3:5). Here is Satan's ultimate plan. This is why God responded to the enemy by underscoring Job's steadfast faithfulness: "He still holds fast his integrity, although you incited me against him to destroy him without reason" (Job 2:3). Believers must be careful not to fall into Satan's temptations. They should never lash out against God in accusations whenever they suffer, because this is precisely Satan's ultimate goal.

Third, God uses even the suffering Satan brings into the Christian's life for His good purposes and glory. While Job engaged in tense dialogue with his friends and posed many painfully honest questions before God (Job 2:11–37:24), the final chapters of the book of Job focus on the Lord's unparalleled sovereignty and goodness (Job 38–42). God is in control during all of life's circumstances. Whether believers are soaring over the mountain peaks or struggling as they walk through the valleys, God is sovereign. Furthermore, He is always worthy of praise. This is a message repeated throughout Scripture (Psalm 103) and powerfully illustrated in Job 1:1–2:10.

31

NEGATIVE AND POSITIVE SIDES OF MINISTRY

~ Jeremiah 1:9–10 ~

Everyone in ministry wishes that circumstances could always move forward and be positive. However, this is simply not possible, especially in established ministry settings. Leaders who enter established ministries even have to move backwards sometimes before they can move forward. Some aspects of long-standing ministries become entrenched over time. At some point, ministries may move away from God's design and continue to move further off course. Ministers who come into these settings have to help restore God's people to a proper focus. They oftentimes have to go back to the place where a ministry stumbled and redirect the work forward from there.

This usually takes courage and is oftentimes a lonely venture. Nevertheless, God desires for His people to follow Him in authentic commitment. This means that every faithful leader will have to deal with both the negative (removal and rebuilding) and positive (building) sides of ministry.

Context

Such is the case with the prophet Jeremiah. Jeremiah 1:1–3 supplies the historical time span for Jeremiah's prophetic ministry. This time frame included two extremely different spiritual climates. Jeremiah entered his prophetic office during the reign of Josiah (Jeremiah 1:2). This was one of the brightest spots of Judah's history. During his reign, Josiah sought to reform the Lord's wayward people. Also, the book of the law was rediscovered, and the Passover was celebrated on a very large scale (2 Kings 22:1–23:27; 2 Chronicles 34:1–35:19).

However, Jeremiah unfortunately witnessed the other end of the spiritual spectrum as well. The last king mentioned in Jeremiah 1:3, marking the ending point of Jeremiah's prophetic tenure in Judah, was Zedekiah. Like most of the other kings of Judah, he was an ungodly ruler. He reigned "until the captivity of Jerusalem" (Jeremiah 1:3, *see* also 2 Kings 24:18–25:7; 2 Chronicles 36:9–21).

Even though Jeremiah 1:1–3 mentions both Josiah (a positive period of spiritual renewal) and Zedekiah (a negative period of spiritual deterioration), the bulk of Jeremiah's prophetic ministry dealt with Judah's sinfulness until its demise into captivity. In fact, one commentator summarized what a human evaluation of Jeremiah's ministry might look like:

> An evaluation of Jeremiah by most standards of success would brand him an abysmal failure. He preached for forty years without convincing the people that he was God's prophet. He was threatened, ridiculed, and physically abused by his own people. Jerusalem was finally destroyed, and Judah ceased to exist as a nation

because the people refused to accept Jeremiah's remedy for deliverance—to turn back to God and submit to the Babylonians.[35]

In light of the above human summary, someone could easily gather the impression that Jeremiah was a failure as a prophet. But the same commentator also added:

> However, Jeremiah must not be judged by human standards. God has a different measuring stick by which he judges a person's life. His is the test of obedience. God only required that Jeremiah obey him by proclaiming his message. Jeremiah was not responsible for a favorable response or lack of response. One who is an obedient servant of the Lord today is not held accountable for lack of response from those who hear his message.[36]

Thus, God's evaluation of His prophet is different from how the world views His servant. The world measures success by looking at the bottom line. The Lord looks at His prophet's heart. As long as His servant sought to trust Him in faithful obedience, God deems his ministry a success.

With this said, Jeremiah's ministry involved negative and positive aspects, and the Lord alerted His prophet to this reality at the time of his call. Jeremiah 1:4–10 describes God's call to Jeremiah to serve Him as a prophet to the nations. After the Lord reassured Jeremiah (Jeremiah 1:4–8), He explained the destruction and construction aspects of his ministry. In other words, Jeremiah had to deal with the negative aspects of long-standing rebellion in God's people. Then he would be in a position to deal with the positive aspects of renewal in his ministry. Although confronting the negative side of ministry is incredibly

---

35. F. B. Huey, *Jeremiah, Lamentations*, vol. 16 of *The New American Commentary*, (Nashville: Broadman and Holman, 1993), 24.

36. Ibid.

challenging (Jeremiah 20:7–10), it is nevertheless essential. It is a necessary part of serving as the Lord's leader because every ministry includes both negative and positive aspects.

The Illustration

The biblical illustration in Jeremiah 1:9–10 is basically a record of Jeremiah's call to prophetic service. When God called His servant, He revealed to him what was coming for God's wayward people (Jeremiah 1:11–12, 13–18). Jeremiah 1:9–10 indicates that Jeremiah was going to be involved in both negative and positive aspects of dealing with God's people.

For example, the negative aspects of Jeremiah's ministry are captured in the words: "to pluck up and to break down, to destroy and to overthrow" (Jeremiah 1:10). These four verbal ideas are negative because they point to a message of judgment for God's people.

Along this same line, the positive aspects of Jeremiah's prophetic ministry are presented in the words: "to build and to plant" (Jeremiah 1:10). These two verbal ideas are positive because they signal the message of future hope for God's people. But this would only come after the hard work of confronting sin and calling for repentance.

These verbal ideas paint an agricultural type of picture. Before a harvest is produced in a field, its soil must be prepared. This often involves removing obstacles such as rocks and roots which prevent the growth of the seeds sown in the ground. However, after removing impediments from the soil, seeds must be sown. Then, after preparation and planting have taken place, a harvest is just a matter of time.

As Jeremiah served faithfully in his prophetic ministry for approximately four decades, he was involved in both the negative and positive sides of ministry just as God foretold. For example, he proclaimed God's certain judgment on His people in Jeremiah 27. He also proclaimed the hope of God's certain restoration in Jeremiah 29:10–11: "For thus says the Lord: When seventy years are completed for Babylon, I will visit you, and I will fulfill to you my promise and bring you back to this place. For I know the plans I have for you, declares the Lord, plans for welfare and not for evil, to give you a future and a hope."

Jeremiah is remembered as the weeping prophet who languished under the burden of announcing God's judgment. Yet, God used him to pen the powerful proclamation of the coming new covenant in Jeremiah 31:31–34. The writer of Hebrews quoted this passage from Jeremiah to show the hope of God's forgiveness in Christ (Hebrews 8:8–12). The book of Jeremiah contains some of the sharpest messages of rebuke and the most moving declarations of hope. Truly, Jeremiah was involved in both the negative and positive sides of ministry as he faithfully obeyed the Lord's call.

Suggestions for Use

The fact that Jeremiah was involved in the negative and positive aspects of ministry can prove useful as a biblical illustration for pastors and teachers. In some important ways, times have not changed from the period in which God called Jeremiah to service and to today. The Lord's servants are still called to confront sin and proclaim the hope of salvation in Christ alone who instituted the new covenant in His blood (Luke 22:14–23).

For example, if a pastor was preaching from 1 and 2 Timothy and was making the point that Paul challenged Timothy to deal with false teaching (*see*, for instance, 1 Timothy 1:3–4; 2 Timothy 4:1–5), he could appeal to Jeremiah as an example. He was a prophet whom God called to confront sin and false teaching in the Old Testament. Pastors who begin a ministry at an established church will have to deal with long-standing traditions. Some of these practices will be helpful for the ministry's progress forward. Others may be an impediment for spiritual growth among God's people.

But how is a ministry leader in this common situation to lead effectively? One way is through the faithful preaching and teaching of God's Word. Paul wrote, "All Scripture is breathed out by God and profitable for teaching, for reproof, for correction, and for training in righteousness, that the man of God may be complete, equipped for every good work" (2 Timothy 3:16–17). He also instructed Timothy to deal with false teaching and those who are negatively impacted by it in the following way:

> Have nothing to do with foolish, ignorant controversies; you know that they breed quarrels. And the Lord's servant must not be quarrelsome but kind to everyone, able to teach, patiently enduring evil, correcting his opponents with gentleness. God may perhaps grant them repentance leading to a knowledge of the truth, and they may come to their senses and escape from the snare of the devil, after being captured by him to do his will (2 Timothy 2:23–26).

Both of these passages from 2 Timothy teach that the Lord's servants must appeal to the truth of God's Word as they seek to deal with the negative aspects of ministry. And this is precisely what God illustrated in Jeremiah's call and prophetic ministry.

Of course, leading the Lord's people forward does not only involve the confrontation of false teaching. Just as God also called Jeremiah to proclaim a message of hope, every preacher and teacher is called to hold forth the glorious truths of the gospel. In fact, the previous point can only be adequately accomplished by contrasting false teachings with the truth of the gospel.

Paul's letter to the Galatians could serve as another instance where the biblical illustration in Jeremiah 1:9–10 could prove useful. As in other letters Paul penned, he confronted the negative aspects of false teaching in Galatians. Specifically, he proved how the legalistic message of the Judaizers completely contradicted the message of salvation through Christ alone. In addition to disproving the lies about the law promulgated by false teachers (Galatians 3), he also emphasized the freedom believers have in Christ, and he urged his audience to understand and walk in their spiritual liberty as Christians: "For freedom Christ has set us free; stand firm therefore, and do not submit again to a yoke of slavery" (Galatians 5:1).

Pastors and teachers could use the story of God's call to Jeremiah to illustrate how those who share the message of Scripture today must engage in the same type of ministry. Ministry leaders will always have to confront false teaching. While this is challenging, it is essential. And the best way to do this is to proclaim the truth of the gospel. Jesus said, "If you abide in my word, you are truly my disciples, and you will know the truth, and the truth will set you free" (John 8:31–32).

32

PROCLAMATION AND REJECTION

~ Jeremiah 36:1–32 ~

Many times people receive God's message, and many times they do not. Although people reject the Lord's message to their own detriment, they nevertheless harden their hearts and turn deaf ears to the truth. Such is the case with the biblical illustration involving King Jehoiakim and the message God sent to him and the people of Judah through Jeremiah. The prophet proclaimed the Lord's message, but this ungodly ruler rejected it.

Context

Commentators on the book of Jeremiah have noted that its contents are not arranged chronologically. Rather, they appear to have a theological order. Maybe the theme of God's judgment provides the best way to

205

understand the flow of the book.[37] This theme certainly fits the overall message of the book as it relates to the negative side of ministry (*see* previous chapter). Also, it fits the specific story of how King Jehoiakim rejected God's message in Jeremiah 36:1–32.

Although two other kings ruled Judah after Jehoiakim before the nation fell into captivity, the Lord had already pronounced judgment on His people for their sins. Yet, even though they heard this message, they refused to repent. They instead persisted in their disobedience to God. They trusted in political alliances more than in the Lord. All this led to their destruction because even when God sent His message of impending doom to His people, they completely rejected it. This is why the story of Jehoiakim and Jeremiah's scroll in Jeremiah 36:1–32 can be called "Proclamation and Rejection."

The Illustration

During Jehoiakim's reign, God sent a message to Jeremiah. It was a rebuke for the people of Israel, Judah, and other nations (Jeremiah 36:1). This had largely been the Lord's message through Jeremiah for the duration of his prophetic ministry (Jeremiah 36:2). The Lord's intention for sending His message was for His people to repent (Jeremiah 36:3).

Jeremiah obeyed the Lord by dictating God's message to Baruch, his trusted secretary, who wrote each word on a scroll (Jeremiah 36:4). Next, since Jeremiah was banned from the temple at this point in his prophetic ministry, he asked Baruch to deliver the word of the Lord. Baruch went into the temple and read aloud the scroll in the hearing of all the people on a particular day when they gathered for a fast (Jeremiah 36:5–10). Jeremiah indicated that the intention of this public

---

37. Charles Dyer, "Jeremiah," in *The Bible Knowledge Commentary: An Exposition of the Scriptures by Dallas Seminary Faculty*: Old Testament, ed. by John F. Walvoord and Roy B. Zuck, (Wheaton: Victor Books, 1985), 1128.

proclamation was for the people to turn their hearts back to the Lord (Jeremiah 36:7).

When Baruch went to the temple to read the scroll, a certain man named Micaiah heard this message and immediately reported it to the king's officials (Jeremiah 36:11–13). Then a man named Jehudi asked Baruch to bring the scroll (Jeremiah 36:14). After Baruch read God's message to the king's officials, they were all afraid and told the king (Jeremiah 36:15–16). They, however, were obviously not confident that King Jehoiakim would respond in a favorable way because they instructed Baruch to go into hiding along with Jeremiah (Jeremiah 36:19).

The king's officials proved to be correct. In fact, Jehoiakim's calloused and calculated rejection of God's message could not be described in more vivid detail. As the scroll was read to Jehoiakim, he sliced the scroll into pieces with a knife. He severed a few columns at a time as they were read to him. Then he tossed them into a fire as he sat to warm himself in his winter house (Jeremiah 36:22–23). Although others urged the king not to destroy the scroll, he and his officials showed no fear or godly remorse in burning it (Jeremiah 36:24–25). Instead, he issued an order to have Baruch and Jeremiah apprehended, "but the Lord hid them" (Jeremiah 36:26).

Even when men reject the proclamation of God's message, their rejection does not void the truth and certainty of His message. The Lord simply reissued His message to Jeremiah, and this time it was rewritten, along with additional words (Jeremiah 36:28, 32). Until this point in the story, the reader is not given any information about the actual contents of God's message. But Jeremiah 36:29 provides some insight on this front. The Lord revealed here that Jeremiah's message was a proclamation of God's impending judgment on His people via the Babylonians. In light of this, Jehoiakim's response revealed his prideful defiance of the Lord since he primarily spent his time as Judah's king relying on political alliances as opposed to God.[38]

---

38. Huey, 20–21.

However, the Lord's message of judgment was clear and certain. After Jehoiakim led the way in rejecting God's call for repentance, the Lord's second rebuke was even more pointed. Specifically, He told Jehoiakim: "He shall have none to sit on the throne of David, and his dead body shall be cast out to the heat by day and the frost by night. And I will punish him and his offspring and his servants for their iniquity. I will bring upon them and upon the inhabitants of Jerusalem and upon the people of Judah all the disaster that I have pronounced against them, but they would not hear" (Jeremiah 36:30–31). Thus, even though God's message was rejected, it still came to pass.

Suggestions for Use

The biblical illustration of how King Jehoiakim rejected the proclamation of the Lord's message through Jeremiah is helpful on several fronts. First, God's message proves true even if it is rejected. Although the context is different, Paul made the general point that human unfaithfulness does not discount God's faithfulness (Romans 3:1–4). He declared, "Let God be true though every one were a liar" (Romans 3:4). This basic idea can be seen in the story of Jehoiakim's rejection of God's message. Even though he made a brazened attempt to deny the validity of the Lord's judgment, God's truth nevertheless prevailed just as He proclaimed.

Second, the Lord's servants proclaim His message out of obedience to Him and not according to an audience's favorable or unfavorable response. Jeremiah surely knew that his message would not be received well. He had been announcing God's judgment for approximately two decades by this time in Jehoiakim's reign (Jeremiah 36:1, 9),[39] and he

---

39. Jeremiah's prophetic ministry began in 627 B.C., and Jehoiakim reigned from 609-597 B.C. Given the time frames mentioned in Jeremiah 36:1, 9, Jeremiah would have preached for approximately 22–23 years by this time. See Dyer, 1122, and Huey, 20.

was apparently banned from the temple at this point because of his lack of "popularity."[40] Yet, Jesus called His followers to focus on God and not people when He sent them out to preach. Christ concluded His instructions to His seventy-two emissaries with these words: "The one who hears you hears me, and the one who rejects you rejects me, and the one who rejects me rejects him who sent me" (Luke 10:16). Likewise, Paul urged Timothy:

> I charge you in the presence of God and of Christ Jesus . . . Preach the word; be ready in season and out of season . . . For the time is coming when people will not endure sound teaching, but having itching ears they will accumulate for themselves teachers to suit their own passions, and will turn away from listening to the truth and wander off into myths. As for you, always be sober-minded, endure suffering, do the work of an evangelist, fulfill your ministry (2 Timothy 4:1–5).

It is clear from the above passages that God's servants are to focus on Him and to be faithful to Him when delivering His message. People may accept the message or reject it, but this does not influence whether or not God's servants proclaim it. This was true for Jeremiah, and it is true of every preacher or teacher today.

Third, leaders can either set the pace for obedience or disobedience, and they will be accountable before God accordingly. While it is apparent that some people wanted to respond differently to the Lord's message (Jeremiah 36:25), Jehoiakim was a leader who defied God. For this reason, God reissued His message and directed a particular word of judgment to Jehoiakim. The Lord also announced that the king's sin would have a devastating impact on his descendants (Jeremiah 36:30–31). God is just in all His dealings with people regardless of their ranks or positions in life, and leaders will incur stricter judgments. This is

---

40. Dyer, 1180, and Huey, 320.

true especially for leaders in the church (1 Timothy 5:17–21; James 3:1), and it is apparently true for leaders in general as the story of Jehoia-kim in Jeremiah 36:1–32 indicates. This point emphasizes why every-one should respond in obedient submission to God's message instead of defiantly rejecting it.

33

CONSIDERING OPTIONS

~ Daniel 1:3–21 ~

Some believers only see one way ahead whenever they are faced with temptations to compromise. For a host of reasons, such as legalism, self-righteousness, or pride, they think that the only way forward is the way that they have known in the past. However, Daniel 1:6–21 teaches that different options for obedience are available when believers face compromising situations. While God's call to obedience is always the best path, there may be various options to walk that path. In light of this, Christians should always be open to considering such options.

Context

The background for the biblical illustration in the opening chapter of the book of Daniel is twofold. It has a historical background in Daniel 1:1–2 and a canonical background in the Old Testament law. First, the setting for the book of Daniel is Judah's Babylonian captivity. The deportation of treasures and people described in Daniel 1:1–4 took place during the first wave of Babylonian victory over Judah.[41] Promising young men from the land of Judah lost their land and their liberty. They were stripped of everything they held sacred and dear, and they were hauled off to a strange, pagan society. In a word, they were captives.

Second, the canonical context of the book of Daniel, especially as it relates to the law of Moses in general, is important to understand. The book of Leviticus reveals that the Lord gave various laws to His people so they might see their need for Him (Galatians 3:10–29) and so they might be witnesses before other nations (Deuteronomy 4:1–14). The Old Testament laws, including the dietary laws, served as a way for the Israelites to show covenant loyalty to God. This is precisely the situation which emerged in Daniel 1:3–21. But the question remains: How did Daniel and his friends deal with the temptation to compromise God's guidelines? Their story demonstrates how all believers need to consider options when facing temptations to compromise.

The Illustration

Daniel 1:3–21 begins with a description of Daniel and his friends. Obviously, they were young men who were already distinguished in Judah (Daniel 1:3–4). Daniel may have even had royal blood pulsating through his veins.[42] However, he and his friends were brought to Babylon to be completely submerged in Babylonian culture. For example, they were taught the literature of the Babylonians as opposed to God's law. They were fed the food the Babylonian king assigned to them rather than

---

41. Dwight J. Pentecost, "Daniel," in *The Bible Knowledge Commentary: An Exposition of the Scriptures by Dallas Seminary Faculty: Old Testament*, ed. by John F. Walvoord and Roy B. Zuck, (Wheaton: Victor Books, 1985), 1326.

42. Stephen R. Miller, *Daniel*, vol. 18 of *The New American Commentary* (Nashville: Broadman and Holman, 1994), 59–60.

their preferred kosher diets, and they were given new names. Their Babylonian names drew attention to pagan deities instead of to the Lord (Daniel 1:3–7).

It was the issue of their diet that became the primary focus of the rest of the first chapter of Daniel. Simply put, "Daniel resolved that he would not defile himself with the king's food, or with the wine that he drank" (Daniel 1:8). Speculation abounds as to why Daniel refused to partake of the king's food and wine. It seems most probable that the Babylonian food and drink was simply unclean and/or associated with idolatry. Either way, Daniel did not want to become unclean by partaking of the king's food and drink. This would require Daniel to break covenant with the Lord.[43]

So what was Daniel to do? He could have simply refused to eat in a blatant act of disrespect. Or he could consider other options. While any valid choice had to align with Daniel's commitment to covenantal faithfulness, other avenues were available. Daniel made a polite request to the one in authority over him for an alternative diet (Daniel 1:8). God honored Daniel's actions because the Scripture says, "God gave Daniel favor and compassion in the sight of the chief of the eunuchs" (Daniel 1:9).

However, the chief of the eunuchs did not initially embrace Daniel's plan. He had to think of his own safety. If Daniel and his friends consumed a different diet and did not perform well before the Babylonian king, the chief of the eunuchs risked his own life (Daniel 1:10–11). But once again, Daniel evidenced politeness and patience by suggesting the idea of a testing period. Daniel asked the chief of the eunuchs to try his plan for ten days. If they did not fare as well as the others who were eating the king's food and drinking his wine, he could do with them as he saw fit (Daniel 1:12–13). This plan seemed like a good option to the chief of the eunuchs. He implemented it, and Daniel and his friends

---

43. Ibid., 66–67.

fared so well that they were allowed to continue to eat a kosher diet (Daniel 1:14–16).

Some may wonder what Daniel and his friends would have done if they did not fare well on their alternative diet. While such a question may make for interesting speculation, the reality is that God honored Daniel and his friends. They were able to continue living in obedience to Him because He had further plans for them. However, the careful reader familiar with the other stories of Daniel and his friends must conclude that they would have been faithful to their deaths (consider, for example, narratives in Daniel 3 and 6).

Of course, the biblical illustration in Daniel 1:3–21 does not conclude with the chief of the eunuchs' decision to allow Daniel and his friends to refrain from the king's food and wine. Instead, the Scripture says that "God gave them learning and skill in all literature and wisdom, and Daniel had understanding in all visions and dreams" (Daniel 1:17). So when Daniel and his companions stood before the Babylonian king for evaluation, "he found them ten times better than all the magicians and enchanters that were in all his kingdom" (Daniel 1:20). Basically, God blessed Daniel and his friends so that they stood head and shoulders above others by comparison.

Suggestions for Use

This scriptural story illustrates various biblical principles about living in obedience to God in the trenches of life. For example, He calls Christians to be set apart from the world for His glory. Daniel sought to live differently before others, and God was glorified in his obedience. In a similar way, Jesus said the following about His disciples in Matthew 5:13–16:

> You are the salt of the earth, but if salt has lost its taste, how shall
> its saltiness be restored? It is no longer good for anything except to

be thrown out and trampled under people's feet. You are the light of the world. A city set on a hill cannot be hidden. Nor do people light a lamp and put it under a basket, but on a stand, and it gives light to all in the house. In the same way, let your light shine before others, so that they may see your good works and give glory to your Father who is in heaven.

However, Christians are not to live as just any type of witnesses. They should always seek to live as respectful witnesses in the world. This is a key point in Daniel 1:3–21. Daniel was respectful in his appeal to the chief of the eunuchs, and all believers should emulate this in their lives. This principle is both illustrated in the story of Daniel 1:3–21, and it is taught in other places in Scripture.

For instance, Peter urged Christians to be ready to give a reason for their faith in Christ "with gentleness and respect, having a good conscience, so that, when you are slandered, those who revile your good behavior in Christ may be put to shame" (1 Peter 3:15–16). Paul told believers to "walk in wisdom toward outsiders, making the best use of the time. Let your speech always be gracious, seasoned with salt, so that you may know how you ought to answer each person" (Colossians 4:5–6). Peter also emphasized the need for showing respect to those in authority when he wrote:

> Be subject for the Lord's sake to every human institution, whether it be to the emperor as supreme, or to governors as sent by him to punish those who do evil and to praise those who do good. For this is the will of God, that by doing good you should put to silence the ignorance of foolish people. Live as people who are free, not using your freedom as a cover-up for evil, but living as servants of God. Honor everyone. Love the brotherhood. Fear God. Honor the emperor (1 Peter 2:13–17).

Another important point from Daniel 1:3–21 is that believers must commit to purity even while living in a pagan society. Daniel's commitment to purity is evident in the fact that "he would not defile himself" (Daniel 1:8). In like manner, believers are called to follow Christ in purity (Matthew 18:7–9; John 17:15–19).

One final way Daniel 1:3–21 may be helpful as a biblical illustration for pastors and teachers is captured in the title of this chapter, namely, "Considering Options." Disobedience should never be an option for believers. However, they must understand that they can be polite and respectful in fulfilling their commitment to Christ, even to the point of death. Put another way: Believers are to live as Christ died. For instance, Peter's following admonition to slaves applies to all Christians who are mistreated because of their commitment to Christ: "For to this you have been called, because Christ also suffered for you, leaving you an example, so that you might follow in his steps. He committed no sin, neither was deceit found in his mouth. When he was reviled, he did not revile in return; when he suffered, he did not threaten, but continued entrusting himself to him who judges justly" (1 Peter 2:21–24).

Daniel politely persevered in his pursuit of purity, and Christians should find options to do so for God's glory as well.

34

LIMITLESS GRACE

~ Hosea 1:2–3:5 ~

The familiar saying, *It's too good to be true*, usually is true when spoken in the human realm. But when God's grace is in view, it is utterly false. The message of God's limitless grace is incomprehensible but entirely true. God provided the way for sinners to be forgiven fully through Christ. By the cross, God made Jesus "to be sin who knew no sin, so that in him we might become the righteousness of God" (2 Corinthians 5:21). Through the empty tomb, Jesus "was raised for our justification" (Romans 4:25). In light of Christ's finished work of redemption, Paul declared that believers "have redemption through his blood, the forgiveness of our trespasses, according to the riches of his grace" (Ephesians 1:7). In fact, Christians receive even more than God's free and full forgiveness in Christ (*see*, for example, Ephesians 1:3). While this all sounds "too good to be true," it is true because of God's limitless grace.

Context

Many people read the Bible incorrectly and falsely conclude that the Old Testament is about God's judgment, while the New Testament is about God's grace. But the book of Hosea clearly shows why this thinking is wrong. There is hardly a more powerful portrait of God's grace in all of Scripture than in the opening of Hosea. The first verse in the book provides the reader with the historical background for its prophecies. Hosea prophesied during a time before Israel and Judah were taken into captivity. However, as the content of Hosea's prophecies and history unfolded, God's judgment on His people for their spiritual infidelity was just a matter of time. Still, the Lord promised to redeem and restore His people because of His great love for them and His covenant faithfulness. This is the message of Hosea, and it explains why God's love can only be described as limitless grace.

The Illustration

Hosea 1:2–3:5 weaves together both narrative and poetic language. The storyline in these opening chapters is nothing short of shocking to the reader. In a very brief and straightforward way, God told Hosea what to do and why to do it: "Go, take to yourself a wife of whoredom and have children of whoredom, for the land commits great whoredom by forsaking the Lord" (Hosea 1:2).

In rapid succession, the Lord next told Hosea what to name his three children who were born to his wife of whoredom. Concerning his first child, God said, "Call his name Jezreel, for in just a little while I will punish the house of Jehu for the blood of Jezreel, and I will put an end to the kingdom of the house of Israel" (Hosea 1:4). Concerning Hosea's second child, the Lord said, "Call her name No Mercy, for I will no more have mercy on the house of Israel, to forgive them at all" (Hosea 1:6).

Concerning his third child, God said, "Call his name Not My People, for you are not my people, and I am not your God" (Hosea 1:9).

While the above names convey a message of judgment, the closing verses of the first chapter of Hosea read like a shaft of light piercing a dark sky. Hosea 1:10 summarizes this ray of hope well: "Yet the number of the children of Israel shall be like the sand of the sea, which cannot be measured or numbered. And in the place where it was said to them, 'You are not my people,' it shall be said to them, 'Children of the living God.'"

The second and third chapters of Hosea basically repeat the message of Hosea 1:2–11. Just as that message focused on God's judgment but concluded with a theme of restoration, Hosea 2:2–3 focuses on the Lord's judgment, while Hosea 2:14–23 sounds the note of God's redemption. Also, Hosea 3:1–5 is a further elaboration of the opening narrative. The Lord directed His prophet to buy back his wife who apparently returned to her prostitution (Hosea 3:1–2). God's message of hope through His demonstration of grace was communicated in the final two verses of the chapter: "For the children of Israel shall dwell many days without king or prince, without sacrifice or pillar, without ephod or household gods. Afterward, the children of Israel shall return and seek the Lord their God, and David their king, and they shall come in fear to the Lord and to his goodness in the latter days" (Hosea 3:4–5).

Thus, the theme of God's limitless grace is powerfully presented in Hosea 1:2–3:5. First, the Lord sent Hosea to take a wife from a house of prostitution. This revealed how God's love for His people was not based on any merit of their own. It was based on His unconditional mercy for them.

Second, even after Hosea's wife returned to her house of prostitution, the Lord instructed His prophet to sacrifice in order to redeem her from her sinful ways again. This revealed even more of the incomprehensible depths of God's great grace for His people. The Lord's love and mercy knew no bounds for His people because His grace is limitless, indeed.

Suggestions for Use

The story of God's limitless grace as revealed in the opening of the book of Hosea can illustrate important truths about grace in general. First, in terms of salvation, God's grace is limitless in that He redeemed sinners when they were completely undeserving. If a teacher was dealing with Romans 5:8, the story of the Lord's grace in Hosea could be a powerful illustration. Just as Hosea took a prostitute to be his wife, the Lord takes completely unlovable and unworthy sinners unto Himself.

Furthermore, the story of God's limitless grace provides an example of the extent to which the Lord's love can reach sinners in their rebellion. For instance, if an expositor is handling a text like 1 Timothy 1:12–16, he could appeal to Hosea 1:2–3:5 to illustrate how far God's grace could go to rescue sinners in their rebellion against him. Paul himself taught, "I received mercy for this reason, that in me, as the foremost [sinner], Jesus Christ might display his perfect patience as an example to those who were to believe in him for eternal life" (1 Timothy 1:16). Paul knew that if the Lord's grace could reach him in the pit of his sinfulness, the Lord's grace could reach anyone.

Second, the message of God's limitless grace in Hosea 1:2–3:5 could also be used as an example of the Lord's great love in terms of the sanctification process. For instance, Hebrews 12:5–6 reads, "Have you forgotten the exhortation that addresses you as sons? 'My son, do not regard lightly the discipline of the Lord, nor be weary when reproved by him. For the Lord disciplines the one he loves, and chastises every son whom he receives.'" In light of this text, believers can be confident that their heavenly Father's great love for them knows no bounds. Regardless how far they wander away from Him, He will always be motivated by love for them when He chastises them.

Even though the people of Israel and Judah experienced the pain of captivity and exile, they heard the Lord's message of hope and restoration.

In a similar way, God's children today will doubtlessly experience the pain of the Lord's chastisement because "all discipline seems painful rather than pleasant" (Hebrews 12:11). Yet, this does not mean that God has ceased to love them. It actually means the exact opposite. Since the Lord's great love is *limitless*, He will always and only deal with His children in love, regardless of how much they disobey Him. Sometimes God's discipline may become so severe that it results even in death (*see* 1 Corinthians 5:1–5; 11:17–31). However, this only reveals that the Lord loves His children too much to allow them to continue living in a way that dishonors Him and damages their own lives.

35

GOD'S PERSISTENT CALL

~ Jonah 1:1–3; 3:1–3 ~

It may be incorrect to say that God is the God of second chances, especially if the one speaking is literally limiting His long-suffering to only one "do over" in life. The reality more often than not is that God is the God of many, many chances. He patiently works with His servants through their struggles and failures. He allows them more than two opportunities to grow through their mistakes and even disobedience. This biblical principle is crystal clear in the story of Jonah.

Context

The prophet Jonah is the poster child of a runaway preacher, quite literally. While the opening verse of the book of Jonah does not locate him within a specific historical period, scholars date Jonah's prophecies to a time prior to Israel's fall to the Assyrians. This is important background information, considering the fact that Nineveh was a large city in the

Assyrian empire at the time of Jonah. In addition to this, the Ninevites were also known for their brutal cruelty. This means that God called Jonah to preach a message of repentance to a violent, pagan nation.[44]

Jonah doubtlessly loved the idea of God's call on his life to preach against the city of Nineveh (*see* Jonah 1:2). Frankly, he wanted the Lord to destroy the city without allowing any opportunity for its inhabitants to repent and escape His wrath. Yet, he had a suspicion that if the Ninevites turned from their sinful ways, God would extend mercy to them. And this is exactly what happened. In fact, this is the very reason why Jonah tried to run away from the Lord's call in the first place (Jonah 4:2).

Ironically, just as the Lord showed mercy to the pagan Ninevites, He also extended mercy to His rebellious prophet. The very attributes that Jonah complained about—God's grace and mercy—were the very attributes that saved his life. Apparently, Jonah was not opposed to the Lord's grace as long as it was extended to him, but he was adamantly opposed to God's grace when it was shown to those whom Jonah considered unworthy. But every person is unworthy of God's grace. This is why His grace is grace. Grace has been classically defined as God's unmerited favor. Whether the rebellious Ninevites or the renegade prophet Jonah is in view, every person throughout history needs the Lord's grace and mercy.

The Illustration

The biblical illustration of God's persistent call in Jonah 1:1–3 and 3:1–3 is simple and straightforward. First, the Lord called Jonah to preach against the city of Nineveh, but Jonah tried to run in the opposite direction (Jonah 1:1–3). If God were not gracious, this could have been the end of the book of Jonah and the end of Jonah. However, the Lord

---

44. Billy K. Smith and Franklin S. Page, *Amos, Obadiah, Jonah*, vol. 19B of *The New American Commentary* (Nashville: Broadman and Holman, 1995), 209, 225.

acted in His great mercy and sent a large fish to swallow His disobedient prophet. He essentially saved Jonah's life from certain death (Jonah 1:4–17). After Jonah cried out to the Lord for deliverance (Jonah 2:1–9), God commanded the fish to release him. At this point, Jonah once again heard the Lord's call to preach to Nineveh (Jonah 2:10).

Second, when the Lord repeated His call to Jonah, the prophet responded in obedience—at least in a surface type of obedience (Jonah 3:1–3). Here the reader must understand two interesting aspects of God's repeated call to Jonah. The first aspect is that God's call issued in Jonah 1:2 and 3:2 are basically the same. With the exception of the final few words in each verse, both calls are largely verbatim. The second aspect is that the way God worked in Jonah's life between Jonah 1:2 and 3:2 positioned him to hear God's call. In other words, after Jonah first heard the Lord's call, tried to flee from God's presence, was thrown overboard into a tumultuous sea, was swallowed by a large fish, cried out for the Lord's mercy, and was vomited onto land, he heard God's call a second time. It is almost as though one could imagine the following setting for the Lord's repeated call to Jonah: Jonah is lying on the shore with the waves gently lapping on his body. He is exhausted after spending time in the belly of a fish and living to see another day. As he struggles to push himself up on all fours, he removes seaweed from his head and ears. Using his little finger, he wrings his right ear to release the water clogged in his head. At precisely this moment, he hears something. A voice. An unmistakable voice. God's voice, and His message is a familiar one. To paraphrase a popular cell-phone commercial, the Lord asks: *"Can you hear Me now? Good! Go to Nineveh!"*

Suggestions for Use

The story of God's persistent call to His prophet in Jonah 1:1–3 and 3:1–3 is a helpful illustration for preachers in at least two ways. First,

God's long-suffering patience is amazing. Just as the story of Jonah lasts beyond the report of his initial disobedience, even so the story of the lives of believers lasts beyond their acts of rebellion and resistance against God. Other scriptural stories and teachings like Jesus's words to Peter prior to his betrayal, "Simon, Simon, behold, Satan demanded to have you, that he might sift you like wheat, but I have prayed for you that your faith may not fail. And when you have turned again, strengthen your brothers" (Luke 22:31–32), find an example here as well of the Lord's long-suffering.

Second, the ways God worked to reposition Jonah to hear His call a second time is a powerful demonstration of how He uses various circumstances to accomplish His will. Romans 8:28 teaches, "And we know that for those who love God all things work together for good, for those who are called according to his purpose." The Lord can and oftentimes does use all types of situations to help His servants hear His call more clearly. His purpose is to cultivate obedience in them. This is how He worked in Jonah's life, and it is how He works in the lives of His people even today.

36

OVERCOMING SATAN'S LIES WITH GOD'S TRUTH

~ Matthew 4:2–11 ~

Believers never have to wonder *if* temptations will come. They only have to wonder *when* temptations will come. Peter described the enemy as the "adversary the devil [who] prowls around like a roaring lion, seeking someone to devour" (1 Peter 5:8). From Satan's very first introduction in the Bible, he is sketched as "the serpent [who] was more crafty than any other beast of the field" (Genesis 3:1). From the moment of his initial interaction with Adam and Eve to his present-day activities, Satan is constantly tempting God's people. His sinister desire is for them to fall prey to his lies rather than to stand victorious in God's truth.

Context

In light of the above thought, there is no surprise that Jesus's temptation occurred early in Matthew's Gospel. The first chapter of Matthew describes

226

Jesus's Israelite heritage as the Messiah (Matthew 1:1–17) and His supernatural birth as the Son of God (Matthew 1:18–25). The second chapter of Matthew provides insight into how Christ fulfilled messianic prophecy even from His birth (Matthew 2:1–6), how others worshipped Him (Matthew 2:7–12), and how the Lord protected Him as Scripture predicted (Matthew 2:13–23). Although the attention seems to shift to John the Baptist in Matthew 3, John the Baptist is simply a foil, accentuating how Jesus fulfilled all messianic expectations (Matthew 3:1–12) and enjoyed the public declaration of His heavenly Father's favor (Matthew 3:13–17).

As Matthew began to tell the story of Jesus's public ministry, he described how Christ overcame Satan's lies with God's truth. The first Adam succumbed to the Devil's temptation because he believed the Enemy's lie. God plainly gave Adam and Eve this singular command when He placed them in the garden of Eden: "You may surely eat of every tree of the garden, but of the tree of the knowledge of good and evil you shall not eat, for in the day that you eat of it you shall surely die" (Genesis 2:16–17). However, when the Serpent tempted Eve, he directly contradicted God's earlier command when he said to Eve, "You will not surely die" (Genesis 3:4). Eve and Adam listened to Satan's lie instead of God's truth and ate of the forbidden fruit. As a consequence, death came upon the whole world (Romans 5:12–14). But Jesus did not succumb to the Devil's deception. He perfectly obeyed God's Word according to Matthew 4:2–11. Jesus, the last Adam, brings salvation to believers through His righteous life, death, and resurrection (Romans 5:18–21). In this way, Christians today understand how Jesus overcame Satan's lies with God's truth, and they seek to walk in their Master's footsteps by the power of the Holy Spirit.

The Illustration

Matthew's description of how Jesus overcame Satan's lies with God's truth is straightforward. In each of the three temptations presented, the

Devil set a trap for Jesus (Matthew 4:3, 5–6, 8–9, respectively). But in each temptation, Christ overcame the Devil's lies with a quotation from Scripture (Deuteronomy 8:3 in Matthew 4:4; Deuteronomy 6:16 in Matthew 4:7; and Deuteronomy 6:13 in Matthew 4:10).

Only one variation to the above pattern surfaced in the second temptation. Here Satan also appealed to Scripture. However, he twisted it according to his deception (Psalm 91:11–12 in Matthew 4:6). So each temptation in Matthew 4:2–11 follows a relatively simple pattern, and it provides a powerful illustration for how believers can follow Christ's perfect example in overcoming Satan's lies with God's truth. Jesus did not rely on the truth of God's Word a third of the time to slice through the darkness of the Devil's deception. He did not even rely on God's Word two-thirds of the time when He faced temptation. Christ relied on the truth of Scripture without fail 100 percent of the time! Matthew's message is clear: Christ is the perfect, victorious Messiah who came to save sinners and whose perfect example shows His disciples how to walk in victory over Satan's lies by relying on the truth of God's Word.

Suggestions for Use

The story of how Jesus overcame Satan's lies with God's truth is serviceable to pastors and teachers in a host of ways. For instance, this narrative puts flesh and bones on two of the main themes in Psalm 119. This psalm is the classic text focusing on the powerful truth of God's Word. In Psalm 119:9, the psalmist both asked and answered a key question all believers pose: "How can a young man keep his way pure? By guarding it according to [God's] word." The psalmist went on to say two verses later: "I have stored up your [God's] word in my heart, that I might not sin against you" (Psalm 119:11). While all Christians desire to live as the psalmist outlined in Psalm 119:9, 11, the reality is that they all stumble and fall in many ways (James 3:2). They invariably listen to the Enemy's lies rather than God's truth from time to time. However, Christ demonstrated by His perfect example in Matthew 4:2–11 that the only way to assure victory over the Enemy's deception is to rely on God's truth in every temptation. It should also be noted at this juncture that Jesus quoted the Scripture. This implies that He first memorized it. God's truth was "stored up . . . in [His] heart" as the psalmist indicated in Psalm 119:11. Jesus was not walking around the wilderness with a little pocket-sized scroll of the Gideon Old Testament. He first learned God's Word by heart so that He could live in line with it from the purity of His heart.

Also, the psalmist declared in Psalm 119:105, "Your [God's] word is a lamp to my feet and a light to my path." The Enemy doubtlessly attempts to spread a cloak of darkness over the pathway of believers with his temptations. He wants them to stumble in their blindness. Yet, the truth of God's Word is like a shaft of brilliant light, dispelling his deceptive darkness. This is particularly clear in Jesus's second temptation in Matthew 4:5–7. Here Satan sought to couple his temptation with a twisting of God's Word. He compounded his sinister scheme. The Devil not only lied, but he also sought to validate his lie with the façade of appealing to Scripture. But Jesus saw through Satan's deceptive strategy because He truly trusted the Word of God. He used it as a lamp and a light to illuminate the pathway before Him.

In the same way, believers can walk in the liberating freedom of God's truth rather than the debilitating bondage of the Devil's lies as they walk in the light of Scripture. Jesus taught, "If you abide in my word, you are truly my disciples, and you will know the truth, and the truth will set you free" (John 8:31–32). Christ also went on to warn others about the destructive nature of the Devil's lies: Satan "was a murderer from the beginning, and does not stand in the truth, because there is no truth in him. When he lies, he speaks out of his own character, for he is a liar and the father of lies" (John 8:44). As Christians follow Christ's example by the Spirit's power, they too can experience the freedom of God's truth instead of the bondage of Satan's lies.

Finally, the story of how Jesus's victory over temptation in Matthew 4:2–11 powerfully illustrates Paul's teaching about "the sword of the Spirit" in Ephesians 6:17. Only one offensive weapon is mentioned in Paul's description of the armor of God in Ephesians 6:14–17: The belt of truth, the breastplate of righteousness, the shoes of readiness, the shield of faith, and the helmet of salvation are all defensive types of armor. However, the final weapon named—the sword of the Spirit— is the only offensive weapon. It clearly refers to "the Word of God" (Ephesians 6:17). This was certainly the case in the biblical illustration of Jesus's temptations in Matthew 4:2–11. He wielded the sword of the Spirit faithfully and flawlessly as He overcame the Enemy's assaults through his lies. Even so, believers can also overcome Satan's lies with God's truth—"the sword of the Spirit, which is the word of God."

37

THE SIGNIFICANCE OF SOLITUDE

~ Mark 1:35–39 ~

Many times the world is so fast paced that believers seem to meet themselves coming and going. The flurry of constant activity does not lessen in ministry settings. Apparently, many churches and/or ministry leaders feel that *spirituality* is spelled A-C-T-I-V-I-T-Y. But this is simply not true. While being active is not inherently wrong, solitude is significant. This is seen very early in Mark's account of Jesus's life and ministry.

Context

The biblical illustration of the significance of solitude in Christ's life surfaces even before the first chapter of Mark comes to a close. In the span of just thirty-four verses, Mark summarized the ministry of John the Baptist (Mark 1:1–8), described the baptism of Christ (Mark 1:9–11), the temptation of Jesus (Mark 1:12–13), and the beginning of Christ's public ministry (Mark 1:14–15). Mark then outlined how Jesus called some of His first disciples to follow Him (Mark 1:16–20) and how He ministered with authority over unclean spirits (Mark 1:21–28). Next, after Christ performed another miracle of healing (Mark 1:29–31), His ministry activity only increased (Mark 1:32) to the point that "the whole city was gathered together at the door. And he healed many who were sick with various diseases, and cast out many demons" (Mark 1:33–34).

This summary highlights the heightened activity of Jesus's ministry. As Mark was likely writing to a Roman audience, he described Christ's power and activity. Although the Romans had conquered the known world at this time in history, Jesus's power and authority was greater than all the political and military prowess of Rome. Christ taught with authority, and even disease and demons obeyed Him.

In addition to pointing to Jesus's powerful activity, Mark revealed the urgency of Christ's ministry. For example, the word typically translated *immediately* occurs many times throughout Mark's Gospel. Mark used it eight times before Mark 1:35–39 (Mark 1:10, 12, 18, 20, 21, 23, 29, and 30). This type of language emphasized Jesus's authority to move forward in His ministry with unparalleled power. And this resonated well with Mark's Roman audience who viewed themselves as the most powerful people in the world.

Yet, even in the midst of all this activity, Jesus demonstrated the significance of solitude in Mark 1:35–39. His example illustrates a profound biblical truth: God desires for His people to be active in serving Him, and He also wants them to experience the refreshing and revitalizing impact of solitude.

The Illustration

Mark 1:14–34 describes a seemingly unending flow of ministry activity for Jesus. But, even though the crowds wanted more of His time and attention, Jesus arose "very early in the morning, while it was still dark" for a time of solitude (Mark 1:35). Although His disciples searched for Him, found Him, and told Him that everyone was looking for Him (Mark 1:36–37), Christ still took time to get alone with God. He made solitude a priority before the proverbial waves of ministry activity and human need crashed into the coast of His life again.

Then, being energized by His personal time in prayer, Jesus continued His public ministry with renewed vigor. Christ knew that the time was now for Him to preach the gospel, and so He set off to the next towns in order to continue to fulfill His mission (Mark 1:38). Jesus's powerful preaching and miracle-working ministry was fueled by His time alone with God (Mark 1:39).

Several truths surface for the careful reader in light of Christ's focus on solitude. First, ministry activity is not automatically sinful. Jesus, the sinless Son of God, engaged in much ministry activity.

Second, both ministry activity and personal time in prayerful solitude must be incorporated for a ministry to remain healthy. Activity and solitude are not either/or options for the believer. They are both/and mandates from the Lord.

Third, solitude requires discipline. While everyone else was doubtlessly sleeping, Jesus arose early in the morning for prayer even though His ministry schedule was the busiest.

Fourth, solitude has a way of helping the main thing remain the main thing in life and ministry. When Jesus responded to His disciples from His quiet place, it was with a laserlike focus on His mission to preach the gospel.

Fifth, when pastors and teachers understand the balance of both activity and solitude, they are in a position to focus on the twin pillars of effective ministry—the Word and prayer (Acts 6:4). Although their activity level may remain high, they do not focus on activity for the sake of activity alone. All their activity is focused on God's purpose to teach Scripture with a prayerful dependence upon the Lord gained through solitude.

Suggestions for Use

All the truths mentioned above reveal the ways that the significance of solitude can be a useful biblical illustration. For instance, ministry activity is good. Paul exhorted believers to "be steadfast, immoveable, always abounding in the work of the Lord, knowing that in the Lord your labor is not in vain" (1 Corinthians 15:58). He also urged Christians, "Do not be slothful in zeal, be fervent in spirit, serve the Lord" (Romans 12:11). God desires for believers to be fully engaged in His service. But He wants them to do this as they rest in Him through times of prayerful solitude. This is a crucial truth that Jesus revealed in His public ministry.

Second, a biblical balance calls for ministry leaders to incorporate both activity and solitude in their ministries. As preachers emphasize one or the other of these biblical truths, they can appeal to Jesus's example in Mark 1:35–39 to show how a balance must exist in both of these areas of life and ministry. An emphasis on one point without a helpful reminder about the other will result in imbalance.

Third, the importance of discipline in order to engage in prayerful solitude is presented clearly in this biblical illustration. It has been said that anything in life worth anything will be costly. And this point is certainly appropriate here. While believers should never seek to engage in early morning prayerful solitude because of legalistic motives, they nevertheless understand that making time for concentrated prayer does require a deep commitment. But the attitude of the heart is everything on this front. If believers try to rise early because they think this makes them more holy or more loveable to God, their actions are repulsive to Him. However, if they carve out time for prayerful solitude because of their love for God, they will experience the power that comes from resting in Christ because of God's great love for them.

Fourth, times of prayerful solitude help ministry leaders cut through the clutter of activities and to focus on the real reasons for service—spreading the gospel throughout the world. Jesus responded with energy rather than exhaustion to Simon's statement that everyone was looking for Him (Mark 1:37–38). And ministry leaders who spend time in solitude enjoy the same energy and insight to remain focused on God's goal for their service. They keep their fingers on the pulse of His heartbeat—making disciples of all nations (Matthew 28:18–20).

Fifth, in a way similar to the previous point, times of prayerful solitude help ministry leaders concentrate on their key responsibilities. Leaders will always feel the relentless pressure to meet people's demands. But just as Jesus gave Himself to prayer and the Word, ministry leaders must do the same if their impact will be genuine and sustained. Activity for the sake of activity is draining. Activity with purpose because of the insights gained through prayerful solitude is invigorating. From the very beginning, God called His people to reverent rest on the Sabbath (Genesis 2:1–3; Exodus 16:1–30; 20:8–11), and He still desires for His people to rest in Him as they engage in ministry service. This is what Jesus illustrates in Mark 1:35–39. It is the significance of solitude.

38

RELEASING DISCIPLES ON MISSION

~ Mark 6:6–13 ~

An important part of training others for any endeavor is hands-on participation. People cannot learn to swim in a classroom. They may be instructed in some crucial safety pointers, while sitting at a desk on dry ground, but if they are going to learn to swim, they will have to get in water at some point. Furthermore, they are going to have to take the plunge into deep water. They may dip their toes or take baby steps in the kiddy pool to confront their fear of water. However, they will never learn to swim in this situation. Sooner or later, they will have to get into deep water.

Of course, teaching people to swim should involve a planned process. Throwing them into deep water and watching them gasp for air is hardly an effective strategy. This may have been the old school method of swimming instruction, but a more deliberate, multistep teaching process is definitely more desirable (at least, from the viewpoint of the beginning swimmer).

Context

The above example of teaching people to swim is a good way to think about how Jesus taught His disciples. Christ gathered disciples around Him during His public ministry. His goal for them from the beginning was for them to help others become disciples. For instance, when He called Peter and Andrew in Matthew 4:18–20, He told them right from the start, "Follow me, and I will make you fishers of men" (Matthew 4:19). The underlying message in the second half of His call ("fishers of men") signaled Jesus's ultimate purpose: He did not have designs to impact Peter and Andrew's lives alone. He also planned to use them to impact others. In fact, before Jesus ascended to heaven, He commissioned His followers to "make disciples of all nations . . . teaching them to observe all that I have commanded you" (Matthew 28:19–20). In light of His overarching plan, Jesus taught His disciples to be disciple makers.

In order to accomplish His strategy, Jesus trained His followers with a hands-on approach. They did not simply hear Jesus preach about repentance. Christ sent them to preach about repentance. They did not merely observe Jesus's healing ministry; they laid their hands on the sick with His authority. This is the focus of Mark 6:6–13. While others voiced their opposition to Jesus (Mark 6:1–6), He persevered. He engaged in His itinerant teaching ministry abroad (Mark 6:6), and He released His disciples through hands-on participation in His mission.

The Illustration

The biblical illustration of releasing disciples on mission begins with Mark 6:6. These words actually describe Jesus's ongoing preaching ministry. For example, the verb translated *went about* is in the imperfect tense, indicating an ongoing action in the past. The verbal idea translated *teaching* is a present active participle, signaling how Christ continuously instructed others. One writer made a similar observation while commenting on Matthew's parallel account in the following words: "He [Jesus] never asked anyone to do something that he was unwilling to do. So as the disciples went out, the Master likewise 'departed thence to teach and preach in their cities' (Matt. 11:1)."[45] Thus, Jesus persistently modeled before His disciples what He taught them, and this emboldened them to advance courageously even in the face of opposition.

In addition to Christ's example, Mark 6:7 furnishes two more important insights concerning Jesus's training strategy. First, Christ sent out His disciples in pairs, and second, He sent them out with His authority. The first point helped the disciples practically. In going forth in pairs, Christ's followers could share the load of ministry. They could encourage one another when disappointments arose, and they could share counsel with one another as they needed wisdom along the journey. The second point hints at the inadequacy of the disciples to fulfill Christ's mission without His divine power. Jesus's disciples were not up to the task in their own strength. They were never to view their call to ministry through the lens of their inability. Rather, they were to go forth in Christ's all-sufficiency.

The next four verses (Mark 6:8–11) basically summarize Jesus's verbal instructions to His disciples for this particular mission in terms of three key points. First, the disciples were not to be preoccupied with the material aspects of life (Mark 6:8–9). In essence, they were to focus first and foremost on the kingdom of God and trust God to supply their material needs (Matthew 6:33).

---

45. Robert E. Coleman, *The Master Plan of Evangelism*, 2nd ed., abridged (Grand Rapids: Revell, 1993), 86.

Second, when the disciples encountered advocates for their mission—someone who was willing to provide hospitality for them—they were to remain under the umbrella of their kindness and support as long as it was available (Mark 6:10).

And third, when the disciples faced opposition for their mission, they were not to take it personally (Mark 6:11). Instead, they were to point to the fact that they were unaltered in their commitment to proclaim the gospel. Also, they were to realize that everyone is accountable for their personal response to the gospel. Simply put: There is no median on the two roads stretching out into the horizon of eternity. People will either receive the gift of eternal life through Christ alone, or they will reject Jesus and face eternal condemnation. When they reject Jesus's emissaries, they really reject Christ Himself.

Mark 6:12–13 reveals that the disciples did, in fact, experience all that Christ sent them to accomplish. They preached the same message of repentance that Jesus preached (Mark 1:15; 6:6), and they witnessed the Lord's power at work through them to impact others. All of the elements of Jesus's discipleship strategy were fulfilled. He taught and trained them effectively through a hands-on approach as He released them to serve in His mission.

Suggestions for Use

The way Jesus taught and trained His disciples is the same way contemporary believers should teach and train others to serve in Christ's mission to make disciples of all nations (Matthew 28:19–20; Acts 1:8). For example, Christians are to equip and exhort other believers to share the gospel throughout the world (Colossians 4:5–6; 2 Timothy 4:5; Philemon 6; 1 Peter 3:15). They are to live before others and speak to them as Christ's ambassadors. As Jesus modeled these truths before His disciples, believers should model these practices before one another.

Also, Christians should partner with others on mission and realize that their strength comes ultimately from the Lord who is at work in and through them. Paul had his partners in ministry (see, for example, 2 Corinthians 8:23; Philemon 17), and Proverbs admonishes believers to connect with others in a way that nurtures wisdom in their lives (Proverbs 13:20). Any teaching on the power of partnerships in life and ministry could easily appeal to Jesus's strategy of sending out His disciples in pairs as an illustration. Also, if teachers are emphasizing the need for Christ's strength to empower His servants (Psalm 127:1; John 15:5; 1 Corinthians 3:5–7; Colossians 1:28–29; 1 Thessalonians 5:24), they can find a useful example in the way Jesus released His disciples to serve on mission in Mark 6:7.

Next, several other important truths are illustrated in Mark 6:8–11. For example, the scriptural teaching that believers should prioritize God's kingdom above material possessions is evident in these verses. The fact that Christians should appreciate the hospitality of advocates who support Christ's mission is plainly presented in this passage. The point that believers should not be discouraged nor deterred in their service because of disappointments is illustrated here as well. In light of this, a teaching from Matthew 6:33 (the priority of God's kingdom over material concerns) could find an example here. A message on Philippians 1:27–30 (the joy of gospel partnerships) could be illustrated here. And an exposition on texts such as Exodus 16:8 and 2 Corinthians 5:20 (the fact that God's servants really represent Him) could be demonstrated here.

Lastly, those who follow Christ and serve Him do not labor in vain. They will see either in this life or in the next the fruitfulness of their work. Any teaching on persevering in the Lord's work such as 1 Corinthians 15:58 could use Mark 6:12–13 as an illustration. Also, messages on Christ's promise that He will build His church in Matthew 16:18 or that God will grow the seed planted and watered by His various servants in 1 Corinthians 3:5–9 could be illustrated in this text. As the above suggestions reveal, how Christ taught and trained His followers to be disciple-making disciples by releasing them in service is a fertile biblical illustration.

39

God's Different Ways
of Healing

~ Mark 7:31–37 ~

Believers commonly wrestle with the various ways God does or does not seem to work in their lives. This struggle is particularly heightened during seasons of sickness. The questions (or even accusations) that erupt to the surface of suffering hearts are: *God, why don't You heal? You healed others in the past, and You continue to heal others now. Yet, You are not bringing wholeness and health to this specific situation. Or, You are at least not bringing deliverance quick enough and in the way You could.*

Context

The biblical illustration of Jesus's healing in Mark 7:31–37 provides insights into the above struggles. While all of Christ's acts of healing were meant in some way or another to confirm His messianic identity and deity as the Son of God, they also reveal another truth: God works in various ways, especially in the area of healing.

As Jesus continued to face opposition and rejection from His own people (Mark 7:1–23), He spent time on occasion ministering in predominately Gentile territories. Mark first reported how Christ healed the demonized daughter of a Syrophoenician woman in Mark 7:24–30. Then in Mark 7:31–37, he described how Jesus healed "a man who was deaf and [had] a speech impediment."

These stories occurred one after another, and when they are viewed together, something interesting surfaces. Their juxtaposition emphasizes how Christ healed in different ways. For example, Jesus healed the daughter of the Syrophoenician woman from a distance. With just a spoken word—without even traveling to lay hands on the little girl—Christ exorcised the demon (Mark 7:29–30). However, Jesus took more than one step when He healed the man who suffered with deafness and speech problems (Mark 7:33–34). Again, the above observations show how God heals in different ways. In fact, sometimes He does not bring about a restoration of health. He simply deems it best to allow death to pursue its natural course.

The Illustration

As Jesus ministered in Gentile territory (Mark 7:24, 31), some people brought a man who had been suffering with deafness and a speech impediment in hopes that Christ would heal him (Mark 7:32). However, Jesus did not heal the man in an instant. In Mark 7:32–37, Mark described how Christ moved through a six-step process to restore the man's health. First, Jesus took the sick man aside. Second, Christ put His fingers into the man's ears. This may seem natural since one of the main ailments the man was suffering from was deafness. Third, Jesus spit and touched the man's tongue. Christ's actions here also make sense because the man suffered from a speech problem. Thus, in two of the first three steps of the healing process, Jesus physically touched the areas of suffering.

Mark continued to describe the fourth step in the healing process, which was Jesus's upward gaze toward heaven. This is a clear indication that God provided the healing. Fifth, Jesus sighed. As with the short verse in the story of Christ raising Lazarus from the dead, "Jesus wept" (John 11:35), the reader comes across two words that convey the depth of Christ's compassion. It's been well-said that John 11:35 is one of the shortest but also deepest verses in Scripture. This thought could also be shared about the brief but deep description of Jesus's emotions in the words "he sighed." Sixth, Christ spoke words of healing. Jesus healed the sick man by His authority.

While the sixth step alone is needed for healing to occur, Mark nevertheless took the reader through a lengthy and detailed process in Mark 7:31–37. There is no doubt that Jesus could have healed the ailing man as He healed the demonized girl. Christ's divine power knew no bounds. However, He chose to heal in different ways. On other occasions, He did not bring physical healing at all. For example, Jesus healed only one person at the pool of Bethesda in John 5:1–9, although many sick people were present.

Suggestions for Use

Mark 7:31–35 is useful as a biblical illustration on several fronts. First, since this miracle occurred on Gentile soil, it shows how God's healings were not reserved for certain people. Although the Lord did not heal everyone during His public ministry, He healed both Jews and Gentiles. Just as God healed Naaman, a Syrian commander, in the Old Testament (2 Kings 5), He could heal anyone He chooses. As previously mentioned, the underlying purpose in all of Christ's healings was to reveal His messianic identity (John 20:30–31; 21:25; Acts 2:22–24). He oftentimes used a healing as an opportunity to communicate the gospel.

This is evident on several occasions in the book of Acts (*see* Acts 3:1–26; 5:12–16). The healing miracle in Mark 7:36-37 confirms how it attracted attention to Jesus's messianic identity, although many misunderstood the true nature of His role as the Messiah.

Second, Jesus chose to heal different people in different ways. This aspect of Mark 7:31–37 could be useful to preachers and teachers as they deal with various passages of Scripture. For instance, Paul instructed Timothy to "no longer drink only water, but use a little wine for the sake of your stomach and your frequent ailments" (1 Timothy 5:23). Paul's advice was likely medicinal in nature. Paul knew that God could use the unique properties of the wine to help Timothy with his stomach problems. This implies how the Lord sometimes uses natural remedies to accomplish His healing purposes.

However, James gave the following instructions to believers dealing with illness: "Is anyone among you sick? Let him call for the elders of the church, and let them pray over him, anointing him with oil in the name of the Lord. And the prayer of faith will save the one who is sick, and the Lord will raise him up" (James 5:14–15). While the oil in this passage could serve medicinal purposes, James' emphasis seems to focus on the supernatural side of healing. This observation is supported by his strong concentration on prayer. Of course, God alone brings healing. He simply can use different natural means or no intermediate means at all. This is clear from the healing stories of Mark 7:24–30 and 7:31–37.

Third, the bondage and negative impact of sin (as evidenced in sickness) moves God's heart with compassion for people. Christ's sigh in Mark 7:34 may not refer exclusively to His compassion. But it seems to say something about His love for people and His burden for them in their suffering.[46] Just as the Lord was concerned for Israel as they languished

---

46. John D. Grassmick, "Mark," in *The Bible Knowledge Commentary: An Exposition of the Scriptures by Dallas Seminary Faculty: New Testament* , ed. by John F. Walvoord and Roy B. Zuck (Wheaton: Victor Books, 1985), 136.

under Egyptian slavery (Exodus 2:23–25; 3:7–10), He is concerned for people today. Yet, it is important to note that God's compassion is not only manifested when He chooses to heal. He is always compassionate toward His people (Psalm 103:8–19), even when He allows them to die. Although the psalmist wrote about how God delivered him from the threat of death (Psalm 116:1–14), he indicated in verse 15 that "precious in the sight of the Lord is the death of his saints." Spurgeon insightfully commented on this verse: "They [the Lord's saints] shall not die prematurely; they shall be immortal till their work is done; and when their time shall come to die, then their deaths shall be precious. The Lord watches over their dying beds, smooths their pillows, sustains their hearts, and receives their souls. Those redeemed with precious blood are so dear to God that even their deaths are precious to him."[47] Scripture is clear: At times the Lord demonstrates His mercy in healing, but His mercy is present in death as well. The story of how God healed different people in different ways in Mark 7:31–37 reveals that His ways are mysterious, but they are always good (Psalm 119:67–68).

---

47. C. H. Spurgeon, *The Treasury of David*, vol. 3 (McLean, VA: MacDonald Publishing Company, n.d.), 71.

40

THE DANGER OF DOUBTING

~ Luke 1:5-22 ~

While people naturally think some sins are not as offensive to God as others, He sees all sin the same. Depraved human hearts will always try to rationalize the severity of their sins, but the Lord's holy character never allows such a compromise. As the saying goes, "Sin is sin" to God. This is why the danger of doubting as described in Luke 1:5–22 is so shocking.

Context

As Luke began his Gospel account, he informed his audience that he had conducted research into the life and ministry of Jesus (Luke 1:1–4). In his words, "it seemed good to me also, having followed all things closely for some time past, to write an orderly account" (Luke 1:3). It is no surprise then that Luke included several details about the background of Jesus's life and ministry that the other Gospel writers did not mention. Luke's approach provides the setting for the biblical illustration concerning the danger of doubting.

Before he detailed anything about the ministry of Christ, Luke discussed important aspects of the family and life of John the Baptist, the forerunner of Jesus the Messiah. In the context of this section of his story, Luke focused on the parents of John the Baptist. Specifically, he concentrated on John's father whose name was Zechariah. Although Zechariah was a priest and lived a righteous life (Luke 1:5–6), he was still a fallen man. This is clear in Luke's first chapter. Zechariah's struggle to believe God's message about his son's miraculous birth in Luke 1:5–22 illustrates the danger of the sin of doubt.

The Illustration

The first description of John the Baptist's parents is that his father was a priest, and both he and his wife, Elizabeth, were "righteous before God, walking blamelessly in all the commandments and statutes of the Lord" (Luke 1:6). Although Zechariah and Elizabeth were righteous, they were not perfect. Other than the Lord Jesus, God incarnate, no person who walked this earth in flesh and blood was perfect (Hebrews 4:15). This fact is clear from the account of Zechariah's doubt (Luke 1:11–22). The basic point is that Zechariah and Elizabeth sought to live according to God's ways. They wanted to please God and honor Him in their lives.

However, all was not well with this godly couple. On the heels of Luke's thumbnail sketch of their piety, he wrote, "But they had no child, because Elizabeth was barren, and both were advanced in years" (Luke 1:7). The first word in this sentence, the conjunction *but*, points the reader to a problem for this faithful couple. In that society, barrenness was not only viewed as a physical challenge but a spiritual crisis. Since the Lord knits life together in the womb (Psalm 139:13), the obvious question in the face of barrenness was always, *Why has God withheld the blessing of a child?*

Couples wrestle with painful speculations regarding the reason for their barrenness. However, the Lord always seemed to accomplish some of His greatest works in the midst of this agonizing struggle. For example, careful readers would likely think of aged Abraham and Sarah holding little Isaac (Genesis 17:15–21; 21:1–7) when they read about Zechariah and Elizabeth in Luke 1:6–7. Also, while the aspect of advanced years does not factor into the following accounts of barrenness, the births of Samson (Judges 13) and Samuel (1 Samuel 1) also come to mind in light of Zechariah and Elizabeth's struggle with barrenness. So it is not surprising that an angel appeared to Zechariah as he served at the temple (Luke 1:11). In light of all the ways God worked in the past to use barrenness as a backdrop for some of His greatest works, the student of Scripture anticipates His powerful work in the lives of Zechariah and Elizabeth.

Now, although Zechariah's fear is understandable when he saw an angel standing before him, his doubt was clearly unacceptable (Luke 1:13–20). One of the interesting aspects of this story surfaces in the angel's initial words to Zechariah in Luke 1:13–17. The angel told Zechariah that his "prayer has been heard" (Luke 1:13). Presumably, Zechariah's prayer was for a child in spite of his wife's barren state. Zechariah, a Jewish priest, no doubt knew the stories of God's powerful works of old in relation to barrenness.

Yet, even though Zechariah surely had heard these stories, he still responded in doubt to the Lord's angelic messenger (Luke 1:18). His question and statements to the angel betrayed his doubt. This is clear because the angel later rebuked Zechariah with these words, "You did not believe my words" (Luke 1:20).

While the reader might be surprised at the severity of the consequence imposed on Zechariah for his doubt, this may hint at two important points. First, some people may not consider doubt as a bad offense. However, as previously mentioned, sin is sin. Scripture even teaches that an entire generation died because of their unbelief (Numbers 13:1–14:38; Psalm 78:21–22; 106:24–27; Hebrews 3:19).

Second, some may be tempted to compare the responses of Zechariah in Luke 1:18 and Mary in Luke 1:34. But they would be incorrect to conclude that these responses were essentially the same. The Lord knows the hearts of people. Although their words were similar, Mary's heart was surrendered to the Lord in faith. Her final words to the angel indicated this, "Behold, I am the servant of the Lord; let it be to me according to your word" (Luke 1:38). Zechariah's words betrayed his doubt, and for this reason, the Lord brought a remedial consequence into his life.

Suggestions for Use

The story of the danger of doubting in Luke 1:5–22 is useful for illustrating important biblical truths. For instance, readers should not judge Zechariah for his doubt. All believers struggle with doubt in some form on occasion. Zechariah's doubt should not subtract from the overall portrait of his godliness mentioned in Luke 1:5–22, especially verse 6. Just like the man who brought his demonized son to Jesus and desperately cried, "I believe; help my unbelief!" (Mark 9:24), all Christians wrestle with faith and doubt at innumerable points in their spiritual journeys. The story of Zechariah is yet another illustration of this common struggle.

Also, the Lord's disciplinary actions in the lives of His people are remedial in nature as opposed to punitive. The angel told Zechariah about the consequences of his unbelief, but he also assured him that his speech would be restored in due time (Luke 1:20). Perhaps one of the most important words in this verse (at least from Zechariah's perspective) was the preposition *until*. Although Zechariah suffered a serious consequence for his offense, it did not last forever. This aspect of the story illustrates the biblical principle that God's discipline, even though painful and not pleasurable, is profitable. It teaches and trains His children in righteousness (Hebrews 12:4–11).

Next, God takes doubt, like all sins, seriously. James teaches that "if any of you lacks wisdom, let him ask God, who gives generously to all without reproach, and it will be given him. But let him ask in faith, with no doubting, for the one who doubts is like a wave of the sea that is driven and tossed by the wind. For that person must not suppose that he will receive anything from the Lord; he is a double-minded man, unstable in all his ways" (James 1:5–8). Doubt is serious because it is a denial of God's character and ability. It is a denial of His character because it calls into question the truthfulness of His promises. And it is a denial of His ability because it casts suspicion on His power to fulfill what He promises. The reality is that God fulfills all His promises because He is the God of truth (Titus 1:2). He has the omnipotence to accomplish all He declares (Luke 1:37). For at least these reasons, doubting is a serious danger.

Lastly, since doubt is a struggle all believers experience, the Lord always looks upon the heart. Both Zechariah and Mary responded to God's announcement with questions (Luke 1:18, 34), but only one of them received a consequence. This was the case because the Lord knew Zechariah communicated doubt with his words, but Mary did not. God knows every heart.

This aspect of the story could illustrate an important point in other scriptural stories. For example, Saul was removed from serving as Israel's king for his sin (1 Samuel 15:24–28), but David was not (2 Samuel 12:7–15). Why? David was "a man after [God's] heart" (Acts 13:22). So the Lord sees deep into the motives of the heart, and He responds to His people with appropriate consequences. A doubting heart has dangerous consequences, but God does not abandon His people. Paul wrote these reassuring words to believers in the midst of their struggles: "If we are faithless, he remains faithful—for he cannot deny himself" (2 Timothy 2:13).

41

Breaking Barriers
~ John 4:4–38 ~

In terms of sharing the gospel, it has been said that while the message never changes, the methods must always change. Jesus said, "I am the way, and the truth, and the life. No one comes to the Father except through me" (John 14:6). Also, Peter proclaimed that "there is salvation in no one else, for there is no other name under heaven given among men by which we must be saved" (Acts 4:12).

So there is only one message of good news, and it is the message of Jesus's death, burial, and resurrection for the sins of the world (1 Corinthians 15:1–4). Yet, Paul taught that Christ's ambassadors share this message in creative ways as they connect with different audiences. For example, he described his own methodology of personal evangelism in 1 Corinthians 9:19–23:

> For though I am free from all, I have made myself a servant to all, that I might win more of them. To the Jews I became as a Jew, in order to win Jews. To those under the law I became as one under

the law (though not being myself under the law) that I might win those under the law. To those outside the law I became as one outside the law (not being outside the law of God but under the law of Christ) that I might win those outside the law. To the weak I became weak, that I might win the weak. I have become all things to all people, that by all means I might save some. I do it all for the sake of the gospel, that I may share with them in its blessings.

Paul's clear focus in the above words was the gospel. He never compromised this message. Yet, he adjusted his methods of sharing the message with different people so that he might be most effective in his personal witness. Christ Himself demonstrated this truth in John 4:4–38.

Context

The background for Jesus's encounter with the woman at the well in John 4 is two-pronged. First, a geographical aspect of the story comes into play. Christ performed His first miracle in Cana of Galilee (John 2:11). Then He journeyed to Jerusalem for the Passover (John 2:13). After spending some time in and around Jerusalem, He "left Judea and departed again for Galilee" (John 4:3).

A direct route from Judea to Galilee would be a path through Samaritan territory. However, many Jews did not travel this way because of their extreme animosity toward the Samaritans. In an effort to avoid Samaritan territory completely, some Jews crossed the Jordan River in the south, traveled on the east side of the river until they cleared Samaria, and then crossed the Jordan again in the north to enter Galilee. They basically added a considerable distance to their journey in order to avoid contact with any Samaritans.

Therefore, when John 4:4 begins with the statement that Jesus "had to pass through Samaria," the focus here was not about geography. He could have easily taken the alternate route to Galilee described above.

Rather, John's statement in John 4:4 was about theology. Jesus had to pass through Samaria because He had a divine appointment with a woman at a well in Sychar. And through her transformed life, He was going to impact an entire village for God's glory (John 4:39-42).

Second, a cultural aspect of this biblical illustration is important. This aspect surfaces within the story itself. As mentioned above, the Jews and Samaritans despised one another. This point is obvious from both the way the Samaritan woman responded to Jesus's request for water and in John's parenthetical remark in John 4:9, "For Jews have no dealings with Samaritans." Further evidence of the barrier separating Jews and Samaritans may be detected in the shock the disciples voiced when they found Jesus talking with the woman at the well (John 4:27). Both here and in other passages, the New Testament highlighted the deep rift that divided the Jews and the Samaritans (see also Luke 10:25–37).

But Christ did not live with prejudice in His heart. He broke through barriers of discrimination to touch and transform lives by His power. He did not travel traditional routes; He lived to fulfill His Father's will (John 4:34). He also did not shun people who were rejected by others; He engaged them, embraced them, and evangelized them. Simply put: Jesus broke barriers and changed lives for God's glory.

The Illustration

Jesus's conversation with the woman at the well teaches insightful lessons concerning how He revealed Himself to others. First, Christ did not allow exhaustion to keep Him from being sensitive to ministry opportunities (John 4:6).

Second, no one was off-limits to Jesus. Although this woman was likely an outcast because of the time of day she went to draw water (John 4:6) and because of her past (John 4:16–18), Christ touched and transformed her life.

Third, Jesus shared the same message about Himself with others but in different ways, depending on their particular backgrounds. For example, when Christ spoke with Nicodemus, He told this religious leader about the new birth and appealed to the Old Testament (John 3:1–15). When Christ called some fishermen to follow Him, He told them He would make them "fishers of men" (Matthew 4:18–20). When Jesus responded to a wealthy man's question about obtaining eternal life, He challenged him to leave everything because no one can serve two masters (Matthew 6:24; Mark 10:17–22). So when Christ interacted with the woman at a well, He offered her living water because her soul was parched for something more than earthly water (John 4:10).

Fourth, Jesus broke through every barrier in order to change the Samaritan woman's life (John 4:9–10). Fifth, Christ showed the inadequacy of everything but Himself to give eternal life (John 4:10–14). Sixth, Jesus revealed to others their sin and desperate need for Him (John 4:15–18). Christ did not try to make things easy for people; He called them to a complete abandonment of themselves to His sufficiency (Matthew 16:24–26; John 4:28–29). Seventh, Jesus kept people focused on the main issue—the salvation He offered through Himself (John 4:19–24). Eighth, Christ confronted people with His true identity as the Messiah and the Savior of the world (John 4:25–26). Lastly, Jesus challenged His disciples to see the opportunities before them and to join Him in breaking barriers to be part of God's mission throughout the world (John 4:27–38).

Suggestions for Use

Communicators can use the biblical illustration in John 4:4–38 in a variety of ways. They can direct attention to this story to illustrate James's call for believers to live without discrimination (James 2:1–13). They can incorporate this narrative as an example of how Jesus urged

His followers to pray for God to send laborers into His harvest (Matthew 9:35–38). Obviously, John 4:4–38 is a demonstration of the Lord's great love in sending His only Son to be the Savior of the whole world (John 3:16). Paul's urgent exhortation for believers to make the most of every opportunity in how they act towards outsiders (Colossians 4:5) finds a great example from the life of Jesus in John 4. As mentioned above, Paul's philosophy of being all things to all people in order to win some (1 Corinthians 9:22) is illustrated here. Jesus's encounter with the Samaritan woman shows the power of the gospel to save all who believe (Romans 1:16). The fact that Jesus shared the same message about Himself in different ways illustrates the truth that He alone offers salvation (John 14:6; 17:3; Acts 4:12; 1 Timothy 2:3–6).

42

FALSE FAITH

~ John 8:31–59 ~

Things are not always as they appear. This is true of both things and people. Numerous illustrations of this principle occur in the Bible. For example, Jesus warned about false teachers in Matthew 7:15, "Beware of false prophets, who come to you in sheep's clothing but inwardly are ravenous wolves." Also, Paul appealed to this basic idea when he described potential church leaders in 1 Timothy 5:24–25, "The sins of some people are conspicuous, going before them to judgment, but the sins of others appear later. So also good works are conspicuous, and even those that are not cannot be hidden." Both Jesus and Paul confirmed the biblical truth that things or people are not always as they appear.

Context

John 8:31–59 likewise illustrates this principle. From the beginning of the Gospel of John, Scripture assures us that there has always been more to people than what meets the eye. For instance, John 1:11 says, "He [Jesus] came to his own, and his own people did not receive him." Next, at the end of his second chapter, John reported, "Now when he [Jesus] was in Jerusalem at the Passover Feast, many believed in his name when they saw the signs that he was doing. But Jesus on his part did not entrust himself to them, because he knew all people and needed no one to bear witness about man, for he himself knew what was in man" (John 2:23–25). The people John described as those who believed in Jesus's name did not have true faith, however. Jesus knew that what was in them was not the same as what was on the surface of their lives. This is the dangerous irony of false faith. Simply put: Things are not as they appear.

Other examples of this opening theme in John emerge at various points in his narrative. For instance, Nicodemus is presented as a teacher of Israel, but he does not understand Jesus's teachings about eternal life (John 3:1–15). Furthermore, after Christ healed the invalid at the pool of Bethesda, He warned him about his sin, which could lead to future problems (John 5:1–17). Along the same lines, after Jesus fed the five thousand in John 6:1–14, He preached to the crowds, but many rejected His message (John 6:22–66). In fact, so many people turned from Christ on this occasion that John 6:67 says, "So Jesus said to the Twelve, 'Do you want to go away as well?'"

Then in John 7:5, the reader learns that "not even his brothers believed in him." Of course, Christ's brothers were not the only ones who struggled with their opinion of Him. John 7:40–44 reports, "When they [those hearing Jesus preach] heard these words, some of the people said, 'This really is the Prophet.' Others said, 'This is the Christ.' But some said, 'Is the Christ to come from Galilee? Has not the Scripture said that the Christ comes from the offspring of David, and comes from Bethlehem, the village where David was?' So there was a division among the people over him. Some of them wanted to arrest him, but no one laid hands on him."

All of these examples combine to reinforce the notion that not everyone who looked as if they believed in Christ possessed true faith. Again, they were not what they appeared to be. This recurring theme is powerfully illustrated once more in John 8:31–59.

The Illustration

John 8:31 profiles Jesus's audience for the remainder of this chapter (John 8:31–59): "So Jesus said to the Jews who had believed in him." However, even though these Jews were described as believing in Christ, their faith was not genuine, saving faith. This is clear from what Jesus eventually says about and to them. He called them "children of the devil" (John 8:44), and He plainly implied twice that they did not believe in Him (John 8:45, 46). Their faith was not a true faith. It was false faith.

But the obvious question is: How can one distinguish false faith from true faith? John 8:31–59 reveals several ways. First, those with false faith do not abide or remain in the Word of Christ (John 8:31). They may live according to their own spiritual or religious thoughts, but they do not live according to Jesus's teachings as revealed in His Word.

Second, false believers live in sin (John 8:34). While all believers struggle and stumble in sin daily (James 3:2), sin does not mark the lives of true believers as the ongoing pattern of their behavior (Romans 6:1–4). The verbal idea translated "who practices sin" in John 8:34 is in the present tense, indicating a continuous course of action. Those with false faith may talk the talk, but they do not walk the walk.

Third, those who do not have true faith reveal that they are actually children of the Devil because they live like the Devil (i.e., they reject Christ and His teachings, John 8:41). They do not love Jesus (John 8:42). They do not understand His Word (John 8:43), and they do not believe what Jesus says (John 8:43, 45).

Fourth, those who are false believers do not honor Christ (John 8:49). Other insights about false faith and true faith can be gleaned from John 8:31–59, but these points distinguish between those who truly know Christ from those who do not.

Suggestions for Use

The biblical illustration in John 8:31–59 is useful in painting a picture of one major scriptural principle and several other biblical truths. First, the major truth illustrated here is the theme of living and dead faith in James 2:14–26. James 2:19 says, "You believe that God is one; you do well. Even the demons believe—and shudder!" In other words, readers must remember that Jesus was speaking "to the Jews who had believed in him" (John 8:31). As members of the Jewish nation, these people in Jesus's audience were doubtlessly firm monotheists. Yet, they rejected Christ precisely because they viewed His claim to deity as heresy— worthy of nothing short of capital punishment (John 8:58–59). While these Jews claimed to believe in the one and only God, they simultaneously refused to submit to Christ's lordship. Hence, their faith was false rather than true.

Second, several other sub-points could be offered as ways to use this narrative to illustrate additional biblical truths. For instance, those who walk according to Scripture give evidence that their faith is genuine (Ephesians 4:20–24). Those who do not live in light of God's Word reveal that they are not truly trusting in Him (Psalm 1:1–2, 5–6). Also, those who walk in righteousness are truly God's children (1 John 3:9–10). Those who live in sin without any sense of conviction or signs of correction are spiritually illegitimate (Hebrews 12:4–11). Next, those who truly know Christ enjoy a growth in spiritual perception (1 Corinthians 2:13; 1 John 2:26–27). Those who do not know Jesus lack godly insight (1 Corinthians 2:14; 1 Timothy 1:6–7; Jude 8–10, 17–19). Lastly, those who know Christ seek to acknowledge and honor Jesus as Lord in both their words and their works (Matthew 5:16). Those who do not truly know Him have no regard or desire to honor Him (1 Corinthians 12:3).

All of the above points (both positive and negative) can be found in those who are members of churches. This means that true and false believers are mixed together. While Christians will not always be able to distinguish those who are genuine from those who are false (Matthew 13:24–30, 36–43, 47–50), Christ is never deceived. He will one day declare that He never knew some who claimed to know Him (Matthew 7:21–23). This will be the ultimate revelation that will separate those with true faith from those with false faith.

43

Powerful Restoration
~ John 21:1–22 ~

Stories of restoration move readers because every believer needs restoration at numerous points in life. Salvation is the first and ultimate experience of restoration. In conversion God redeems rebellious sinners through the finished work of His Son. He adopts them into His spiritual family by the power of the Holy Spirit (Romans 5:6–11; Ephesians 2:1–10; Titus 2:11–14; 3:3–7). However, since Christians often succumb to temptation as they learn to walk in the Spirit (Galatians 5:16–6:5), they need to experience God's ongoing restoration in their walk.

Context

This is why the story of Peter's encounter with Christ in John 21:1–22 is a portrait of powerful restoration. The background for this touching passage is the dark curtain of Peter's utter failure—his notorious public denials of Christ (John 13:36–38). Peter pledged that he would die for

Christ, but instead he denied Him three times (John 18:15–18, 25–27). However, all the disciples claimed that they would never forsake Jesus before they all, in fact, did (Mark 14:31, 50).

In light of this, careful readers may ask: Why was there an emphasis on Peter's failures, if all the disciples denied Jesus? One reason may follow from the way Peter is presented in the Gospel accounts. He appears to have been a spokesman for the disciples. For better or for worse, Peter often spoke on behalf of the disciples on various occasions. For example, Jesus asked His disciples about His identity in contrast to the crowds, but Peter responded (Matthew 16:15–16). On this occasion, Peter swung the proverbial hammer and hit the nail right on the head. However, Peter asked Jesus (apparently on behalf of all the disciples) to explain one of His parables to them. Christ met this request with a rebuke for His disciples' lack of understanding (Matthew 15:15–16). This is an occasion where Peter verbalized a question on behalf of all the disciples that precipitated a less than positive response from Christ.

Even in view of all this, many believers identify more with Peter than with the other disciples. The reason does not primarily have to do with the fact that he is mentioned often in the Gospels. Instead, it has to do with the fact that both Peter's victories as well as his failures are in the open for all to see. Since all Christians stumble and fail in many ways (James 3:2), readers find comfort when they witness Peter's restoration in John 21. They understand that all believers need moments of restoration over the course of their spiritual journeys.

The Illustration

The story of powerful restoration in John 21:1–22 begins with Peter and some others going fishing (John 21:1–3). At first glance, this activity may appear benign. But when the reader remembers that Jesus called Peter from a life of fishing to a life of discipleship (Matthew 4:18–19), the question arises as to whether or not there might be more than meets the eye in Peter's decision to go fishing. Was this an innocent fishing venture? Or was this a signal that Peter was returning to his previous vocation because of his recent failure as a disciple? The latter idea may be the motivating factor behind Peter's decision, and this may be why Jesus chose this particular occasion to restore him.

While Peter did not immediately recognize Jesus (John 21:4–8), all the details of this story thus far recall Christ's work in Peter's life on a previous occasion (Luke 5:1–11). But although Peter played a huge role in this narrative, Jesus must be in primary focus for the reader. Just as the disciples caught nothing apart from Christ's directives and power, believers can do nothing without Christ (John 15:5). Also, just as Jesus did not need the disciples' fish since He already had breakfast for them when they arrived on the shore (John 21:9), He still invited His followers to be a part of His supernatural work (John 21:10–14).

Of course, the most memorable moments of Jesus's encounter with Peter occur in John 21:15–22. At this point in the story, Jesus restored Peter three times. Many commentators have noted that Christ's three restorations likely corresponded to Peter's three denials. For every time Peter failed miserably, Christ restored him gently and deeply.

In light of this, a fascinating play on words appears in John 21:15–17. Jesus used a word for *love* that typically describes God's love in His first two questions to Peter (John 21:15–16). However, when Peter answered Jesus's first two questions, he responded with a different word for *love* (John 21:15–16). The word Peter used in his replies referred to a brotherly type of affection. Then in Jesus's third question to Peter in John 21:17, Christ adjusted His word for *love* to the same word Peter had used in his first two answers. This is likely why "Peter was grieved" (John 21:17). He was not simply burdened because of his three interchanges with Jesus. He was burdened because Jesus changed His word. At this poignant moment in the narrative, readers wait with baited breath for Peter's response. And he responded without changing his word for *love*. He still used the word that referred to a brotherly type of love (John 21:17).

The message of this interesting exchange between Christ and Peter is not that Jesus came down to Peter's level. Rather, it demonstrates Peter's humility. No longer was Peter boasting about his courage to stand for Christ as he did prior to his public denials (Luke 22:31–34). Instead, he was humble about his ability to love Christ as he should. And all this highlights Peter's brokenness and more effective usefulness in the hands of God for His purposes.

In the closing phase of this story, Jesus predicted Peter's martyrdom, and He exhorted him to remain focused on his personal walk of faithfulness (John 21:18–22). Christ's challenging words here reveal that He was not calling Peter to a lesser commitment but to a higher one.

In other words, even though believers fail, God desires to restore them to even greater usefulness. Although the nature of their failures could result in a change of service dynamics, God's plan is always to deepen His work in and through His people for His glory. He uses both the moments of rebellion and restoration in their lives to accomplish His plans and purposes.

Suggestions for Use

Pastors and teachers can use the biblical illustration in John 21:1–22 in a number of helpful ways. For example, Christians should persevere in line with God's call in their lives even though they may be tempted to give up because of their failures. While certain failures could yield a radical adjustment in ministry (1 Timothy 5:20), believers should never cease committing themselves to the work of the Lord (Romans 12:11; 1 Corinthians 15:58). Paul realized he was not perfect, but he made this resolution: "But one thing I do: forgetting what lies behind and straining forward to what lies ahead, I press on toward the goal for the prize of the upward call of God in Christ Jesus" (Philippians 3:13–14). In the same way, believers should embrace God's call to service even through difficulties and discouragement.

Also, God often uses failures to teach His servants about their inability and His all-sufficiency. Peter failed in his attempt to stand for Christ when he publically denied Jesus three times (John 18:15–18, 25–27). He also failed in his attempt to return to fishing because he caught nothing (John 21:1–3). However, after Jesus appeared and instructed Peter and the others concerning how to make a catch, they hauled in a large number of fish (John 21:4–6). All of this illustrates how believers can do nothing apart from Christ (John 15:5).

Furthermore, this story demonstrates that as long as Christians are living in disobedience to God's call, they will not experience all that the Lord has in store for them (James 4:1–10). God's blessings will not always come to His servants in the form of abundant provisions. Sometimes they will suffer greatly even to the point of death for their commitment to obey Christ (Matthew 13:20–21). Nevertheless, this narrative confirms that blessings will come (Proverbs 3:5–10; Matthew 6:33). Some rewards, however, will not become visible until the light of eternity shines on them (Matthew 6:19–21).

Next, the Lord often uses failures to humble His servants and to nurture them for greater usefulness. Peter did not preach the inaugural message of the church on the day of Pentecost on the heels of his perfect stand for Christ in the face of hostility. Rather, he preached the gospel on the day the church was born in the wake of his bitter failure and subsequent restoration. In other words, Peter was most useful in his humility and brokenness. His personal experience described in John 21:1–22 illustrates his own words in 1 Peter 5:5–7: "Clothe yourselves, all of you, with humility toward one another, for 'God opposes the proud but gives grace to the humble.' Humble yourselves, therefore, under the mighty hand of God so that at the proper time he may exalt you, casting all your anxieties on him, because he cares for you." (Interestingly, Peter experienced Jesus's prediction concerning Satan's desire to "sift [him] like wheat" (Luke 22:31). So he issued the warning of 1 Peter 5:8 from trenches of his own life: "Be sober-minded; be watchful. Your adversary the devil prowls around like a roaring lion, seeking someone to devour.")

The main point here, however, is that Peter learned about humility as Christ powerfully restored him. He was humbled. He was broken, and He was modest in his self-assessment. In this way, Jesus postured Peter for greater usefulness as evidenced on the day of Pentecost that soon followed.

Lastly, restoration is an opportunity for believers to move forward in their commitment to Christ rather than backward. Peter initially declared that he was willing to die for Christ before he actually denied Jesus (Luke 22:33). Christ assured Peter after he experienced His restoration that he would have the opportunity to fulfill that promise (John 21:18–19). Jesus's call to Peter before and after his denial and restoration did not change. Some of Christ's first words to Peter were, "Follow me" (Matthew 4:18-–19). Some of Christ's final words to Peter were, "Follow me" (John 21:19, 22). The Lord always calls His servants to deeper levels of commitment (2 Peter 1:3–11). This is one of the truths from the trenches of powerful restoration in John 21:1–22.

44

Scripture, Prayer, and Faith in the Decision-Making Process

~ Acts 1:15–26 ~

Many times believers struggle with making critical decisions. Those who earnestly desire to live in alignment with God's will want to wait on the Lord, but they also understand that action is necessary at some point. Striking a balance between patience and practical planning is oftentimes difficult.

Context

Jesus's disciples faced a struggle like this in Acts 1:15–26. Christ's post-resurrection appearances doubtlessly soothed the pain of His recent crucifixion to an extent (Acts 1:1–3). Nevertheless, the disciples were anxious to do something, even though they were commanded to "wait for the promise of the Father" (Acts 1:4). They already asked the resurrected Jesus about the timing of the restoration of the kingdom of Israel (Acts 1:6), and they heard Christ's call to take the gospel to the ends of the earth reiterated (Acts 1:8; see also Matthew 28:18–20). They stood in amazement as Jesus ascended to the Father (Acts 1:9–11), and they obeyed the Lord's command to wait for the Father's promise by joining others in continual prayer (Acts 1:12–14). But the balance between waiting and acting was difficult.

Furthermore, this was not a quick time of waiting, especially in light of the timing of the events mentioned in Acts 1–2. It's been well-noted that Jesus was crucified on the Passover (Matthew 26:2), and the Feast of Pentecost (Acts 2:1) is fifty days from the Sunday following Passover (Leviticus 23:15–16). Christ appeared for forty days after His resurrection (Acts 1:3). When His forty days of postresurrection appearances are subtracted from the fifty days between Passover and Pentecost, it is clear the disciples engaged in prayerful waiting for approximately ten days.

Yet, as the followers of Christ patiently prayed for the promise of the Father to come, they also realized their need to take certain practical actions. This is what is vividly illustrated in Acts 1:15–26. In this situation, Jesus's disciples demonstrated how believers can engage in prayer, Scripture, and faith in their decision-making processes as they wait on God.

The Illustration

Peter first led the disciples and other early believers to focus on Scripture in light of their need of a replacement for Judas. To begin with, the betrayal and death of Judas fulfilled David's prophetic words in Psalm 69:25 and Psalm 109:8. Peter's language in Acts 1:16 conveyed his belief that Scripture sheds light on the significance of various events (Psalm

119:105). As the disciples moved forward in making a crucial decision, they stepped out on the rock-solid foundation of God's Word. They did not trust their own interpretation of history, but they turned to Scripture as their compass and guide (Proverbs 3:5–7).

After two men were presented who satisfied certain general criteria for taking Judas's place as an apostle (Acts 1:21–23), the disciples continued their prayerful focus. Although they had been engaged in prayer for days, they sought God's guidance on this particular matter too. They acknowledged God's omniscience when they confessed His ability to know human hearts (Acts 1:24). While they operated according to a basic set of criteria, the disciples prayerfully relied upon God's direction.

Christ's followers also took a step of faith at the conclusion of their decision-making process by casting lots. The practice of casting lots in order to determine the Lord's will is rooted in the Old Testament. For instance, one writer references Proverbs 16:33 as a possible background for Acts 1:26. Proverbs 16:33 says, "The lot is cast into the lap, but its every decision is from the Lord." While some may question whether or not the apostles acted in line with God's will at this particular point, the above writer notes, "One thing that is clear is that the casting of lots was firmly believed to have indicated the divine choice of Matthias."[48] In other words, the casting of lots was a demonstration of faith in God. The disciples believed God used the lots to direct His people according to His sovereign will in their decision-making process.

Suggestions for Use

In light of the above points related to Scripture, prayer, and faith in the decision-making process, Acts 1:15–26 could be useful as a biblical

---

48. Donald Guthrie, *The Apostles* (Grand Rapids: Zondervan, 1975), 23.

illustration for several scriptural principles. First, the length of time the disciples waited on God in prayer and unity is a powerful portrait of the importance of prayer (Matthew 26:40–41; Philippians 4:5–7; 1 Thessalonians 5:17).

Second, Peter's appeal to Scripture as the beginning point of the disciples' decision-making process undergirds the Bible's call to live all of life in alignment with God's Word (Psalm 119:9–11, 105; Proverbs 3:5–7).

Third, the emphasis on faith in this text is an example of how the Lord calls all His followers to walk by faith (Hebrews 11; James 1:5–8). Christians should prayerfully search the Scriptures in their efforts to make decisions according to God's will. As they do this, they will ultimately come to the time when they must take a step of faith. They must trust the Lord's sovereign direction as He has revealed it to them (Proverbs 16:3; 19:21). All these truths are sharply presented in Acts 1:15–26, which describes how the disciples engaged in Scripture, prayer, and faith in their decision-making process.

45

GOD AND GENTILES

~ Acts 10:1–48 ~

The natural inclination of the depraved human heart is to always look inward. Of course, believers have new hearts. God's indwelling Spirit leads Christians to see the world through His eyes and His heart. And the heart of God bleeds for the whole world. When believers are not focused on spreading the gospel throughout the world, they are living out of sync with God's heart. This is why Christians need to grasp the lessons of the powerful story of God and Gentiles in Acts 10:1–48.

Context

Acts 9–10 can be viewed as hinge chapters in the storyline of the book of Acts. In Acts 1:8, Jesus told His followers, "But you will receive power when the Holy Spirit has come upon you, and you will be my witnesses in Jerusalem and in all Judea and Samaria, and to the end of the earth." The narrative flow of Acts is a fulfillment of Jesus's prediction in this verse.

In Acts 2, the Holy Spirit came upon and took residence within believers, and the church was born. In Acts 3–7, the church flourished in Jerusalem and spread into various environs. This accomplished Jesus's words that His followers would be His "witnesses in Jerusalem and in all Judea." After the martyrdom of Stephen in Acts 7, God used persecution to mobilize Christians (Acts 8:1–3). As a result, they proclaimed the gospel in Samaria (Acts 8:4–25). This completed Christ's statement that His followers would be His witnesses in Samaria. Then, in Acts 9, Saul of Tarsus was converted to faith in Jesus, and he became the apostle "entrusted with the gospel to the uncircumcised, just as Peter had been entrusted with the gospel to the circumcised" (Galatians 2:7). However, before Paul took center stage in the storyline of Acts, Peter had an initial and unique opportunity to preach the gospel to the Gentiles. This fulfilled in a significantly symbolic way the final words of Jesus's statement in Acts 1:8, "You will be my witnesses . . . to the end of the earth."

So one of the aspects of the background for the story of God and Gentiles in Acts 10:1–48 can focus on Acts 1:8, specifically. But it can also concentrate on the overall narrative flow of Acts 1–9 as well. Either way, the bottom line remains the same: Jesus sends His followers to make disciples of all nations (Matthew 28:19–20). Not everyone will respond favorably to the gospel, but the Lord still wants His people to bear witness to His salvation among the nations because "there is salvation in no one else, for there is no other name under heaven given among men by which we must be saved" (Acts 4:12).

Yet, even though God's plan to share the gospel with the whole world is crystal clear in Scripture, Christ's followers still struggle with being mobilized on mission. As implied above, the tendency of even believers is always to look inward instead of outward. For this reason, the Lord works in powerful ways to move His people outward. This point is powerfully presented in Acts 10:1–48.

The Illustration

The story of God and Gentiles in Acts 10:1–48 opens with God confronting Cornelius through His angelic messenger (Acts 10:1–8). Several points are immediately clear at this early stage of the narrative. The most important is the fact that Cornelius was a Gentile. According to the first two verses of Acts 10, Cornelius was a "centurion of what was known as the Italian Cohort." But he also "feared God." This is probably an indication of Cornelius's relationship to Judaism. While he had not converted to Judaism by submitting to the Jewish rite of circumcision, he nevertheless empathized with the monotheistic theology of Israel. Lastly, Cornelius was known as a generous man who devoted himself to prayer. Evidently, God was at work in Cornelius's heart to draw him to true faith because apart from the work of God's Spirit in the human heart, "no one seeks for God" (Romans 3:11).

After the Lord instructed Cornelius to send for Peter, Christ's witness to preach the gospel, God also worked in Peter's heart to go to Cornelius's house. Interestingly, the Lord was already at work in Peter's life. For example, Peter had previously witnessed God's salvation come to the Samaritans (Acts 8:14–25). This is important because Peter would not likely have been open to ministry among the Samaritans, since the Jews and Samaritans had deep-seated animosity towards one another (John 4:9).

Also, on this particular occasion, Peter was "lodging with one Simon, a tanner, whose house is by the sea" (Acts 10:6). This is important because scrupulous religious leaders considered tanners unclean since they worked constantly with dead animals. Hence, God was preparing Peter for a ministry opportunity among the Gentiles. He previously had involved Peter in His work among the Samaritans (Jewish half-breeds). The Lord was moving Peter gradually towards the place where he would be more open to obey Christ's call to be His witness to "the end of the earth," i.e., among the Gentiles.[49]

But the main experience God used to mobilize Peter toward his ministry at Cornelius's house occurred while Peter was staying at the home of Simon, the tanner. It was a vision God gave him prior to the arrival of Cornelius's messengers (Acts 10:9–16). Basically, the Lord showed Peter a vision of all types of animals and instructed him to "rise . . . kill and eat" (Acts 10:13). The description of the animals in verse 12 coupled with Peter's reply about not eating anything unclean reveals that these animals were not permissible for a Jew to eat. This was another way the Lord opened Peter's heart to embrace His mission to the Gentiles (Acts 10:17–23). This point became unmistakable when the Holy Spirit told Peter as he heard Cornelius's men ask for him, "Behold, three men are looking for you. Rise and go down and accompany them without hesitation, for I have sent them" (Acts 10:19–20). The Holy Spirit told Peter not to hesitate to go with these men because Peter would have been reluctant. God assured Peter that He was divinely orchestrating everything that was taking place, even though it was out of his comfort zone.

Peter obeyed the Lord and journeyed to Cornelius's house. He listened to the great work God had been doing to draw these Gentiles to Himself, and he preached the gospel to them (Acts 10:23–48). The Lord moved in their hearts, and salvation came to the Gentiles. In summary, the account of God and Gentiles in Acts 10:1–48 followed a fascinating storyline. The Lord drew Gentiles to Himself. He opened Peter's eyes and heart to His desire to bring His salvation to Jews and Gentiles alike, and He saved those Gentiles who responded favorably to the gospel.

---

49. Walter A. Elwell and Robert W. Yarbrough, *Encountering the New Testament: A Historical and Theological Survey*, 2nd ed. (Grand Rapids: Baker Academic, 2005), 227–228, 231–232.

Suggestions for Use

This biblical illustration is helpful to ministry leaders as they seek to affirm several scriptural principles. First, the Holy Spirit must work in the hearts of people in order for them to come to know God's salvation in Christ. Jesus said in John 6:44, "No one can come to me unless the Father who sent me draws him." This does not negate the human response to the gospel (Matthew 4:17). It emphasizes what Christ taught concerning the Spirit's ministry of conviction in the world (John 16:4–11). In Acts 10, before Peter even arrived at Cornelius's house, the Lord was already opening hearts to hear and respond to the gospel.

Second, believers are called to be a part of God's work throughout the whole world. Along the lines of the previous point, God was at Cornelius's house before Peter arrived there. The Lord did not begin to move at Cornelius's house after Peter was courageous enough to enter the home of a Gentile. Rather, God called Peter to be a part of His work that was already underway in Cornelius's life and home. This point illustrates the fact that the Lord is not only with us as we seek to make disciples of all nations (Matthew 28:19–20). He is actually going before us to prepare hearts by the power of His Spirit (John 16:4–11).

Third, the Lord works in the lives of His servants in order to cultivate Christlike compassion in them for the world. Peter moved through stages of growth in the book of Acts. He first preached the gospel in Jerusalem. Then he witnessed God's work among the Samaritans. And he also lodged as a guest in the home of Simon, the tanner, who was ritually unclean. After all this growth took place, God opened a door for Peter to preach the gospel in the home of a Gentile. The Lord promises to work in the lives of all His people (Romans 8:28–29; Philippians 1:6). He cultivates their hearts to share the gospel with diverse people groups just as the story of God and Gentiles in Acts 10:1–48 indicates.

Fourth, God's heart bleeds for the whole world. Believers sometime encourage others to read verses such as John 3:16 in a personal way. For example, they may ask them to include their names in John 3:16 where the word *world* occurs. They do this in order to underscore the Lord's love for each individual. However, the reality is that this verse and others like it (see, for instance, 2 Peter 3:9) emphasize the Lord's heartbeat for the whole world. Although many will not surrender their lives to Christ, the call of Scripture is to live as Christ's witnesses everywhere (Matthew 28:19–20; Acts 1:8). Christians must always be careful not to focus inwardly and turn their hearts away from God's call to make disciples of all nations. He has compassion for the whole world. The story of God and Gentiles in Acts 10:1–48 illustrates this important scriptural truth.

46

Dealing with Disagreements

~ Acts 15:1–35 ~

Disagreements will always abound in the world and even within the church. Sometimes people have honest disagreements about peripheral issues. In these cases, they simply agree to disagree without being disagreeable, and they move forward in unity. Other times, disagreements concern nonnegotiable issues. These situations require lines to be drawn in the sand. There is no option to agree to disagree. To do so would result in a compromise of the gospel, and this is never a good solution (Galatians 1:6–9).

Context

A nonnegotiable issue arose in Acts 15:1–35. The background for this passage is really twofold. First, stretching far back into the Old Testament, God gave circumcision as a sign for the covenant He formed with Abraham (Genesis 17:1–14). This sign was nonnegotiable because God said, "Any uncircumcised male who is not circumcised in the flesh of his foreskin shall be cut off from his people; he has broken my covenant" (Genesis 7:14). Thus, one of the distinguishing marks between Jews and Gentiles from Abraham to the church was circumcision. For this reason, the disagreement concerning whether or not circumcision was necessary for salvation was a heated debate. This is clear in Acts 15:1–35.

Second, the immediate background for Acts 15 is the first missionary journey recounted in Acts 13–14. As Paul and Barnabas preached the gospel in synagogues, they often met with hostility from Jews. This led them to turn their attention to the Gentiles. The first time this happened, Paul and Barnabas told the Jews, "It was necessary that the word of God be spoken first to you. Since you thrust it aside and judge yourselves unworthy of eternal life, behold, we are turning to the Gentiles" (Acts 13:46). But this was not an isolated incident. Paul and Barnabas continued to preach the gospel to both Jews and Gentiles, and the Lord saved both Jews and Gentiles.

Yet, disagreements arose concerning how to handle Gentile converts in particular. Some argued that they were saved by God's grace through faith just like the Jews. Nothing else was needed. Others argued that Gentiles had to be circumcised in order to be saved. This is how the biblical illustration in Acts 15:1–35 opens.

So the narrative of Acts 15 focused on the nature of salvation. This is why it is a nonnegotiable issue. For example, the central theme of the book of Galatians is salvation by God's grace through faith and not by works of the law. In light of this, Paul argued early in the first chapter of Galatians, "But even if we or an angel from heaven should preach to you a gospel contrary to the one we preached to you, let him be accursed. As we have said before, so now I say again: If anyone is preaching to you a gospel contrary to the one you received, let him be accursed" (Galatians 1:8–9). These are extremely serious words about an extremely serious subject. For this reason, Acts 15:1–35 provides helpful insights on how to deal with disagreements.

The Illustration

As mentioned above, the biblical illustration in Acts 15:1–35 opens with a clear presentation of the main topic of debate: "Unless you are circumcised according to the custom of Moses, you cannot be saved" (Acts 15:1). Paul and Barnabas could not disagree more vehemently with this statement (Acts 15:2). So they journeyed to Jerusalem to deal with the issue of God's salvation among the Gentiles apart from the works of the law (Acts 15:2). At this point, the lines had been drawn: Paul and Barnabas preached the gospel—the message of salvation by grace alone through faith alone. But "some believers who belonged to the party of the Pharisees rose up and said, 'It is necessary to circumcise them [Gentile converts] and to order them to keep the law of Moses'" (Acts 15:5).

After various people argued different sides of this issue, Peter described how he saw God's salvation come to the Gentiles (Acts 15:7–11). Here Peter referred back to God's work in the lives of Cornelius and others in Acts 10. Peter had already explained or defended his actions in preaching to the Gentiles in Acts 11:1–18. In light of this, the debate in Acts 15 was old news.

Next, Paul and Barnabas "related what signs and wonders God had done through them among the Gentiles" (Acts 15:12). Then James concluded the debate with his view. Based on the evidence of God's saving work among Gentiles as reported by Peter, Paul, and Barnabas (Acts 15:13–21), James said, "Therefore my judgment is that we should not trouble those of the Gentiles who turn to God" (Acts 15:19). While Gentile believers needed to be sensitive to Jewish believers in some general areas (Acts 15:20), the basic disagreement was resolved. The purity of the gospel by God's grace alone through faith alone was safeguarded. A short letter describing the church's decision was sent out, and this news brought joy and encouragement to Gentile believers (Acts 15:22–35).

Suggestions for Use

The story of how to deal with disagreements in Acts 15:1–35 illustrates several key points in Scripture. First, while believers are encouraged to live at peace with others as much as possible (Romans 12:18), certain nonnegotiable issues make disagreements unavoidable. The nature of the gospel is one such issue. Even in these situations, however, Christians can disagree without being disagreeable. Believers are called to speak God's truth in love when dealing with the onslaught of false doctrines (Ephesians 4:14–15). This scriptural principle of speaking the truth in love in an agreeable manner is vividly portrayed in Acts 15:1–35.

Second, issues that deal with the true nature of the gospel are nonnegotiable issues, as mentioned above. Sometimes believers may wonder when it is appropriate to take a stand and disagree with others vehemently. Proverbs 27:5 teaches, "Better is open rebuke than hidden love." But this verse hints at two facts: There is a time to speak open words of rebuke, and there is also a time to be quiet in love. Like all aspects of applying God's wisdom in the trenches of life, this is an art not a science.

However, Acts 15:1–35 reveals an occasion when open rebuke was necessary. It is when God's truth was under assault and being polluted by false teaching. Paul instructed both Timothy (1 Timothy 1:3–5) and Titus (Titus 1:10–11) to confront false doctrines courageously. The story of the Jerusalem council in Acts 15 is a picture of this reality.

Third, the best way to deal with disagreement is to have an orderly discussion focused on the clear facts and undisputed evidence of God's work. In Acts 15, Peter testified first, Paul and Barnabas bore witness third, and James, along with the whole church, made a corporate decision (Acts 15:6–22).

In the same way, believers should always seek to handle matters decently and in order. This approach gives everyone an opportunity to hear evidence and embrace God's direction as they move forward. These aspects of the story illustrate scriptural truths about how believers ought to handle themselves in church assemblies. For example, God desires organization as opposed to chaos when believers gather (1 Corinthians 14:26–33). Also, every Christian has a role in discerning Christ's direction for His church (1 Peter 2:4–10).

Lastly, news about important decisions must be shared widely and clearly. Not everyone will accept decisions. But everyone must be given the facts so that truth is safeguarded from false accusations as much as possible. Acts 15 reveals how the early church sought to accomplish this. They sent at least two well-respected men along with Paul and Barnabas to deliver the announcement of their resolution on this important issue. Their actions here likely follow Old Testament directives. Two or three witnesses were required to establish the truthfulness of any claim made on crucial matters (Deuteronomy 19:15).

47

PROVIDENCE AND PERSONAL CONFLICTS

~ Acts 15:36–40 ~

God's providential workings are mysterious. Many times believers see their lives as a chaotic twisting and turning with no rhyme or reason. However, when they look back on their journeys, hindsight allows them to see the beauty and brilliance of God's providence. The Lord's providence appears particularly amazing against the backdrop of struggles. Joseph's story captured this truth in a nutshell. He explained to his brothers why he would not seek revenge against them in the following words: "Do not fear, for am I in the place of God? As for you, you meant evil against me, but God meant it for good, to bring it about that many people should be kept alive, as they are today" (Genesis 50:19–20). God's providence often works through painful struggles.

Context

The brief account of the intense conflict between Paul and Barnabas in Acts 15:36–40 is another illustration of this scriptural truth. Several aspects of this story are important in order to understand its context. First, the time frame mentioned in Acts 15:36 ("after some days") is interesting. It refers to how Paul and Barnabas, along with many other leaders in the church, had walked through a time of serious disagreement. Acts 15:1–35 describes the occasion of the Jerusalem council. At this crucial gathering, believers resolved a debate concerning the true nature of God's salvation in Christ (Acts 15:1–21). Then they shared the news of this resolution to the delight of Gentile Christians abroad (Acts 15:22–35). Even though a time of corporate peace settled upon the church, the potential for conflict continued to lurk around every corner. And it quickly struck again! This time, conflict violently erupted on a personal level as Paul and Barnabas locked horns in a sharp disagreement.

Second, Paul suggested to Barnabas in Acts 15:36, "Let us return and visit the brothers in every city where we proclaimed the word of the Lord, and see how they are." Here Paul referred to their first missionary journey recorded in Acts 13–14. Ironically, the issue that led to the skirmish between Paul and Barnabas focused on their mutual commitment to missions. Clearly, the Devil uses anything he can to drive a wedge of disunity between God's servants in an effort to weaken their effectiveness (Matthew 12:25).

Third, a particular struggle which Paul and Barnabas experienced on their first missionary journey is alluded to in Acts 15:37–38: "Now Barnabas wanted to take with them John called Mark. But Paul thought best not to take with them one who had withdrawn from them in Pamphylia and had not gone with them to the work." The actual account of John Mark's premature departure during the first missionary journey is described in Acts 13:13. While the details for John Mark's early exit are not provided, Paul viewed his actions as unacceptable. So he adamantly opposed Barnabas' suggestion to include him on the second missionary journey (Acts 15:39).

Thus, the three points above set the stage for Acts 15:36–40: The debate and resolution of the Jerusalem council (Acts 15:1–35), the first missionary journey of Paul and Barnabas in general (Acts 13–14), and John Mark's lack of perseverance during the first missionary journey in particular (Acts 13:13). God used these positive and negative elements to lead His servants forward. In this way, Acts 15:36–40 reveals how the Lord providentially used even the personal conflict between Paul and Barnabas to accomplish His purposes.

The Illustration

The crux of the narrative in Acts 15:36–40 focuses two items: Paul and Barnabas's disagreement over John Mark and what occurred as a result of this disagreement. First, Paul and Barnabas disagreed on whether or not John Mark should be welcomed back to their mission team after he prematurely left their earlier work (Acts 13:13). As noted above, although the reasons for John Mark's departure are not given, they were clearly questionable at best. The description of Paul's opposition to Barnabas' recommendation makes this point undeniable.

Second, the results of the disagreement between Paul and Barnabas about this issue are threefold. To begin, such a sharp conflict erupted between Paul and Barnabas over this issue that they parted company. This is the sad result of disunity. It divides God's servants.

Also, Barnabas decided to give John Mark a second chance by taking him on another mission venture. In some ways, Barnabas's actions are not surprising. After all, his name means "son of encouragement" (Acts 4:36). He also stood by Paul after his conversion and gave him a recommendation to other believers who were skeptical of Paul's claim to be a Christian (Acts 9:26–30). So Barnabas had a proven track record of coming alongside others who were marginalized and supporting them. This is what he did for Paul, and this is what he did for John Mark.

Lastly, Paul chose another partner, Silas. As any reader would expect, Paul's selection would likely be someone who would remain committed to the cause at all costs. This is precisely what becomes clear in their mission work together. For example, in the next chapter, Paul and his new partner persevered through finding God's direction for them (Acts 16:6–10). Later, Paul and Silas were imprisoned together in Philippi (Acts 16:16–24). Yet, even in this incredibly painful situation, they offered prayers and praises to God (Acts 16:25). Paul had selected a partner who persevered through every trial by God's grace, indeed.

Suggestions for Use

The biblical illustration in Acts 15:36–40 is fertile soil for preachers and teachers. For example, this story demonstrates how believers must remain vigilant on the heels of victory. Peter admonished Christians to "be sober-minded; be watchful. Your adversary the devil prowls around like a roaring lion, seeking someone to devour" (1 Peter 5:8). Paul and Barnabas experienced a great victory at the Jerusalem council, but they soon found themselves at odds with one another. And believers today must always be aware of the Devil's plan to attack them at every turn.

Also, Satan's age-old strategy to "divide and conquer" is still alive and well. Jesus identified the Devil's scheme in Matthew 12:25 when He said, "Every kingdom divided against itself is laid waste, and no city or house divided against itself will stand." This may be one of the main reasons why Christ prayed for unity among His followers (John 17:20–21). Jesus knows that disunity leads to dysfunction. In turn, this is detrimental to the church's witness in the world. The enemy's plan on this front ultimately failed as it related to Paul and Barnabas in Acts 15:36–40. They continued their mission work effectively. However, it is nevertheless an important scriptural warning for Christians today to keep in mind.

Furthermore, believers should always be ready to restore others and seek to incorporate them back into God's work in whatever ways are permissible. There has always been an obvious question about who was right between Paul and Barnabas in regard to this conflict. While Scripture does not present a straightforward answer to this question, the last letter Paul wrote may provide a pivotal clue. In 2 Timothy 4:11, Paul made the following request of Timothy: "Get Mark [John Mark] and bring him with you, for he is very useful to me for ministry." Apparently, Paul came to a place where he was willing to trust John Mark again and to see him as useful in the ministry. Perhaps in Acts 15:36–40, Paul's wounded heart could not trust John Mark because his recent failure (Acts 13:13) was too fresh in Paul's mind. But Paul healed, and he came to a different conclusion about John Mark. Through this whole ordeal, Paul learned to practice the restoration he preached in Galatians 6:1–5.

Lastly, God expanded His work even through the less than ideal circumstances of conflict among His servants. This is where the idea of how the Lord works providentially even in the midst of human failures comes into sharp focus. Paul wrote in Romans 8:28 that "we know that for those who love God all things work together for good, for those who are called according to his purpose." He later commented in Romans 8:37 that "in all these things we are more than conquerors through him who loved us." Now, the "all these things" referenced here can be found in both the verses that proceed and follow Paul's statement—things such as "tribulation, or distress, or persecution, or famine, or nakedness, or danger, or sword" (Romans 8:35) and other things such as "neither death nor life, nor angels nor rulers, nor things present nor things to come, nor powers, nor height nor depth, nor anything else in all creation" (Romans 8:38–39). Clearly, most of the "all these things" mentioned here are not positive. They are negative. This confirms that God is at work victoriously in the lives of His people even as they experience trials and troubles because He has already secured victory through Christ (John 16:33). This is the message in Acts 15:36–40 and in other places throughout Scripture: The Lord accomplishes His providential plan even in the face of conflicts and struggles.

48

DISCERNING GOD'S DIRECTION

~ Acts 16:6–10 ~

A critical question all believers ask is: How does one discern God's direction? This question is important because the Christian life is about following Christ. Jesus plainly says in John 10:27, "My sheep hear my voice, and I know them, and they follow me." But this only brings the critical question all believers ask back into focus: How does one discern God's direction? The biblical illustration in Acts 16:6–10 provides an example of how Paul and others learned to follow the Lord's guidance in their service.

Context

In Acts 16:6–10, Paul and his missionary team were fully engaged in the second missionary journey. After completing the first missionary journey (Acts 13:1–14:28), Paul and Barnabas confronted questions about God's work among the Gentiles at the Jerusalem council (Acts 15:1–29).

They then shared the church's decision with others who rejoiced with them (Acts 15:30–35).

However, difficult dynamics often appear in ministry. A sharp disagreement erupted between Paul and Barnabas. They argued over whether or not to take John Mark on their second missionary journey (Acts 15:36–41). But the Lord worked even through this conflict. Barnabas partnered with John Mark, and Paul connected with Silas (Acts 15:39–40).

As Paul and Silas embarked on their mission, they encountered a young disciple named Timothy. Paul invited him to join their mission venture (Acts 16:1–5). As Paul's missionary team strengthened the churches (Acts 16:4–5), he pressed on to share the gospel in other cities. This led to Acts 16:6–10 and the story of how Paul and others discerned God's direction.

The Illustration

Four principles emerge from Acts 16:6–10 which illustrate how Paul and his mission team learned to discern God's direction for their journey. First, Paul and his partners focused on God's call to be Christ's ambassadors, proclaiming the message of reconciliation to the world (2 Corinthians 5:17–20). While they had to discern the Lord's specific directions for their journey, they were certain of God's general call to make disciples of all nations (Matthew 28:18–20). Paul already demonstrated his commitment to this call in the first missionary journey and in his interaction with Timothy. And he continued to live a missional lifestyle of discipleship as he labored to proclaim Christ in unreached places.

Second, Paul and his missionary team learned to trust in God's sovereign direction. No less than three times in Acts 16:6–10, God directed His missionaries. Luke reported that the Holy Spirit forbade Paul and his team from entering into Asia (verse 6). Next, "the Spirit of Jesus" did not allow them to go into Bithynia (verse 7). Yet, Paul and his fellow missionaries concluded that God issued a compelling call for them to go to Macedonia (verses 9–10). It probably seemed that God closed every door for new ministry. But the Lord was actually directing His servants through His providential guidance to His open door.

Third, Paul and the others had to be sensitive to the leadership of God's Spirit. They could have easily thrown in the proverbial towel and concluded that they had missed God's direction. But this would have been a bad mistake. Instead, Paul and his fellow workers were convinced of God's call to proclaim the gospel throughout the nations. So they remained sensitive to the Lord's direction. They knew the need to continue their missionary work was not open for discussion. They also knew God's particular direction was something they needed to discern with constant sensitivity.

Fourth, Paul and his coworkers tested the possibility of God's call to Macedonia before they simply launched out to that area. Although they were ready to move in the Lord's direction, they nevertheless took time to discern if Paul's vision was indeed from God's Spirit. Luke wrote that "when Paul had seen the vision, immediately we sought to go on into Macedonia, concluding that God had called us to preach the gospel to them" (Acts 16:10). Both Paul's commitment to immediate obedience and his care in discernment in decision-making are evident in this verse. A. T. Robertson insightfully touched on the balance of Luke's language here when he wrote:

> A very striking word [the word translated "concluding" means] to make go together, to coalesce or knit together, to make this and that agree and so to conclude . . . This word here gives a good illustration of the proper use of the reason in connection with revelation, to decide whether it is a revelation from God, to find out what it means for us, and to see that we obey the revelation when

understood. God had called them to preach to the Macedonians. They had to go.[50]

Suggestions for Use

Like all of God's inspired Word (Romans 15:4; 2 Timothy 3:16–17), Acts 16:6–10 is a passage rich with insights for teaching biblical principles about discerning God's direction. These verses can be used to illustrate a wide variety of scriptural truths. For example, this text presents a powerful portrait of being fully committed to God's general call, while being sensitive to His specific directions. Every believer who seriously studies Scripture is aware of Christ's commission to make disciples of all nations (Matthew 28:18–20). Yet, all believers have to discern how obedience to this command takes shape in their individual lives. Every disciple of Christ can and should be looking for ways to invest in others. Also, every Christian should be prepared to embrace Jesus's commission to make disciples of all nations. But obedience to God's call to live as Christ's ambassador is uniquely expressed in the life of each believer.

Also, the issue of persevering trust in the Lord's providential leadership is obvious in Acts 16:6–10. As noted previously, Paul and his missionary team could have grown weary in what they considered failed attempts to sow the seed of the gospel among the nations. And Christians today can likewise faint in their struggles. However, this passage illustrates how a closed door in one direction does not mean a closed door in every direction. In fact, the easiest way to discern God's direction is through providential guidance. When the Lord dismisses one option, it only means He repositions His people for another option for service. Believers should never give up in their labors for the Lord.

---

50. A. T. Robertson, "The Acts of the Apostles," vol. 3 of *Word Pictures in the New Testament* (Grand Rapids: Baker, 1930), 248.

They can rest assured of God's providential guidance, and this passage clearly illustrates His call to perseverance (1 Corinthians 15:58).

Lastly, Acts 16:6–10 is a great example of the biblical balance between discerning God's direction and being fully ready to obey His call. For instance, Paul wrote in 1 Thessalonians 5:19–22, "Do not quench the Spirit. Do not despise prophecies, but test everything; hold fast what is good. Abstain from every form of evil." Believers may struggle striking the balance between taking action steps and taking time to evaluate ministry options carefully.

Some quench the Spirit's direction by claiming to be cautious in making decisions. Others cast all caution to the wind as they claim to "let the Spirit lead them" in any and every direction. Biblically, believers are called to be open to the Spirit's leadership, but they are to exercise discernment by testing what they sense to be the Spirit's promptings. This testing occurs when ministry options are measured against the standard of God's Word. If any sense of direction does not align with Scripture, the Lord is not leading in that direction. God does not and will not contradict His Word. Believers can be sensitive to the Spirit's guidance and confidently discern His direction by filtering every decision through the truth of Scripture.

49

THE PRACTICALITY
OF PRIVILEGES

~ Acts 22:22–29 ~

Sometimes God works in ways that are obviously miraculous. For example, when God held the sun still for a time (Joshua 10:12–14), the Lord did not use any mediating means. This was simply a supernatural act and involved the suspension of natural laws. Other times God works in ways that do not seem so miraculous. For instance, Paul counseled Timothy to use a little wine to help his frequent stomach ailments (1 Timothy 5:23). Although the Lord alone is the ultimate healer, He used the natural benefits of wine for His healing purposes. Regardless of how God chooses to work, either through supernatural actions or through natural mediating means, God Himself is the source of power for accomplishing His plans.

Context

The biblical illustration in Acts 22:22–29 is an example of how God accomplished His plans in ways that might initially appear ordinary. In Acts 21:17–26 Paul journeyed to Jerusalem and entered the temple. However, hostility against Paul had been mounting because of his conversion to Christ and missionary work among the Gentiles. So, some Jews who saw Paul in the temple incited a riot and began to beat him (Acts 21:27–32). The Lord used the intervention of the Roman authorities to save his life (Acts 21:33–36). As they were taking Paul away, he asked for permission to speak, and he used even this dangerous situation to preach the gospel (Acts 21:37–22:21). This is the series of events that forms the background for Acts 22:22–29—a story illustrating how God worked through the practicality of privileges to save His servant.

The Illustration

Paul's message in Acts 21:37–22:21 was prematurely interrupted. When Paul declared that God called him "far away to the Gentiles" (Acts 22:21), his Jewish listeners had heard enough and called for his execution (Acts 22:22). In light of the disturbance that others created about Paul, the Roman authorities wanted to know why he was so controversial. So they decided to interrogate him in a brutal way—by flogging (Acts 22:23–24). But as Paul's body was being secured for the flogging, he asked an attending centurion: "Is it lawful for you to flog a man who is a Roman citizen and uncondemned?" (Acts 22:25).

Paul already knew the answer to his own question. He simply wanted the centurion to realize that he was not an average Jew. He was a man with the privileges of dual citizenship in Israel and Rome. After the centurion reported this to his superior, another conversation took place. Acts 22:27–28 reads, "So the tribune came and said to him, 'Tell me, are you a Roman citizen?' And he said, 'Yes.' The tribune answered, 'I bought this citizenship for a large sum.' Paul said, 'But I am a citizen by birth.'" At this point, Paul was immediately released from his bounds. He was not flogged (Acts 22:29) because this would have been a severe violation of Roman law.

What is interesting about the above biblical illustration is that it reveals how God works in different ways in the lives of His servants. This point is particularly evident when readers consider how God worked during times when His servants were imprisoned. For instance, when Peter was jailed in Acts 12, God saved him by sending an angel to lead him out of his cell. Of course, this took place as the church earnestly prayed for his release (Acts 12:1–17). When Paul and Silas were incarcerated in Acts 16, the Lord delivered them by an earthquake. The foundations of the prison rattled locked doors opened, and they were freed (Acts 16:16–34). These two episodes describe the miraculous ways God worked to liberate His servants from experiencing even more suffering than they had already endured.

However, the Lord still worked in a miraculous way in Acts 22:22–29. But this time He accomplished His purpose through a less than sensational means. He used Paul's dual citizenship as a Jew and a Roman to protect him from further persecution, at least on this occasion. Of course, God providentially positioned Paul in a family where he would be born a Roman citizen. Paul certainly could not take credit for orchestrating the family of his birth. And the Lord clearly knew how his Roman citizenship would be beneficial to him in this difficult circumstance. Also, Paul did not hesitate to appeal to his citizenship rights to avoid unnecessary suffering. While he was prepared to die for Christ (Acts 21:13; Philippians 1:21), he still wanted to serve Jesus in this life as long as he could (Philippians 1:21–24). In light of this, he employed his privileges as a Roman to work in his favor so he could continue his ministry. Simply put: God used the practicality of Paul's privileges to preserve his life and to sustain his ministry.

Suggestions for Use

The story of Acts 22:22–29 illustrates at least three core principles in Scripture. First, God is sovereign. He positions His servants and uses various circumstances to accomplish His will. For example, Proverbs 16:4 says, "The Lord has made everything for its purpose, even the wicked for the day of trouble." God knew everything about Paul even before he was born. The Lord knit him together in his mother's womb (Psalm 139:13). So God knew Paul would one day be in the situation described in Acts 22:22–29, and He used the privileges of his dual citizenship to mitigate his suffering and prolong his ministry.

Second, believers should use wisdom and the practical benefits of God's provisions as they minister in hostile environments. When Jesus sent out His disciples on one occasion, He knew that they were going to face hostility and opposition. He told them, "Behold, I am sending you out as sheep in the midst of wolves, so be wise as serpents and innocent as doves" (Matthew 10:16). As Christians minister with integrity and courage, they must also use good judgment. They must realize that God may have arranged certain options to benefit them in difficult circumstances. Paul modeled how believers can walk in wisdom as they honor the Lord in the face of persecution.

Third, although Christians are willing to suffer for the sake of the gospel, they are not sadistic in their approach to life and ministry. Paul mentioned on his way to Jerusalem that he was willing to not only be imprisoned there but to die there as well (Acts 21:13). Paul did not appeal to his Roman citizenship because he was not willing to suffer for Christ. However, he did not want to suffer needlessly. He understood the value of having more time on earth to preach the gospel. For this reason, he wanted to live as long as possible so he could proclaim the gospel (Philippians 1:21).

The previous observation presents a good balance between two points demonstrated in Paul's life. He was in Jerusalem because He was not afraid to go anywhere for the cause of Christ, even to walk right into the lion's mouth. Yet, he was not reluctant to employ the practical privileges of his citizenship to escape the clutches of suffering and death. To paraphrase Paul's stance: When it would be God's time for Paul to die, he was ready to die. But until that time, he wanted to use every day to proclaim the gospel. This is why he used the practicality of his privileges.

50

Open Rebuke

~ Galatians 2:11–21 ~

Everyone who is familiar by experience with the need for tough love understands that applying this principle is more of an art than a science. Sometimes believers should remain silent, and other times they should speak. Knowing when to engage appropriately and wisely in either option is challenging. This is one reason why the biblical illustration in Galatians 2:11–21 is helpful. It shows an example of when open rebuke is necessary.

Context

The entire message of the book of Galatians may be summarized in the following way: Salvation is not by human works but by Christ's finished work alone. No ordinary human being will ever be justified before God by keeping the law. Christ fulfilled all the righteous demands of the law perfectly. Then He died in the place of sinners to satisfy God's just wrath against them. He took their sins upon Himself as their substitutionary sacrifice and offered them His righteousness in its place.

The following verses confirm the above points in broad brushstrokes. Jesus said in Matthew 5:17, "Do not think that I have come to abolish the Law or the Prophets; I have not come to abolish them but to fulfill them." Paul explained in 2 Corinthians 5:21, "For our sake he [God] made him [Jesus] to be sin who knew no sin, so that in him we might become the righteousness of God." Paul wrote in Romans 8:3–4, "For God has done what the law, weakened by the flesh, could not do. By sending his own Son in the likeness of sinful flesh and for sin, he condemned sin in the flesh, in order that the righteous requirement of the law might be fulfilled in us, who walk not according to the flesh but according to the Spirit." In summary: Christ fulfilled the law. He died as the perfect substitute for sinners, and those who repent and trust in Him stand justified before God in Jesus's righteousness. This is why Paul wrote in Galatians 2:16, "We know that a person is not justified by works of the law but through faith in Jesus Christ, so we also have believed in Christ Jesus, in order to be justified by faith in Christ and not by works of the law, because by works of the law no one will be justified."

The above summary is the core of the gospel. It is what Paul both declared and defended throughout the book of Galatians. And it is this idea of defending the gospel which takes center stage in Galatians 2:11–21. Here Peter acted in hypocrisy, and according to Galatians 2:13, he negatively impacted others as well. His behavior "was not in step with the truth of the gospel" (Galatians 2:14). Paul had already declared that anyone (including even an angel) who preached another gospel other than the one he preached should be forever condemned (Galatians 1:8–9). In light of this, he did not hesitate to rebuke Peter publically before others (Galatians 2:11, 14). Clearly, when the truth of the gospel is compromised, open rebuke is appropriate.

The Illustration

The story of how Paul rebuked Peter openly in Galatians 2:11–21 divides neatly into two parts. The first part of the narrative (Galatians 2:11–14) describes the reason for Paul's rebuke. The second part of the story (Galatians 2:14–21) provides Paul's reasoning for why his rebuke was necessary.

In relation to the first part of the story, Paul basically rebuked Peter for an act of hypocrisy. This was a compromise of the gospel, and it negatively impacted others, "even Barnabas" (Galatians 2:13). The situation was straightforward: The scene for the rebuke was Antioch, and Peter was clearly in the wrong (Galatians 2:11). Peter journeyed to Antioch and ate with Gentiles until certain Jews affiliated with James, the apparent leader of the church in Jerusalem (Acts 15:12–21), made an appearance (Galatians 2:12). At this point, Peter stepped out of line. He withdrew from eating with the Gentiles out of fear of what the Jews would think (Galatians 2:12). Then others followed Peter's hypocrisy, even the well-respected Barnabas (Galatians 2:13). It was this action that led Paul to speak an open rebuke to Peter (Galatians 2:14).

This is where the second part of the story begins. Paul's opening words pinpointed Peter's hypocrisy with laserlike accuracy (Galatians 2:14). He basically raised an insightfully straightforward rhetorical question to Peter: "If you understand that Christ has set you free from the Law as a Jewish person, then why would you force Gentiles to live under the Law?" The rest of the story (Galatians 2:15–21) summarizes Paul's theological reasoning for his argument that neither Jews nor Gentiles are justified by the law. No one should live in bondage to the law because righteousness before God is only possible by His grace through Christ's finished work (Galatians 2:15–21).

Suggestions for Use

The brief narrative in Galatians 2:11–21 illustrates three key points in Scripture. First, there is a time for open rebuke. Proverbs 27:5 teaches, "Better is open rebuke than hidden love." Of course, Ecclesiastes 3:1 and verse 7 convey another important nugget of wisdom: "For everything there is a season, and a time for every matter under heaven . . . a time to keep silence, and a time to speak." In other words, believers are not to keep quiet all the time, and they are not to speak their minds on every occasion.

An obvious question is: When can Christians know the times to speak and the times to remain silent? The biblical illustration in Galatians 2:11–21 provides insight for at least one setting in which open rebuke is necessary—when the truth of the gospel is threatened. Just as Paul urged Timothy to "guard the deposit" (1 Timothy 6:20) and to "preach the word" (2 Timothy 4:2), Paul also boldly stood in defense of the gospel, regardless of who needed to be rebuked in the process.

Second, the fear of man will always lead believers astray. Proverbs 29:25 teaches, "The fear of man lays a snare, but whoever trusts in the Lord is safe." An interesting contrast emerges between Paul and Peter in Galatians. For example, Paul indicated that even an angelic messenger should be forever condemned if he preaches another gospel (Galatians 1:8–9). After he made this point, he wrote, "For am I now seeking the approval of man, or of God? Or am I trying to please man? If I were still trying to please man, I would not be a servant of Christ" (Galatians 1:10). Paul did not live in the fear of man but in the fear of God. This led him to declare and defend the gospel at all costs before anyone.

However, Peter withdrew from eating with Gentiles because he feared the circumcision party (Galatians 2:12). So within the first two chapters of Galatians, readers see a sharp contrast between Paul and Peter. Since Paul feared God alone and not man, he boldly stood in defense of the gospel. He would even reject an angelic messenger who tried to preach any other message. But Peter, on the other hand, feared men on this occasion. Consequently, he stepped out of line with the gospel and deserved a public rebuke for his hypocrisy.

This story (and its context) illustrates the dangerous trap that the fear of man creates for God's servants. When believers care more about humanity's opinion than heaven's opinion, they are already caught in sin. Those who see this happen ought to be courageous enough to speak an open rebuke in love. This aspect of the biblical story in Galatians 2:11–21 serves as a good illustration of what Paul taught later in Galatians 6:1, "Brothers, if anyone is caught in any transgression, you who are spiritual should restore him in a spirit of gentleness. Keep watch on yourself, lest you too be tempted."

Third, believers should use every opportunity to present the truth of the gospel. Paul used even the difficult and unpleasant occasions of public rebuke. Even when he rebuked Peter, one of God's servants "entrusted with the gospel to the circumcised" (Galatians 2:7), Paul further explained the truth of the gospel (Galatians 2:14–21). This point is important because it illustrates how rebukes should always be redemptive in nature and focus. All Christians stumble in many ways (James 3:2). As a result, they all need rebukes and corrections from time to time. The truth that will shine the light on a wayward believer is the truth of the gospel. This is the message that shattered the darkness of their lives when they first began to follow Christ (Ephesians 4:17–24). For this reason, Christians should be prepared to share open rebukes with others in love whenever they step out of line with the gospel. The message of Christ should always remain the central focus in the lives of believers.

WORKS CITED

Alden, Robert L. *Job*. Vol. 11 of *The New American Commentary*. Nashville: Broadman and Holman, 1993.

Block, Daniel I. *Judges, Ruth*. Vol. 6 of *The New American Commentary*. Nashville: Broadman and Holman, 1999.

Blomberg, Craig L. *Matthew*. Vol. 22 of *The New American Commentary*. Nashville: Broadman and Holman, 1992.

Cabal, T., C. O. Brand, E. R. Clendenen, P. Copan, J. Moreland, and D. Powell, eds. *The Apologetics Study Bible: Real Questions, Straight Answers, Stronger Faith*. Nashville: Homan Bible, 2007.

Charpentier, Pete. *Reaching the Next Level: Partnering with Others for Spiritual Growth*. Leader Guide. Rapid City, SD: CrossLink Publishing, 2010.

Cole, Dennis R. *Numbers*. Vol. 3B of *The New American Commentary*. Nashville: Broadman and Holman, 2000.

Coleman, Robert E. *The Master Plan of Evangelism*. 2nd ed. Abridged. Grand Rapids: Revell, 1993.

Deere, Jack S. "Deuteronomy." In *The Bible Knowledge Commentary: An Exposition of the Scriptures by Dallas Seminary Faculty: Old Testament*. Edited by John F. Walvoord and Roy B. Zuck. Wheaton: Victor Books, 1985.

Dyer, Charles. "Jeremiah." In *The Bible Knowledge Commentary: An Exposition of the Scriptures by Dallas Seminary Faculty: Old Testament*. Edited by John F. Walvoord and Roy B. Zuck. Wheaton: Victor Books, 1985.

Elwell, Walter A., and Robert W. Yarbrough. *Encountering the New Testament: A Historical and Theological Survey*. 2nd ed. Grand Rapids: Baker Academic, 2005).

Erickson, Millard J. *Christian Theology*. 2nd ed. Grand Rapids: Baker Academic, 1998.

The English Study Bible (ESV). Wheaton: Crossway Bibles, 2001.

Fee, Gordon D., and Douglas Stuart. *How to Read the Bible for All Its Worth: A Guide to Understanding the Bible*. 2nd ed. Grand Rapids: Zondervan, 1993.

Gangel, Kenneth O. *Team Leadership in Christian Ministry: Using Multiple Gifts to Build a Unified Vision*. Chicago: Moody Press, 1997.

Grassmick, John D. "Mark." In *The Bible Knowledge Commentary: An Exposition of the Scriptures by Dallas Theological Seminary Faculty: New Testament*. Edited by John F. Walvoord and Roy B. Zuck. Wheaton: Victor Books, 1985.

Guthrie, Donald. *The Apostles*. Grand Rapids: Zondervan, 1975.

House, Paul R. *1, 2 Kings*. Vol. 8 of *The New American Commentary*. Nashville: Broadman and Holman, 1995.

Howard, David M., Jr. *Joshua*. Vol. 5 of *The New American Commentary*. Nashville: Broadman and Holman, 1998.

Huey, F. B. *Jeremiah, Lamentations*. Vol. 16 of *The New American Commentary*. Nashville: Broadman and Holman, 1993.

Klein, William W., Craig L. Blomberg, and Robert L. Hubbard Jr. *Introduction to Biblical Interpretation*. Nashville: W Publishing Group, 1993.

Lindsay, F. Duane. "Judges." In *The Bible Knowledge Commentary: An Exposition of the Scriptures by Dallas Theological Seminary Faculty: Old Testament*. Edited by John F. Walvoord and Roy B. Zuck. Wheaton: Victor Books, 1985.

Longman, Tremper, III. *How to Read Proverbs*. Downers Grove: InterVarsity Press, 2002.

Merida, Tony. *Faithful Preaching: Declaring Scripture with Responsibility, Passion, and Authenticity*. Nashville: Broadman and Holman Academic, 2009.

Merrill, Eugene H. "2 Chronicles." In *The Bible Knowledge Commentary: An Exposition of the Scriptures by Dallas Seminary Faculty: Old Testament.* Edited by John F. Walvoord and Roy B. Zuck. Wheaton: Victor Books, 1985.

Miller, Stephen R. *Daniel.* Vol. 18 of *The New American Commentary.* Nashville: Broadman and Holman, 1994.

Pentecost, Dwight J. "Daniel." In *The Bible Knowledge Commentary: An Exposition of the Scriptures by Dallas Seminary Faculty: Old Testament.* Edited by John F. Walvoord and Roy B. Zuck. Wheaton: Victor Books, 1985.

Richards, L. O. *The Bible Reader's Companion.* electronic ed. Wheaton: Victor Books, 1991.

Robertson, A. T. "The Acts of the Apostles." Vol. 3 of *Word Pictures in the New Testament.* Grand Rapids: Baker, 1930.

Robinson, Simon J. *Opening Up Judges.* In the *Opening Up Commentary.* Leominster, United Kingdom: Day One Publications, 2006.

Smith, Billy K., and Franklin S. Page. *Amos, Obadiah, Jonah.* Vol. 19B of *The New American Commentary.* Nashville: Broadman and Holman, 1995.

Spurgeon, C. H. *The Treasury of David.* Vol. 3. McLean, VA: MacDonald Publishing, n.d.

Wiersbe, Warren W. *Be Skillful (Proverbs): God's Guidebook to Wise Living.* The BE Series Commentary. Colorado Springs: David C. Cook, 1995.

Zodhiates, Spiros and Warren P. Baker, eds. *The Hebrew-Greek Key Word Study Bible.* Chattanooga: AMG Publishers, 2008.

SUBJECT INDEX

Matthew 5:43-48	117	Mark 1:10	232
Matthew 5:44-45	33	Mark 1:12-13	231
Matthew 5:46-48	35	Mark 1:12	232
Matthew 6:33	266	Mark 1:14-34	232
Matthew 6:7-8	164	Mark 1:14-15	232
Matthew 6:9-13	167	Mark 1:15	239
Matthew 6:13	178	Mark 1:16-20	232
Matthew 6:9-10	164	Mark 1:18	232
Matthew 6:11	167	Mark 1:20	232
Matthew 6:14-15	33, 65	Mark 1:21-28	232
Matthew 6:19-21	266	Mark 1:21	232
Matthew 6:24	255	Mark 1:23	232
Matthew 6:33	238, 240	Mark 1:29-31	232
Matthew 7:7-11	16, 20, 164, 167	Mark 1:29	232
Matthew 7:15	257	Mark 1:30	232
Matthew 7:21-23	261	Mark 1:32	232
Matthew 7:24-27	61	Mark 1:33-34	232
Matthew 8:5-13	165	Mark 1:35-39	231, 232, 234, 235
Matthew 9:35-38	256	Mark 1:35	233
Matthew 10:16	297	Mark 1:37-38	235
Matthew 11:1	238	Mark 1:36-37	233
Matthew 12:25	284, 286	Mark 1:38	233
Matthew 13:20-21	266	Mark 1:39	233
Matthew 13:24-30	261	Mark 1:40-42	165
Matthew 13:36-43	261	Mark 3:1-5	130
Matthew 13:47-50	261	Mark 6:1-6	237
Matthew 15:15-16	263	Mark 6:6-13	236, 237
Matthew 16:15-16	263	Mark 6:6	237, 239
Matthew 16:18	240	Mark 6:7	238, 240
Matthew 16:24-26	255	Mark 6:8-11	238, 240
Matthew 18:7-9	216	Mark 6:8-9	238
Matthew 26:2	269	Mark 6:10	239
Matthew 26:36-46	165	Mark 6:11	239
Matthew 26:39-43	167	Mark 6:12-13	239, 240
Matthew 26:40-41	271	Mark 7:1-23	243
Matthew 26:53	21	Mark 7:24-30	243, 245
Matthew 28:16-20	108	Mark 7:24	243
Matthew 28:18-20	235, 269, 290, 292	Mark 7:29-30	243
Matthew 28:19-20	237, 239, 273, 276, 277	Mark 7:31-37	242, 243, 244, 245, 246
		Mark 7:31-35	244
Mark 1:1-8	231	Mark 7:31	243
Mark 1:9-11	231	Mark 7:32	243

When you buy a book from **AMG Publishers, Living Ink Books**, or **God and Country Press**, you are helping to make disciples of Jesus Christ around the world.

How? AMG Publishers and its imprints are ministries of **AMG (*Advancing the Ministries of the Gospel*) International**, a non-denominational evangelical Christian mission organization ministering in over 30 countries around the world. Profits from the sale of AMG Publishers books are poured into the outreaches of AMG International.

AMG International Mission Statement

AMG exists to advance with compassion the command of Christ to evangelize and make disciples around the world through national workers and in partnership with like-minded Christians.

AMG International Vision Statement

We envision a day when everyone on earth will have at least one opportunity to hear and respond to a clear presentation of the Gospel of Jesus Christ and have the opportunity to grow as a disciple of Christ.

To learn more about AMG International and how you can pray for or financially support this ministry, please visit

www.amgmissions.org

CPSIA information can be obtained at www.ICGtesting.com
Printed in the USA
LVOW04s1142120115

422401LV00003B/6/P

9 780899 573687